MY STORY

JUDITH EXNER

MY STORY

as told to Ovid Demaris

Grove Press, Inc., New York

To my husband, Dan, whose love and strength have given me the courage to be who I am and not what others would have me be.

Judith Exner filed suit against the FBI for the release of their files concerning her. The following is an excerpt from the judge's oral ruling on her case:

IN THE UNITED STATES DISTRICT COURT
SOUTHERN DISTRICT OF CALIFORNIA

HONORABLE EDWARD J. SCHWARTZ, JUDGE PRESIDING

JUDITH KATHERINE EXNER, Plaintiff, -vs- FEDERAL BUREAU OF INVESTIGATION, et al., Defendants.	No. 76-0089 S HEARING MOTION TO STAY PENDING APPEAL

Now, I think I should say that I have no particular concern with Mrs. Exner as a person or what her motives may be. Evidently, it is alleged that she is going to write a book or is in the course of writing a book. She may have other motives. She has alleged that there is some fear of danger to her life because of the statements that have been leaked in the press coverage of possible underworld connections.

She's also stated that she would like to know what's in the file: so that she can set the record straight, so to speak, if the file contains erroneous information. Again, I think that the Court should take into consideration the fact that, for whatever reason or whatever motives, Mrs. Exner kept the information that is now the hub of this controversy to herself for a period of perhaps 15 or 16 years, that she didn't write any books, she didn't publish any of this information, and then she was subpoenaed before a Senate Committee and required to testify.

I'm sure she was informed that the proceedings were secret, and then she found that the proceedings, at least insofar as they pertained to her, had been leaked obviously—and I can't imagine any other way than through some Government source.

Then, when the stories began to hit the press and Mrs. Exner was made the subject of a great deal of notoriety and publicity, she then brought this action to see if she could have a look at the information and materials that are filed.

PROLOGUE

The media attack on Judith Campbell Exner has been one of the most disgraceful performances on record. I can't recall a more vicious onslaught, a more hysterical outpouring of poisoned pen polemic—disguised as hard news wherever possible—all of it slanted to denigrate and assign the blame for untold crimes and misdemeanors in high and low places on the shoulders of one defenseless woman. In Watergate, at least, the shotgun attack was democratic in assessing guilt on a whole gang of felons.

The wrath of a righteous press is a sight to behold. Not one tempered word to be found anywhere. Legends are not easily surrendered. The press will fight to preserve its manufactured illusions, its Camelots and Good Ships Lollipop, and God help anyone who inadvertently threatens them.

Imagine my state of mind when I was invited to meet this pariah, this instant "mob moll" or "tramp" or "party girl" or "hooker"—pick your own epithet, and whatever it is, rest assured it has been reported somewhere as fact. I went to San Diego to have dinner with Dan and Katherine Exner, the name she is now using. She was christened Judith Eileen Katherine Immoor; the Campbell comes from her former marriage to movie actor William Campbell.

Actually, the first time I heard the name Judith Campbell Exner was during a television interview on a morning talk show in Nashville. I was doing the author's bicycle trick: a five-week, twenty-one-city publicity tour to promote my latest book, a biography of J. Edgar Hoover entitled THE DIRECTOR. I was at the tail end of the tour and thoroughly exhausted. I was not paying too close attention to current news. I had been jumping on airplanes and out of cabs, rushing to late evening radio and early morning television shows, and was beginning to think that the whole world was concentrating exclusively on my book.

The morning of this particular show in Nashville, I had not read the story concerning the Exners' press conference in San Diego. My host was one of those intrepid quizzers who loves to impress the home folk with his clever repartee. Always, of course, at the expense of his guests, be they local bumpkins or Nobel laureates.

"I'm going to put you on the spot," he said, "and I want a straight answer." He paused to wink at the camera, a signal to his fans that I was in for it. "Why did your publisher delete the Judith Campbell Exner material from your book?" He waggled an accusing finger at me. "Now, don't deny it. I know all about the publishing game." He was smiling but the glint in his eyes was that of a fox hotfooting it into a henhouse. "Boy, you guys are something else," he said to the camera, shaking his head in great bewilderment. "You don't mind dirtying Nixon, but when it comes to Kennedy, well, that's a whole other ball game."

As it turned out, his scenario of the Exner "expose" was a garbled version of a distorted news service report, and it went something like this: J. Edgar Hoover had blackmailed President Kennedy with information gained from wiretaps that linked Kennedy with a girlfriend of Sam Giancana and John Roselli, two Mafia bosses the CIA had hired to murder Fidel Castro. This liaison with Exner had put them all in bed together, along with Frank Sinatra, who had arranged the introduction, at Giancana's urging, when Kennedy had visited Las Vegas during his 1960 presidential campaign. In other words, the mob had a plant in the White House, a very neat little package that Hoover had exploited to maintain himself in office.

Fascinating. But where had the press gleaned this hot stuff? The answer is easy: from the Senate Committee on Intelligence Operations, chaired by Frank Church, who had done his damnedest to keep the lid on Camelot. The committee's eleven senators had voted unanimously not to reveal the name or even gender of Judith Campbell, as she was known during the years in question. However, the section in the report alluding to her was a little too intriguing to go unnoticed by the press.

A verbatim excerpt, complete with the Committee's footnotes, follows:

> As elaborated in the previous sections of this report, all living CIA officials who were involved in the underworld assassination attempt or who were in a position to have known of the attempt have testified that they never discussed the assassination plot with the President. By May 1961, however, the Attorney General and Hoover were aware that the CIA had earlier used Giancana in an operation against Cuba and FBI files contained two memoranda which, if simultaneously reviewed, would have led one to conclude that the CIA operation had involved assassination.[1] There is no evidence that anyone within the FBI concluded that the CIA had used Giancana in an assassination attempt. The Committee has uncovered a chain of events, however, which would have given Hoover an opportunity to have assembled the entire picture and to have reported the information to the President.
>
> Evidence before the Committee indicates that a close friend of President Kennedy had frequent contact with the President from the end of 1960 through mid-1962. FBI reports and testimony indicate that the President's friend

1. The two memoranda, which are discussed in considerable detail *supra,* were the October 18, 1960, memorandum linking Giancana to an assassination plot (but not mentioning CIA) and the May 22, 1961, memorandum linking Giancana to a CIA operation against Cuba involving "dirty business" (but not mentioning assassination).

was also a close friend of John Roselli and Sam Giancana and saw them often during this same period.[2]

On February 27, 1962, Hoover sent identical copies of a memorandum to the Attorney General and Kenneth O'Donnell, Special Assistant to the President. The memorandum stated that information developed in connection with a concentrated FBI investigation of John Roselli revealed that Roselli had been in contact with the President's friend. The memorandum also reported that the individual was maintaining an association with Sam Giancana, described as "a prominent Chicago underworld figure." Hoover's memorandum also stated that a review of the telephone toll calls from the President's friend's residence revealed calls to the White House. The President's secretary ultimately received a copy of the memorandum and said she believed she would have shown it to the President.

The association of the President's friend with the "hoodlums" and the person's connection with the President was again brought to Hoover's attention in a memorandum preparing him for a meeting with the President planned for March 22, 1962. Courtney Evans testified that Hoover generally required a detailed summary of information in the FBI files for drafting important memoranda or preparing for significant meetings. (Evans, 8/28/75, pp. 70, 72). The FBI files on Giancana then contained information disclosing Giancana's connection with the CIA as well as his involvement in assassination plotting (Memoranda of 10/18/60 and 5/22/61).

On March 22, Hoover had a private luncheon with President Kennedy. There is no record of what transpired at that luncheon. According to the White House logs, the

2. White House telephone logs show 70 instances of phone contact between the White House and the President's friend whose testimony confirms frequent phone contact with the President himself.

Both the President's friend and Roselli testified that the friend did not know about either the assassination operation or the wiretap case. Giancana was killed before he was available for questioning.

last telephone contact between the White House and the President's friend occurred a few hours after the luncheon.

The fact that the President and Hoover had a luncheon at which one topic was presumably that the President's friend was also a friend of Giancana and Roselli raises several possibilities. The first is, assuming that Hoover did in fact receive a summary of FBI information relating to Giancana prior to his luncheon with the President, whether that summary reminded the Director that Giancana had been involved in a CIA operation against Cuba that included "dirty business" and further indicated that Giancana had talked about an assassination attempt against Castro. A second is whether Hoover would then have taken the luncheon as an opportunity to fulfill his duty to bring this information to the President's attention.[1] What actually transpired at that luncheon may never be known, as both participants are dead and the FBI files contain no records relating to it.

On November 16, 1975, four days before the committee released its report, the Washington *Post,* after some heavy agonizing in editorial aeries, decided it had no choice but to identify Judy as the President's "close friend." The story, under the headline: "Probers Doubt Kennedy Knew of Poison Plot Against Castro," appeared on Page 6A. The thrust of the article was directed at what it termed "a bizarre White House episode"—to wit, the relationship between President Kennedy and a woman involved with two Mafia figures, who in turn were involved with the CIA in plots to assassinate Castro. As a result of its prosaic headline and innocuous position, the story slipped by relatively unnoticed.

1. The President, thus notified, might then have inquired further of the CIA. The Presidential calendar indicates that the President had meetings at which most CIA officials witting [sic] of the assassination plot were present during the period from February 27 through April 2, 1962. All of those persons, however, have testified that the President never asked them about the assassination plot.

Having performed its journalistic duty, the *Post,* the fearless vanguard in exposing Watergate, did not further pursue the story.

Others, of course, picked up the cudgel, but the story was a sleeper for nearly a month before it exploded into banner headlines around the world. Like Watergate, its genesis was in leaked documents.

Since that morning in Nashville, the story has gone from bad to godawful. Some of the stories were so outrageous that they would be comical if not so tragic. Being the co-author of this book has been an enlightening experience. It has given me a whole new perspective on the press, one which is not pretty to behold. However, the purpose of this book is not to take issue with the press, but rather to set the record straight, to tell it as it truly happened with Judith Campbell, and not as imagined by those who delight in speculating on the aberrations of the high and mighty. There is no question in my mind that this book would not have been written if the press had given her a fair shake. It is a safe enough assumption, considering that she lived with this knowledge for sixteen years.

It was a pleasant surprise to meet the Exners. They are just about complete opposites from the image presented in the press. She is not "a rather ordinary woman," as Robert Sam Anson described her in *New Times,* but a very beautiful woman, with luxurious raven hair that is always immaculately groomed. She has classic features, with soft blue eyes and a warm, disarming smile. It is easy to see why she attracted the attention of men who had unlimited access to female pulchritude. In those days, she must have been a stunning beauty. Even more important, she is a lady with impeccable taste. She is thoughtful, gentle, well-mannered, intelligent, and properly reserved.

Contrary to reports that he is short and slight, Daniel R. Exner is six feet and weighs one hundred eighty. The press has made great sport of the fact that he is younger than his wife, but Dan is twenty-nine, going on forty-nine. He has crammed in more experiences during those few years than most people do in a lifetime.

Their preoccupation during dinner was that the book be written in good taste. Judith told me she wanted to tell the full story, the whole truth, but without pandering to prurient appetites. I couldn't have agreed more. Later in the evening, over coffee and brandy, I asked them directly why they had decided to write a book. The answer convinced me that their interest involved far more than money.

"When all of this started after her appearance before the Church committee, we had three choices," Dan said. "We could allow it to continue and just suffer with it. We could run and hide. Or we could stay and fight. She was not emotionally, or physically, in any kind of shape to allow it to continue. You can, in fact, run and hide. You can, in fact, disappear. But it has a tremendous price to it. So you come down to staying and fighting. There is no way this is going to continue without our doing a super effort to fight back. I don't care which side is after her, who it is, she can't take it."

Dan placed his hand gently over hers and she nodded in agreement. The expression in her eyes was of pain, not anger, when she spoke: "When the phone call came from my sister that an investigator for the Church committee was at her house, and she was hysterical on the phone because he had threatened to physically drag her to Washington unless she revealed our whereabouts, my remark to Dan was: 'My God, I knew it was going to happen. I knew it was going to come back.' That's just the feeling I had inside. It was like, merciful God, is it ever going to end? And Dan took over. I was at a point where I couldn't function. I don't know what I would have done if I had been alone. I only know that I had reached the end. There wasn't any way I could go through it again. And that was partially because of what had happened before, and partially because of the death of my mother and father, and what I had experienced through that. I knew I was at a point in my life where I could not take up where I had left off. To just have it happen again. And Dan just took over. From his attitude, slowly but surely, I got strength within me. If they shot him, if they took him away from me, I want to tell you, I couldn't continue."

"I talked to my father, who is a physician," Dan said, his hand still covering hers. "He was in the midst of this as it was happening. And emotionally and physically, he said, most candidly, she couldn't do that. She was just about to fall down."

"I'll tell you," Judith said, "sometimes I really think someone is watching over me because within the period of time all this was happening, the sequence of events, and Dan being the kind of person he is, a fighter—just don't push him in a corner because he's going to fight—I just thank God that he and I found each other. That we became what we are to each other. Without him I was absolutely lost. If you agree to write this book, you will get to a point in my story where I gave up. The fact that I was saved, the hospital records will show, is pure accident. It was all due to this—"

She paused and Dan put his arms around her. "Take a deep breath," she said, "I'm okay. While I was carrying my baby—God—" she stopped and turned to Dan, unable to continue.

"While she was carrying her child," Dan said, not taking his eyes from hers, "among all the other things that were happening, the Federal Bureau of Investigation just about put her away. They hounded her, they watched her, they trailed her, they tapped her phone, they bugged her home, they accosted her on the street, they broke into her home, they went to her friends, they went to her parents, without any regard for her, without any regard for her life, for her child's life. And because of that, she tried to kill herself. When she realized that killing herself wasn't the answer, and that her child was going to be born, and that he had nothing to look forward to other than what was being done to her, for his benefit, and his benefit only, she gave him up."

"After a year," she barely whispered, tears running freely down her cheeks.

"It was a long, long hard walk," Dan said. "And it isn't going to happen twice."

"It took a year for me to give him up."

"She could offer him nothing but what was being done to her."

"My brother wanted him, my sister wanted him, but I knew that he could not be near me and not know that I was his mother." She shook her head and closed her eyes. "Sometimes I wish I was stronger. I know I did the right thing for him. My brother Freddie in Tahoe had him for a period of time—you know, this was when he was a tiny, tiny baby. In fact, he was born at seven months. I almost didn't have him. He was in an incubator for many, many weeks. Freddie wanted to adopt him. He had him baptized. My baby had pneumonia while he was up there, and had the last sacraments while he was up there. They were never going to talk to me again because I would not sign the adoption papers. I knew there wasn't a way in the world I could have anyone in my family—my mother and father said, 'keep your child, we'll bring him up'—but the thing that was hounding at me was that this child deserved a mother and father, he deserved to be out of this mess. There was no way he could survive as my son. If he had a mother and father, at least he has a fair chance. If something happened to him then, at least I gave him a chance. The other way, there was so much stacked against him that there wasn't any way he could make it. He had to be so strong to start with, had to have so many built-in resentments that he would grow up with, there was no way he could survive unscarred. It wasn't fair. For his own safety, I could never tell him who his father was. And I would never tell him."

Later that evening, after she had composed herself, we again went into the reasons for writing a book.

"It isn't just the lies of Evelyn Lincoln and Dave Powers and Kenny O'Donnell, and others," she said, "or the leak from the committee. Or that night when I watched the news after my press conference and realized that no one was going to report it fairly. They sensationalized it, and it's been going downhill ever since."

"These things play a large part in our deciding to write a book," Dan said, "but the most important thing is that she just can't sit back and take any more of it. It's time to say halt. Stop, no more. It's time to stand up and fight back the best way we know how. With a book, surely, and with lawsuits wherever necessary. We've been sitting here like clay pigeons for too long. From this time forward, the enemy will be engaged at every turn. If it takes every penny we own, if it takes every ounce of our strength, if it takes our very lives, so be it.

"It's starting up all over again, just like it was before," Judith said. "We have again been followed, as I was followed constantly in the past. You never feel safe. You never know who is following you. That's it, no more. I'm putting my story down. It's going to be published, the whole story. I don't know whether someone's afraid of what I'm going to say. I just don't know why they are still after me.

"*They* could mean anybody. I didn't know anything about the CIA in those days. It's obvious to me now why they did what they did. It wasn't anything that I was doing wrong. Our own damn government was doing something wrong. They were the ones working with the hoodlums. They were the ones with the close association with them, the government. But I was paying the price for it. And I'm not going to pay it anymore without fighting back.

"As I said, the harassment from the FBI was horrendous. There probably was a tremendous conflict at the time. The CIA was protecting Sam and Johnny, the FBI was trying to get them, the White House was scared to death that the FBI might get them—after the White House found out, or even if they knew all along what was going on. I was caught right in the middle of it. The CIA was afraid because I was going to the White House, and because I did know Sam and Johnny. They wanted to know, I guess, what I was doing every time I went to the powder room. I think they all spend their lives looking over their own shoulders. I doubt if they could even trust their own mothers. So it was my association with those two people, and what the CIA connection was with them—I wasn't the one who was paranoid. I think they were. They had to know where I was, what I was doing, what I was saying, who I was seeing, and I can't live through that anymore. I almost didn't live through it then.

"It's hard to describe the feeling I get whenever the FBI stops me on the street. It is usually in a parking lot, and two of them come at me from opposite directions. They call, 'Judy' and hold out their identification. They say, 'We'd like to talk to you,' and I just—I have finally reached a point where I don't even acknowledge them. I just turn around and get in my car and drive off. Just like they are not even there. They say, 'Wait, we'd like to ask you a couple of questions,' and I act like nothing is there. No one is talking.

"I act indifferent but my heart starts to go, and I really get weak-kneed. It's part anger, and part fear, too. And frustration. The feeling is how am I ever going to get it to end? When is it going to end? How will it end? What will eventually happen? I feel I have no control over the situation. That there is just nothing I can do about it. I am at their mercy.

"Of course, the surveillance has slowed down in recent years and for a while I even thought I was free of them. But now, in a sense, it's worse than it was. I'm being called every name in the book. Maybe if I was a different kind of person, if I'd had a different kind of mother and father, I'd be able to shrug my shoulders at some of the things that are being said about me. I can't. That kind of thing is too important to me. The relationships I've had, whether it be Sam, or Jack, are too important to me, there's too much respect wound up in them. It was not just a matter of two people meeting and going to bed together. It was not a fling. But that's the light it's being put in. That isn't me. I didn't live that way. I'm no angel. I didn't have a great many affairs, but, yes, I was single for many, many years, and I also went with a couple of people who were nobodies. And yes I had affairs. You know, I'm forty-two years old. I'm not an old maid. So I don't try to paint myself as an angel, but neither am I a whore. And neither am I a conspirator. They were strictly man-woman relationships. Two people who cared for each other. Because it was Sam Giancana—bull. It was Sam. The remark that I made to the newspapers that he was not the President to me. He was Jack Kennedy. The papers tried to make it sound flippant. I'm sure I thought about the fact that he was President. I'm sure that at times I was thrilled with it, but I'm sure that I was thrilled with it because I was proud of him. I wasn't saying, 'My God, look at me, I'm going with the President.' I was proud of him, proud that he had attained that position.''

As I lay in bed that night, unable to sleep, thinking of all we had discussed, far more, of course, than reported here, I knew I wanted to write this book. I knew there was far more to this story than sensational headlines. This was a woman who had suffered, a woman who understood what had happened to her, in good and bad times, who could articulate her feelings, who was sensitive, and who was so damned vulnerable.

All right, she admits she is no angel, but who wants to write about angels. She has a story to tell that is unique, and I would gladly topple all the Camelots and King Arthurs, or Sir Lancelots, to give her that chance. As Dan would say, sure, there are some bad dudes around, but they don't wear different colored hats. There is no one in a white hat walking through these pages. As far as I'm concerned—and I have spent considerable time chronicling the adventures of hoodlums, as well as the misadventures of businessmen and politicians—Francis Ford Coppola, who directed *The Godfather,* says it best: "Men of power and the criminals in our society are distinguished only by their situation, not their morality." I think some women know this better than anybody. Judith Campbell is one of those women.

I

I remember people, moments and places. I can see Frank and Jack and Sam—so many faces, expressions, images that flash before my mind's eye. But people are really voices. I can feel their sound, their words course through my veins and warm my soul. Moments are love and music; songs that break my heart. Places are light and color, smells and sound, and I feel a great tenderness for the way they were then and will never be again.

Life is but a moment in time, a grain of sand, the blink of an eye. So why does it seem like a millennium? Death alters our perceptions of loved ones. It makes us remember what we should forget. They killed Sam, with bullets, as they killed Jack. But I knew them when the dream of Camelot was real, when life was the moment, when their worlds never collided—or so it seemed.

When I think of my father I hear thunder. He was a tall man with a barrel chest, and the sound would rumble and ricochet off the walls like thunderclaps on a summer night.

I guess I've always been afraid of my father. When I was at a very impressionable age, when I was so shy and timid, and World War II had started, we lived then in a huge twenty-four room house overlooking the ocean in Pacific Palisades, which is a suburb of Los Angeles. The navy was having bombing practice just off the coast and the noise terrified me. My mother and father were arguing a great deal then and his voice became all mixed up with the noise of the guns. His voice always made it sound like the war was right in our house. I became even more timid, more frightened, and I used to dream about the sound of his voice. Even today, at my age, sometimes at night I can still hear the bombing and his voice is part of it.

My father was German and my mother was Irish. They both had explosive tempers. But it was my father that I feared. He was so formidable. I never could get close to him. He wouldn't allow it. He had so little patience. He couldn't help us with school problems because he expected us to understand whatever he was explaining the first time around. He would yell at us, in this booming voice that paralyzed me with fear.

I was a momma's girl. Whenever anything happened, I'd run to my mother. My most vivid impression of my mother is that she lived for her family. I remember when the money was scarce and there was no food in the cupboard, my mother would prepare a magnificent meal. She could bake from nothing. From absolutely nothing. She dressed us three girls alike until my oldest sister Joan was about twelve. Always white starched pinafores over our dresses. She was very finicky about our clothes and our hair. We always looked like we stepped right out of a washing machine. When we didn't have a maid, she did it herself.

Both my parents were born in New York. My father's name was Frederick Immoor and my mother's was Katherine Shea. I never knew my paternal grandfather. He died before I was born. Grandma Immoor lived to a ripe old age, but she was a hard, cold, frugal woman. Grandpa Shea died when I was in my late twenties. He had that Irish temper, but from stories my mother told me, he was a sailor as a young man and lived quite an adventurous life. Grandma Shea was the typical Irish grandmother, the kind the movies used to portray in the old days—the short, heavyset woman with the brogue and the bun in the back or on either side of her head. She was adorable.

My mother was at least five foot eight and she had the most magnificent red hair and soft blue eyes. As a young woman she was a great beauty. She modeled at Bonwit's in the days when that position was something very special. She was quite artistic. She could create marvelous designs with flowers. Whenever her friends gave a luncheon or shower, any special occasion, they would ask for her help in creating decorations. She could take a few pieces of net, some wire and some ribbon and make the most attractive centerpieces. And she loved doing it. She made all our Christmas stockings, and each one was an individual creation unlike any other.

My mother was an extremely loving, outgoing person. You felt her love. But she had that Irish temper. She was outspoken. She wasn't timid for a second. She was a strong woman. There were times when she was stronger than my father.

When things got impossible between them, my father was the one who deserted us. My mother was the one left behind with the five children. She kept everything together, kept everything going. I think she recognized what was happening within my father, the frustrations he felt when he botched it financially. He left us three times but always came back. Divorce was never even mentioned.

My father was an architect, a good one, too, but he had some problems at different times in his life. Part of it was his temper. He was very difficult to work with. He left some firms simply because of his own disposition. He was impossible to be around at times. Yet he was much in demand, for he had a great talent in his field. When he did leave a firm, whether it was because of his temper, or perhaps he didn't like the way things were done, or for any other reason, there were all kinds of firms who wanted his services. He was known as an impossible human being, and still he managed to direct some very important projects. In his later years, he became an expert in the design and construction of hospitals. He was the project director for the building of St. Vincent Hospital in Los Angeles. He built hospitals in San Francisco and throughout the Southwest.

In those days he was associated with Daniel, Mann, Johnson and Mendenhall. Not long before he retired, he was asked to survey veterans' hospitals and recommend which were to be closed down and which were to be kept open. The government had contracted with the Daniel, Mann firm and they assigned the job to my father. At various times in his career, he also worked for major movie studios designing elaborate sets.

The other problem my father had was that he came from an immensely wealthy family. My father was probably the worst money manager that ever was. He never got the hang of living on less than he was accustomed to while growing up. Our life was always an economic seesaw. It was either everything in the world you could ever want, or nothing at all. He had money coming from his father, but he lost most of it in bad investments and high living.

He loved big homes. Our house in Pacific Palisades was a four-story Mediterranean villa built down a hillside with a dazzling view of the Pacific. Later it was bought by Joseph Cotton and featured in the *Los Angeles Times Home Magazine*[1] under the caption: "Elegance, in the grand manner." But the house frightened me. I remember that part of the living room took up two floors. It had a handpainted vaulted ceiling and the room was so massive that if I ever got caught at the other end of it by myself, I wouldn't move until someone came in. I was a very timid child.

I was born in New York City on January 11, 1934. Although my parents were from the east, we moved to California before I was a year old. I was the fourth child in a family of two boys and three girls. Fred, who was named after my father, is the oldest. Then there's Joan, Jacqueline, myself, and Allen, the baby, who is eight years younger.

I don't really know the reason for our moving to California when I was a year old. I don't know whether my father was just transferred or whether it was a problem. It's something that was never discussed. I don't know too much about my family. My mother didn't sit down and tell me the heartaches of the past. She told me only the good things about the family.

[1] May 26, 1957.

When I think back to as far as I can go, I remember always my shyness. I was a shy, introverted child. A very private child. I was not outgoing. I hung onto my mother a good deal. Whatever happened, I'd always run to my mother. Later on I had my outs with my mother, terrible times with her. But when I was young, I didn't want her to be away from me. Not to the extent where it was a problem. But I didn't make friends very easily. I didn't have a great many friends. It took a while for me to cultivate friendships. But when I did find a friend, now that was my friend. You were my friend, if you wanted to be, for life. I never have taken to people easily.

My mother was my friend. My father was not. I don't want to get ahead of my story, but I should state that I did get to know my father before he died. After my mother passed away, he was a beaten man. My relationship with him was far better, far closer than it had ever been. I felt for him. He blamed himself for a lot of things that happened while I was taking care of my mother. The fact that he couldn't handle it bothered him deeply. I used to try to make him feel better about it. I could almost feel what he was going through.

When I was growing up my parents always did everything together, and with the family. They shopped together, we took rides together, we dined out together, we went to the movies together, to various events together. That didn't seem unusual to me then. I don't know how many families are like that. In meeting other people, I've seen the parents doing things without the children, and I have thought that perhaps in some given areas we were an unusual family. In other ways, of course, I guess you could call us Middle America. I don't really know.

My father wasn't the kind of man who had a night out. He was pretty much a homebody. My parents didn't do a great deal of socializing, but they did have some interesting friends. People today wonder why there are so many promi-nent names surrounding my life, but it was not unusual for me to be around notable people. My parents were friends of theatrical and movie people. Bert Lahr was a friend and so were Dolores and Bob Hope, who were also friends of my aunt Jean who was then married to a man named Horton. Dolores's mother was a close friend of my aunt Jean.

My parents enjoyed entertaining at home. They did very little drinking by themselves. And when they did drink, they were both happy drinkers. It wasn't a matter of having a martini before dinner every night. Usually at Sunday dinner there would be wine or champagne. Before the Sunday dinner, which was usually at three or four in the afternoon, my dad would make my mother a whiskey sour, which she always enjoyed so much. It wasn't that they disapproved of drinking, it just wasn't their pattern of living.

My mother's social functions were connected with her church. She did the flowers for the altar, she was very involved with the Catholic schools. She gave luncheons for her women church friends. She was not a social climber. Needless to say, my mother was a staunch Catholic. My father was a Lutheran. Perhaps the best evidence of my mother's strength is that my father was converted to Catholicism when I was about fifteen.

I was brought up a Catholic and taught by the nuns mostly at all-girls schools. We lived in the Los Feliz area when I started school and I went to Mother of Good Council. During my first two years in school we lived in four different places. From the Los Angeles address, we moved to Balboa for about a year, and then to Phoenix for about six months. This moving around didn't help my insecurity and timidity. Jackie could charge right in and make friends right away. I would just sit by myself and brood. I was a very moody child. I experienced many traumas and many of my fears, or phobias, lingered for years. Some, no doubt, will follow me to the grave.

I have a terrible fear of suffocation. I can trace it back to the time we lived in Balboa. A friend of my parents, who was the head of Technicolor (I think his name was Fritche), came to visit my parents one Sunday. He brought his son who promptly pushed me off the end of our pier. I went in very deep and as I struggled to surface, my fear was that I would come up under the pier. That was because of a story my mother had told me about a girl who dove off a floating platform on a lake and was trapped underneath the platform.

20

Her body stayed there for days before they found it. Yet I love the water and love to swim. I just can't stand being submerged. Even when I'm in a boat, I don't want to sleep in the forward cabin, below the water line. I'm sure the boat will sink and I won't be able to escape.

When we moved from Phoenix to Pacific Palisades, I went to Saint Monica's Catholic School. As I look back on it now, I preferred the Catholic schools. I liked the discipline. The one time I attended a public school for a few months, I was shocked at the rowdiness of the students. They ran and screamed in the halls, they talked back to teachers, and to me that was total confusion. I was used to a tight ship, at school and at home.

My father was a strict disciplinarian, but not to the point where it was totally unreasonable. He wanted us to behave properly. It wasn't something he drummed into our heads. It was just something that was expected of us. We were brought up in such a way that we could go out in the world and be in any given situation and handle ourselves properly. And I admire him for that.

There were times when my father yelled just to give us a bad time. He may not have been angry, but I was never quite sure whether he was kidding or serious. I never knew when he was going to jump on me with both feet. He seldom got physical with us children, but he did get physical with my mother a couple of times, and that's when he would leave us. There would be this big blowup and the next morning he was gone.

His temper would flare to the point where he didn't have any control. The reason he didn't spank us a great deal was quite possibly because he knew he couldn't control himself when he reached a certain point. His anger was just overpowering.

Yet there was love there, too, although never a great show of affection. He would kid with us, as I said, give us a bad time. He'd laugh with us, and, of course, he did everything with the family. But even when he was kidding, you could hear him a mile away.

Both my parents were generous. I remember the soldiers'

lookout down the street from our house in the Palisades. During the war my mother would bake a cake and make lemonade every single day for the soldiers stationed there. Every Saturday my mom and dad would pick up a couple of servicemen on the coast highway and bring them home for the weekend. Some of them would return on their own laden down with coffee, sugar, steaks, butter, all scarce items during the war. My dad always loved to tell the story about the time one of the soldiers spilled a can of coffee on the kitchen floor. He was sweeping it up and was about to dump it in the trash bin when my dad came into the room and stopped him. "My God," he boomed. "I don't care what's in it. Don't throw that gold away."

During the war, with the bombing practice on the ocean below us, they couldn't even light a cigarette on the patio at night. All the heavy drapes throughout the house had to be drawn at dusk.

When times were good we lived off the fat of the land. Big houses, servants, the best of everything money could buy. The fights between my parents, like the money, or perhaps because of the money, fluctuated from minor to major. One of the worst fights I can remember happened when we lived in the Palisades. I heard them fighting in the night and the next morning my father was gone. I think I was about nine then because my brother Allen was just a little baby.

After a period of time, we went east to meet my father, who had been in contact with my mother. We went back to be with him. But first we went to visit Aunt Jean in Chicago. Her husband then was Allen Hendricks, and, as I understand it, he started the sprinkler systems used in department stores. They were wealthy and had a lovely home in, I think, Glenview.

When my mother left to meet my father in Long Branch, New Jersey, my sister Jackie and I stayed with my aunt for about a month. I did very badly. I had never been separated from my mother. I hated being there. My mother was my security blanket. I cried every single night. It got so bad that finally they just put us on a train to Long Branch.

Something very traumatic happened in Long Branch, something that completely changed my attitude on school, and quite possibly my whole life. Because of the month of school I had missed while with my aunt, I was held back a grade at the Star of the Sea Academy. From that moment on I hated school. I never got over it. Every day in school was sheer torture. I was so embarrassed about it. I think I was an average student. I never got bad grades. The fact that Jackie was not held back made me wonder about myself, it made me feel inferior, self-conscious to the point where I resented everybody and everything connected with school. But Jackie was brilliant in school. She never had to study, and she never got anything but A's. I admired her greatly, and I suppose I envied her quickness, her ability to learn with such ease that she made others feel like clods.

We lived in Long Branch—actually in West End—about four years. I was fourteen when we returned to California. We lived in North Hollywood for a few months, and this was the only time in my life that I attended a public school. It was only for a few months while I finished the eighth grade.

That summer we moved to a large house on Martel, just off Sunset, and Jackie and I went to Balboa to spend a few weeks with Aunt Jean, Uncle Allen and their daughter Patsy. They had a beautiful summer home on one of the small islands. I was fourteen that summer, and though I was still a momma's girl, I behaved far better than I had in Glenview. And besides, Los Angeles was only fifty or sixty miles up the road.

Balboa was a marvelous place for a vacation. We went swimming and sailing, ate ice cream by the ton, rode our bikes, and generally had a swell time.

Uncle Allen was the world's sweetest and jolliest human being. I just loved him. He was one of those people who could make you feel comfortable with just a look. He had the kindest eyes. Aunt Jean and Uncle Allen were like my parents in that they included Patsy and us in everything they did.

I'll never forget the night he took us out for hamburgers and then to a movie. When we got home that night, Uncle Allen went into the kitchen for a glass of milk, and, as usual,

23

sneaked a little scotch in his milk. Because he had suffered a heart attack, he was not supposed to drink any alcoholic beverages. I remember he was stretched out on the sofa and sipping his milk when I went to bed.

The next thing I remember are my aunt's footsteps coming up the hall to my room. I looked up when she came into the room and I knew without her having to say anything that there was something terribly wrong. I had felt it in the sound of her footsteps.

"I think something's wrong with Uncle Allen," she said, and her face was chalk white.

I jumped out of bed and ran into the living room. Uncle Allen was lying on the sofa with his head turned and his face against the back of the sofa. I called his name but I knew from just the way he was lying there that something horrible had happened. I reached over and gently pressed against his shoulder until I could see his face. God, it was just all blue and the eyes were blank and staring. I couldn't help it. I screamed and ran up the hallway to my room. I think I even locked the door. I never went into that living room again. Two days later I broke out with chicken pox and nearly died. Instead of the poison coming out through the vesicles, it went back into my system. My mother and aunt had gone to Chicago with Uncle Allen's body, and my father and sister Joan took care of me in the Balboa house. For years I dreamed about Uncle Allen, and the dream always started with my aunt's footsteps coming up the hall.

I started at Immaculate Heart that fall. My big dream at Immaculate was to make up the year I had lost back in the fifth grade. Somehow I was able to talk the Mother Superior into letting me take extra courses so that I could complete my education in three years.

During this period my social life was quite limited. For one thing I was still very shy, and for another my dad was very strict about my dating. Believe me, I wasn't a rip-roaring teenager. I was invited into the Tick-Tockers and the Junior Silver Spoons—they are social organizations that work for hospitals and charities.

24

To add insult to injury my first date was a disaster. I remember the incident so well, but I can't recall the boy's name or what he looked like. I was fourteen and this boy had invited me to a dance at St. Charles, which was our church. My father was driving us and I waited in the car while he went into the house to fetch the boy. He came out alone. The boy had gotten into trouble and his parents had refused to let him go to the dance. I was embarrassed to death. I wanted to crawl under the seat. It was so humiliating for me to walk back in our house. The whole family thought it was hysterical. It's just the kind of thing parents get a boot out of, but when you're fourteen, and timid to start with, you want the whole world to cave in right on top of you.

My next date was with Tom Branigan. He was fifteen and six foot four, just one long drink of water, but I had a terrible crush on him. We must have looked like Mutt and Jeff together, but that never occurred to me then. To my young girl's eyes, he was simply divine. We went "steady" for a little while, but we didn't date all that much. I never could go out during the week. I was restricted to either Friday or Saturday night. As it luckily happened, Jackie's boyfriend had a 1934 Ford, a model that was very popular with my generation. My parents allowed us to double date, which meant that I got to ride to a few dances with Tom. I remember going to a big outdoors party that summer at a large estate in Toluca Lake. I remember it because I had such a crush on Tom at that time. It was the kind of love that moves mountains, but I was scared to death every time he looked at me.

Sometimes we went to the movies, but for many years I had a phobia about movies. When I was just a child my mother took me to see *Snow White and the Seven Dwarfs*. The witch so terrified me that for years I couldn't even enter a theater. One Saturday, to get me over this, my mother made it a condition with my sisters that they couldn't go to the movies that afternoon unless they took me. They bribed me with a huge bag of candy. I was sitting there frightened to death with a lapful of candy when suddenly an oil well came in. The candy flew up in the air and I flew out of the theater.

I never heard the end of it. They were furious. I didn't really start going to the movies again until I was about thirteen. I remember watching a movie called *Ten Little Indians* while standing in the back of the theater, ready to run at a moment's notice.

I think that mostly it was a fear of the dark, coupled with my fear of loud noises. I think it all goes back to the bombing practice and my father's voice when he fought with my mother. Even now, if I'm awakened by a loud noise at night, I can't sleep for the rest of the night. My heart just palpitates like crazy, even when I can identify the cause of the noise. The fear is something beyond my control.

I had been at Immaculate less than a year when my mother was almost killed in an automobile accident. She was alone in a car when a man ran a stop sign and hit her broadside. The impact sent her flying out the door on the passenger side and they found her sixty feet away. She had multiple fractures and contusions. To make matters worse, the doctor who worked on her in emergency was drunk. It wasn't until a month later that they found several cracks in her pelvic bone. The fracture in her arm was set incorrectly which resulted in its being permanently deformed.

Because of my affection for her and my rather fragile nature, I became completely irrational at the thought that my mother might die. I was in a state of semishock for weeks. My first visit to the hospital was so traumatic that I can't even remember it. It was at this point that another major decision was made concerning my future.

My father decided that it was best to keep me home from school until I could function normally so he hired a tutor, which seemed to be the perfect solution. The tutor came in the morning and worked with me for two or three hours. He gave me textbooks, a reading list, and plenty of homework. It was the same curriculum used in high school. The only difference was that I received his undivided attention. If I didn't understand something, it was instantly explained to me. I wasn't in a class with thirty other kids where I would have to wait my turn. Besides I never could raise my hand in class and ask a question in front of all the other kids. I hated to be called upon to recite. I still don't like being the center of attention. I don't like all eyes focused on me, waiting to hear what I have to say. That just isn't me. I don't enjoy it. To me that's a performer. Yet I don't mean to convey the impression that I'm wishy-washy. I'm timid and then I'm not. I know I have tremendous strength. Just don't get me mad because I forget about being timid. There are times when I think I have my father's temper. My temper, or whatever strength I do have, has gotten me out of serious trouble on several occasions. It has earned me respect where I don't think I would have gotten any without it—but that's getting ahead of this story.

I'm sure my parents discussed my continuing with the tutor, but I wasn't in on it. As it turned out I just continued that way, and was very happy about it. I completed all my studies within a year and a half. I passed all the tests for my diploma required by the state when you have a tutor. I was only sixteen and I had finally made up the year I had lost in the fifth grade.

In the end, I don't think it was really good for me. I think that if I had gone back to Immaculate Heart, as difficult and as embarrassing as it was, I think I would—well, I probably wouldn't have married Billy Campbell. It's almost a certainty that I wouldn't have married him. The exchange with other students would have helped me develop emotionally. I would have dated more, gaining more experience with boys. Consequently, I would have matured more quickly. As it was, it took a lot longer for me to understand certain basics necessary for a successful relationship with men.

It wasn't that I was completely sheltered. I had a certain social life. I knew people through my sister Jackie. For example, before I met Billy and fell over the deep end I used to date Robert Wagner, who was just beginning in pictures. He was more a good buddy than a boyfriend. I knew his parents well. I had been to their home. They called him R. J. instead of Bob—the ''J'' is his middle initial.

II

It was Bob Wagner who took me to a party at Billy Campbell's house and started me on that bumpy road to romantic disaster. I was sixteen and Billy was in his late twenties, but he told me he was in his early twenties. I didn't discover his real age until I saw a copy of his navy discharge papers after we were married. At the time I met him Billy was living with Danny Arnold, a writer and actor who recently created the Barney Miller television series, and actor John Agar, who was married briefly to Shirley Temple.

That was a peculiar evening. Originally someone had wanted to introduce my sister Jackie to Billy. For some reason she couldn't go to the party and Billy didn't lose any time in asking me for a date. Jackie was furious with me when I started seeing Billy. Later I discovered that Billy was seeing Jackie on the sly—but that was Billy's pattern. He was never without a girlfriend the whole time I knew him. He grabbed anything within reach. As long as it was warm, he was interested.

We dated for two years before our marriage and during that period my mother and father both tried to break it up nine million times. They were in complete agreement on their opposition to him. There was no argument there. At one time they wouldn't even allow him in the house.

How I wish I had listened to my parents. If only I had not been quite so naive, so young, so damned innocent. I can only refer back to the tutor and the fact that I missed something important by not continuing in school. Perhaps I would have been more interested in going to college and then Billy would never have entered my life, or he wouldn't have entered my life the way he did.

I compare myself to Jackie, who had a very active social life in high school. She was into every fad. She did whatever was *in*. She belonged to a sorority and she just had a good time all four years. She was very outgoing and that was the difference between us. She dated Billy behind my back, and she was furious because he dated me first, but she wouldn't have marrid him for anything on earth. She was just a lot sharper than I was. Right away she saw things in him that took me years to discover. By this time Jackie, who is fourteen months older, had already started in pictures. Still she dated Billy for quite a while. Billy would drive her to an appointment or a screen test, or they just happened to be at the same place and he would bring her home, always late. They had numerous flat tires, and you have no idea how little gas that car carried.

My parents could not deter me. I just ranted and raved and fought them at every turn. I just thought they were the worst parents that ever existed. When you have strict parents, it's natural to rebel. Sometimes I think I married Billy to get away from home because the situation had become intolerable. Though they were doing only what any loving parents would do for their children, I couldn't see that at all then.

Many evenings after Billy brought me home and I had gone up to my room on the second floor, I could hear him arguing with my parents. One night they threw him out and told him never to come back. I got absolutely frantic. I don't know what the devil got into me, but I decided to leave home at that very instant and go find Billy. I had a corner bedroom and directly under my window was a cement driveway. I sat on the window ledge facing out and instead of turning myself around and hanging down by my hands before dropping to the ground, I just jumped from that sitting position. I landed on one knee and on my chest. I can still feel the pain when I think of it. I couldn't breathe and I couldn't walk. Finally I crawled to the front door and banged on it, still unable to breathe. And that really terrified me.

My parents were dumbfounded. They didn't know what had happened. One moment they thought I was in my bedroom and the next I'm at the door on all fours, gasping for breath. All they could think of was getting an ambulance. I was taken to Midway Hospital. To this day, if I kneel in a certain way, pain shoots all the way up that leg.

Eventually my parents came around. I guess they decided that it was hopeless—or more to the point, that I was hopeless. After all, what can you do with a silly little girl in love.

Disaster nearly struck the day before the wedding. There were caterers delivering chairs and tables, workmen putting up green and white awnings and installing a dance floor in the garden. It was just at that point when a big wedding is planned that all hell breaks loose: what are we going to do about this and about that, or the cake can't be here until such and such time, and so on. My father blew his stack. He refused to have anything to do with the wedding. He declared to the neighborhood in his booming voice: "I wouldn't walk her down the aisle to marry *him* for anything in the world. She's going to have to do it on her own. And that's final!" By the next morning he was fine. In fact, he cried at the altar.

The wedding was at three o'clock at St. Ambrose in West Hollywood and required special permission because you're supposed to be married before noon in the Catholic church.[1] There was a garden reception at our home with six hundred guests invited. There were white chairs and tables with white and green umbrellas, a small dance orchestra, and ten maids serving champagne and hors d'oeuvres.

My wedding gown was an elaborate three-tiered creation consisting of seventy-five yards of French tulle and chantilly

---

[1] The whole experience has been so distasteful that I can't remember the exact date of our wedding. It was either late October or late November, 1952.

lace. What a waste! When I went up to change before we left on our honeymoon, Billy's mother was crying her eyes out. My mother was so busy trying to make everyone happy that she had held back her tears. Billy's mother looked at her and said: "You have nothing to be unhappy about. You're gaining a son. I'm losing one and gaining nothing in return." She had been drinking and a moment later she vomited all over my mother's bedspread. After that it was all downhill.

Billy was her whole life. He worshipped her. Everything he did he did for his mother. He didn't like his father, who was a martinet, and the feeling was mutual. His mother was weak and his father was a bully, a very coarse man. His father completely overpowered his mother. He ran the whole show, even to doing the grocery shopping. He wouldn't even let his wife make out a grocery list.

Not long after we were married we went back to Belleville, New Jersey, to visit his parents. It was a disaster. His mother took an overdose of sleeping pills. She pulled through but she blamed me for all her troubles.

Billy's father had no respect for his son. He thought Billy was a weakling and in a sense Billy was an extremely weak man. When I knew him he had very little courage. He was a talker, not a doer. Sometimes he talked too much and to the wrong person, and on such occasions he could be backed into a corner so easily that it was embarrassing. Billy was too quick to criticize other actors. I think it's part of what ruined him in the business. He never had a nice word to say about anybody, but he would never criticize people to their faces. Of course, word got back to them and it hurt him. Gossip moves fast in Hollywood. It's a small incestuous town.

Before our marriage, of course, I saw Billy with different eyes. Because of the imperious strength of my father, I interpreted Billy's weakness as gentleness. I think I was impressed with the fact that he was impressed with himself. I thought it showed a certain confidence. His main topic of conversation was himself. The moment I strayed off that subject, he immediately lost interest. As I was to learn, that's a common trait in many actors. They live in a circumscribed world. The only wars they care about are those between New York bankers and studio chiefs. If it's not printed in the *Hollywood Reporter* or *Daily Variety,* it's not worth reading.

In a sense, Billy did the same thing to me that my parents were doing. They didn't want me to see him and Billy always kept me just on the edge where I wasn't quite sure he loved me. In his own way, Billy was keeping me at arm's length. I was fighting with my parents to see Billy and I was fighting with Billy to hang on in a number of crucial areas. Oh, I think he knew what he was doing. He was remote and displayed no jealousy, two attitudes that are very frustrating when you think you're madly in love. Love usually generates a little confusion, but with Billy it was total chaos.

Marrying Billy was like going from one keeper to another. Someone else was going to look after me. I think because of the problems that I had with Billy it took me a longer time to mature, simply because I was such a young eighteen. It was a process of growing up without my mother and father being there, and with Billy being gone most of the time, away either on location or out with the boys or his girlfriends. I was alone a great deal and could have completely withdrawn within myself—God only knows what would have happened to me. Luckily I was strong enough to avoid moving in that direction. It was a process of growing up one tiny step at a time.

I suppose Billy loved me in his own peculiar way, which was the only way he knew. Love to him was sex, and sex was just something you did at every opportunity to prove your manhood. It was strictly a biological function. He got an itch and he scratched it. Instantly! He couldn't have cared less how I felt. I thought I knew a lot about love then, but I knew nothing about sex. At first I was happy to give him that satisfaction. I never gave my own feelings a moment's notice. His happiness was all that mattered. It sounds strange now when I say, "God, if I knew then what I know now, I wouldn't have gone near him." He was such a dull, selfish human being. That was in the days before we knew about chauvinist pigs. I was nothing more than a possession. I was a pretty young girl from a good family who was totally devoted to her husband. He placed a great deal of importance on his position. He liked how we looked together. When we had parties at my parent's beautiful home, he could be very proud of the picture we presented.

Billy's drinking and eating habits had much in common with his sexual appetite. Whatever he drank he gulped right down, whether it was beer or brandy. Down the hatch. When I cooked dinner I had to fix his plate first. By the time I had fixed my plate he was already finished. I don't remember his ever cutting his food, I think he inhaled it. Then he wanted to get away from the table. In the beginning he would say, "Do you mind if I go watch TV?" What was I going to say? "No, you have to sit here with me." Before long, however, he stopped asking and just left me alone at the table.

Once he was full he left the table; once he was physically satisfied he rolled over and went to sleep. His lovemaking meant that he loaned me his body for one minute. There were long periods that he didn't come near me and it wasn't until much later that I learned that those were the times he was involved in hot and heavy romances and was just too exhausted to pay any attention to me. I was his little passive wife. And he assumed that I was happy and satisfied.

I remember what Van Heflin's wife, Frances, told me once. She was a colorful gal who always had a martini in her hand, she was great. She said: "I have the picture that Billy picks you up and sets you on the bed at night, undresses you like a child, slips this little wool flannel nightgown over your head, ties the bow at the neck and tucks you under the covers." I was nothing more than a doll, a toy that he played with when he was bored.

When he wasn't talking about Billy, or criticizing other actors, he talked about sports. When he watched football he would have two games on radio and one on television. It was never a question of "Honey, would you like to see something?" I was so intent on pleasing him that I kept telling myself that things were exactly the way they should be in a happy marriage.

This is a part of my life I hate to talk about. I know that I have to because they were formative years, and I did promise to tell the full story. But I honestly resent giving Billy this much attention. I know what he will do with it. His career is at a low ebb and he needs something to jump on to get publicity. Even if it doesn't help his career, it's all right with him as long as he gets to say something, as long as he gets his picture in the paper. He's already given several interviews in which he said that my dad borrowed money from him, and that my mom was a stage mother, who did nothing but groom Jackie for stardom. He said my mother would have done it to me if he hadn't stepped in. Of course I didn't really have any talent anyway. Oh, I'd tried to be an actress, but it just hadn't worked out. Just plain flat-out lies. Not an ounce of truth in any of it. Like reciting in class, being an actress was the last thing on earth I aspired to.

There was a time, in fact, when I had an opportunity to be a singer. When we lived in Long Branch an Italian girl lived next door to us whose parents were even more strict than mine. She was taking singing lessons and Jackie and I would go over to her house and I just started singing with her. No one knew I could sing. I didn't know it myself. One day I came home and put a Jane Powell record on the phonograph and starting singing the *Italian Street Song* along with her. My mother and father almost fainted. My father was an opera buff. He had a large collection of classical records and every Saturday we would listen to the Metropolitan Opera on the radio. Once you are familiar with classical music, especially with Italian operas, it's easy to sing along with a record and imitate the sound of the words. I loved *Un Bel Di* from *Madame Butterfly*. I liked melodic arias, music from *La Boheme,* that kind of music.

I was a coloratura when I was thirteen. Our large house at 720 Ocean Avenue in West End was right along the ocean front, across from the Colony Surf Club. When I sang people in the homes on both sides of ours would come out, and people walking by would stop and sit for the whole time I was singing. I had a natural voice. I had no training at that time. I guess the expression would be a "God-given" voice.

That summer I sang at the West End Casino a couple of

times. It was an exclusive beach club with a large ballroom. The audience was marvelous. I sang at the Colony Surf Club also and at the Versailles, where I even forgot some of the words but just went on without any embarrassment. It was really strange. There I was standing in front of all those people, their eyes focused on me, their ears attuned to my every note, and it didn't bother me at all. But God knows I couldn't have spoken two words to them. It was as if I could hide behind my voice so that they didn't really see me. They were hearing music that came from inside of me, but that wasn't really me, not the private, innermost, secret me.

On our way to California we drove to Charleston, South Carolina, to pick up my brother Freddie who was being discharged from the army. There was a delay of a few days, and one evening I sang in an auditorium jam-packed with servicemen, thousands of them, and they gave me a tremendous ovation. The next week I got the mumps and we had to stay another two weeks in Charleston.

When I turned fourteen I became very self-conscious. Everybody was going, "My, my, you've got to do something with her. You can't let this talent go to waste. She must study." It was then that I began to be frightened by it and became more and more aware of myself, until finally I wouldn't sing in front of anybody. I'd sing at home, but I wouldn't sing for anyone except myself. My career collapsed before it even got off the ground. Contrary to what Billy said, my parents didn't push it one way or the other.

Not long before I married Billy, one of Jackie's agents, either Walter or Paul Kohner, was talking to my mother on the phone and he heard me singing in the background. He said, "My God, who's that singing?" My mother said, "That's Judy." He said, "That's Judy? Why haven't you told me about her? Can we do something with her?" My mother said, "I don't know, I doubt it.' He said, "I'd like to come over and hear her sing." My mother asked me and I said, "Well, all right." But deep down I knew it would never work. The minute he walked in through the door my throat constricted.

Sometime later, after I married Billy, the Kohners set up

an audition for Joe Pasternak at MGM studios, in a large room in the Thalberg building. I stood by a big grand piano and tried to loosen my voice, but it felt really tight. I did sing for Pasternak but it wasn't right. Pasternak told them, ''She's got a tremendous talent, but she's got to relax. Tell her to continue to study and I want to see her again in four months.'' I did study with a woman but I didn't pursue a singing career, I never went back to Pasternak or anybody else. It was just something I did for my own pleasure.

The strange thing is that when I talk about my life, particularly my life with Billy, it's as if it happened to someone else. Possibly that's because I'm such a different person now. It took me a long time to wake up and discover that I was a person, too. I went through a period during which I became very afraid at night. The minute it began to get dark, I had a feeling inside me that can only be described as panic. When we'd go out to dinner, I couldn't sit in a restaurant for any length of time because I'd start to feel sick to my stomach. Nighttime became unbearable. I thought I was going out of my mind. I couldn't watch any show about mental illness. I think that was a turning point for me. Either I was going to go stark raving mad, or I was going to start to think for myself and grow up.

I was alone so much of the time and I didn't really see a lot of Billy. I wasn't allowed to go on location with him because he always had a new girlfriend to take along, usually one of the actresses in the picture. He went away on vacations by himself. I went on one location only because Jackie had a small part in the picture. Even when he went into Schwab's (a drugstore on Sunset that's a hangout for a certain class of actors and buffs), I always had to wait in the car. I suppose he just didn't want to create the impression that he was tied down to one person.

He was a fight fan and he would go to the fights all the time. ''I'm going to the fights tonight,'' he would say, and before I could reply he was gone. A few times I found there weren't even any fights that night. Needless to say I wasn't invited to any sporting event.

My social life with him was only in people's homes for dinners and parties, and at our home when we entertained. Parties were where Billy would really shine. He always managed to get somebody in the kitchen or hallway for a little party of his own.

The whole group we socialized with was notorious for playing around. I don't say that all of them did, but there were plenty who kept up with Billy. Steve Forest was really a chaser. Once I was supposed to go horseback riding with him and his wife Chris, but he neglected to tell Chris about it. Then he told me she couldn't go, but had asked that we go ahead anyway. The whole day was sheer agony. Steve was one of those relentless pursuers. Luckily I had a horse under me and could get away. It was a constant chase.

When Billy was away and I would have dinner with them, I'd no sooner get back home than the phone would ring and it would be Steve asking me to meet him someplace. He thought he was so charming that I'd give in at some point. He was good looking but he ruined it with this overbearing attitude. He thought he was irresistible, and that makes a man very unattractive.

Others in the group included Mike and Mary Lou Connors (he was known as Touch Connors then), John and Millie Erickson, Hugh O'Brien, Charlton and Lydia Heston, and Lloyd and Dottie Bridges—I just have to laugh when I think about Lloyd Bridges. He was the most persistent of players. His wife Dottie was overweight, but Lloyd didn't care what she looked like. All he cared about was his waistline, the size of his muscles, that he stood up straight, kept his stomach sucked in, his tan the right shade—narcissism in its most basic state.

Gary Morton, who was once married to my sister Jackie and is now Lucille Ball's husband, used to do a hilarious routine about a guy preening and prancing beside a swimming pool with his stomach sucked in, muscles flexed, who would ask, "Any girls around?" When the answer was no, everything collapsed. "Okay," he'd say, "let's go swimming."

We called Lloyd Bridges "Bud." Well, Bud would corner me at every party, and for a while I was flattered by the attention. I didn't get it from Billy and I must say he was a lot smoother than Steve Forest. I visited Bud on the *Sea Hunt* set a few times. My father called him the cross-eyed underwater cowboy. Bud is dreadfully bowlegged, but I didn't care about that or about his physique. In a sense, seeing him gave me a feeling of freedom. He was fun to be with, very pleasant, good-natured, and loved the attention of attractive women. He was Mr. Charm.

One of the most amusing evenings I can remember spending when I was married to Billy was the time we went to dinner at the home of our houseboy. We knew he was gay and we knew he had money, but we had no idea how rich or how swishy he really was until we arrived at his home.

He dropped hints that he worked only because he loved doing it. And only for certain people. I know he took great pleasure in going through my wardrobe. he thought I had the most divine clothes. He came to clean three times a week and he did the catering when we had parties. He was an accomplished cook and he could bake the most magnificent pastries.

Among some of Billy's friends that he worked for was Bobby Van, the dancer, who was then married to Diane Garrett. The Vans were also invited to dinner that evening and we arrived together at this fabulous home, which was on two or three levels and elegantly furnished.

The next shock came when he opened the door. He was wearing a black sheath dress with at that time fashionable sheer material above the bustline and long puffed sleeves of the same material going to the wrist. The dress had a shaped bustline and he wore a strapless bra with falsies. His hair was blond and rather short, but he had the front brushed up so that it looked like the kind of hairdo a woman with short hair might wear. I had an aunt who wore her hair exactly like that. He had flowers pinned around the back so that they just cupped around the real short part of his hair. He had a great pair of legs and wore plastic Springalator shoes that had a sheer plastic strip across the arch and no sling in the back and were very high heeled. His hose were very sheer and their seams perfectly straight.

We were just dumbfounded when he opened that door. Luckily, we had big smiles on our faces and hellos on our lips. It took us a moment to realize that a man had answered the door. Knowing his preference was one thing, but seeing him in drag was another story.

He served a sumptuous dinner but we ate rather quickly. We played it straight because we didn't want to offend him. The fact that we knew he was gay was probably the reason he felt he could do this in front of us, be completely himself without fearing that we might turn around in disgust and walk out. He didn't feel he was offending us by doing it.

After dinner he put on an elaborate fashion show, modeling five different coats: a silver mink, a black diamond, a white, and two others I can't remember. He modeled cocktail dresses, long evening dresses, dressing gowns, and his patter was going a mile a minute as he swished around with material flowing and his arms moving like a Vogue model. He got away with it because he laughed at himself before we had a chance to. He was amused at our being amused at the whole situation, which made it even more amusing, but comfortable. It wasn't at all awkward.

By the end of the fashion show I think the men felt like "Well, okay, we've seen it all. This has gone far enough." But for me it was a perfectly delightful evening.

Far more delightful I might add than most of the evenings spent at the homes of Billy's actor friends. Perhaps I should qualify the word friend. Billy was just a young struggling actor when I met him. He was under contract at Warner Brothers and he went from there to MGM and later to Universal. They all had plans for him at one time or another, but there was a certain something in his personality that really hurt him. He wasn't a bad actor in the beginning, but the big plans never materialized. Yet Billy was working and this was Hollywood in the 1950's. If you were under contract, you were popular, you had friends. I mean if you gave a party, people would come to your party, and you'd be invited to their parties. As long as you were under contract, you were "in" and everyone stayed friendly with the actors who were working. It was survival.

As far as Billy was concerned I could go anywhere I wanted. He didn't care what I did as long as I left him alone. But until my mother taught me to drive I was stranded at home. Home was a modest house in the Hollywood Hills above Chateau Marmonte. After I learned to drive I took his Oldsmobile and he bought himself a Thunderbird. Then I started going places. I started going to the beach with Marlene Wessel, who became my best friend. Her parents owned clothing stores in Whittier and through her I did some modeling for the Anne Fogarty line. The representatives of the Anne Fogarty Company, a very nice couple, didn't like using professional models because of the style of the dresses—more sweet than sophisticated. It was fun, and it was something to do. It was about this time that I began to sketch the faces of children. Later I began to work in charcoal and oil.

I kept busy. I took extension courses at UCLA. Marlene and I went to Palm Springs. Once we went to Las Vegas. Slowly but surely I began asserting myself. I became a fantastic door slammer. I shattered quite a few full-length door mirrors. If there was a mirror on a door that I slammed, it had to go. Thank God I'm not superstitious.

Then one night I finally gathered up the courage to confront Billy at a party. He had been so revolting all evening long. Yet when I walked into the kitchen and found him pawing this girl, I didn't know where to turn. The only thing I could think of was what he was doing. So I said, "I'm going home and you're going with me." You know, Big Gutsy, me. He said, "No, I'm not going home." So then I said something about the girl being a tramp, some ridiculous thing, and he whacked me right across the face. When I think back on it now, I'm grateful to Billy for that blow. It did more to straighten me out than anything that happened in our marriage. I thought, "What are you doing to yourself? Do you like living in torture? Do you like being humiliated?"

As these thoughts flashed through my head, I was driving away from the party which was at a house on top of the Hollywood Hills. My eyes were blurred with tears and the road was steep and narrow and crooked. I don't know how I survived driving down that mountain. It was a scene right out of a Bette Davis movie.

From that time on my life began to change seriously. Actually in the last two years of our marriage I saw very little of Billy. Then one day while Billy was on location in Panama I met someone I had known before, and had disliked for a long while. He went with Jackie at one time and suddenly I really fell for him. His name is Travis Kleefeld, and he used the stage name Tony Travis. He was of medium build and very attractive. He loved to have a good time and he had a great sense of humor. He was crazy about women, a terrible flirt, but discreet about it. If he was cheating, it wasn't done openly to hurt me.

We were both violently jealous. He'd get mad if I even looked sideways, and I'd get mad when he looked straight ahead. That kind of attitude in the player atmosphere we lived in doomed our relationship from the beginning. Yet we lived together nearly two years before breaking up. In the meantime, we had terrible fights but they never lasted for any great length of time although each one added to the tension that was slowly building up.

At first his jealousy fed my ego. The fact that someone could get so mad at me just because I looked at another man was a new experience. Billy never gave a damn where I went or what I did—that is, until he found out I was leaving him. When he first heard that I had fallen for Travis, fallen for another man, he just couldn't believe it. As I was to learn later, his ego refused to accept it.

III

It's almost impossible to describe the exhilaration I felt being out of Billy's house, the great feeling that came over me the day I walked out. It was like the whole world was welcoming me with open arms.

I rented a small apartment in a Regency-style building just off Doheny, near Sunset. I kept some clothes and a few of my things in the apartment because it was my anchor, a place I could call my own. I never again wanted to be totally dependent on a man. My life with Billy made it really impossible for me to completely trust a man for many, many years.

Somewhere in the back of my mind I think I realized that going from Billy to Travis was like going from home to Billy. I was running away, I was seeking shelter, and really not being on my own. I wasn't learning to live with myself. Again I was leaning on someone else. It wasn't until I broke up with Travis that I started dating the way most girls date when they're in high school. But even with Travis, I started to learn more about other people in relation to me, not in relation to my husband. I'd never had any personal contact with people just for myself. I was Billy's shadow for so many years that it took time before I could step out confidently into the light. Gradually, I started to enjoy life and people in a different way, but I still didn't trust them. There wasn't a man alive I trusted.

Meanwhile back in the Hollywood Hills Billy had gone

berserk. Instead of sending him a "Dear John" letter when he was on location in Panama (I think they were shooting a war movie), I waited until he telephoned one night and then suddenly I blurted out that I was leaving him for good. Of course he didn't believe me. He gave it his usual response: "Oh, take it easy. You're just a little upset. You'll calm down."

By the time he got back to town I had flown the coop. I had taken the sterling dishes and trays my parents and relatives had given us for our wedding, my clothes, and my easels and paints. I didn't take another thing, not a dish, not a stick of furniture, not a book, not even a record, and there were many that I treasured.

When I first moved in with Travis he was living in an apartment belonging to Jackie Loughry, who later married Jack Webb. Travis had swapped his New York apartment for it. Then one Sunday morning Billy came looking for me with blood in his eyes.

There was a knock at the door and Travis asked who it was. Billy yelled, "Let me in. I know my wife's in there."

God, I had on only a robe and we were on the second floor and there was no back door. Billy stood in front of the only exit. As I ran toward the back bedroom, I could hear Travis saying, "No, she isn't here." The back bedroom was being used as a storage place and there was junk everywhere. I slipped out of my robe and grabbed my dress. I remember it was a black and white check with a full skirt—the style then was to wear two or three stiff petticoats underneath for a ballooning effect—and a long-sleeved tailored jacket that ended right under the bustline. I managed to slip into the dress but I had nothing else on when the front door opened and Billy came rushing in, ranting and raving at the top of his lungs. I looked under the bed and thought, "You can't hide there, that's the first place anybody looks." I opened the doors of the closet which was loaded with clothes and things piled up on the floor. I got one shoe on and struggled to squeeze myself between the clothes. While doing this, I managed to get a sleeve of the jacket over my right arm. I closed the doors just as Billy burst into the room, screaming bloody murder. But just as the doors shut I got a glimpse of my three petticoats standing stiffly in a corner of the room and I just knew Billy would recognize them.

The first thing Billy did was look under the bed. Then he headed for the closet and threw both doors open. My right arm, the one with the sleeve, was sticking out of the clothes a good three inches, but he was so mad that he didn't even notice it. If he had looked he would have known that it was a real arm in that sleeve. He pushed clothes around and growled viciously. How he didn't even feel me standing there I'll never know. I was close to having a heart attack. I knew that if he found me he'd kill me. He was that violently angry. I don't think there's a worse anger than that derived from a wounded ego. Especially when that ego belongs to an egotist.

Finally, now even more frustrated, he left the apartment, still screaming and yelling, "I'm going to find her." After the door was closed and locked behind him I got out of the closet and dressed. Then I called Marlene Wessel, who lived only two blocks away, to set up an alibi. But as I was talking to Marlene, I heard Billy's voice in the background and it was then that I realized she was carrying on with Billy. While I was still on the phone she told Billy where I was calling from.

The panic was on again. While I was telephoning, Travis's brother-in-law, Jim Wilson, had come into the apartment and Travis had told him what was happening. Jim said, "Come on," and he grabbed me and pulled me down the stairs to his Jaguar sedan parked in the driveway. He pushed me down on the floor of the back seat and put a blanket over me. Just as he was backing out of the driveway, Billy came barreling down the street and skidded to a screeching stop in front of the apartment house. He jumped out of the car and ran up the steps just as I was making my getaway.

Two months later Billy paid us a call in the middle of the night. We were then staying in Bobby Van's apartment. Billy was drunk and violent. When Travis refused to open the door, Billy tore the screen off the window next to the door and began pounding on the glass so hard that Travis had to go out and talk to him. Billy tried to hit him and Travis came back in and called the police. When they arrived Billy started to cry. He said, ''My wife is in there and we're not divorced and I love her. I want her back.'' The cops felt sorry for him. They kept glancing suspiciously at Travis, but Billy was so drunk they had to cart him away.

For two years Billy was a madman. He drank twenty-four hours a day. He called me at all hours of the day and night, and he'd cry on the phone. He promised to take me anyplace in the world I wanted to go if only I would come back to him. He called my sisters and my parents. He even tried to break into my parents' home. He turned into the most pathetic creature. He even married a girl who looked like me. The love and then the hate I had felt for him now turned to pity.

I filed for divorce in April 1958, and it was final on April 24, 1959—that date I do remember. The divorce attorneys wanted to do all kinds of dreadful things to Billy, but I refused to go along with them. They wanted him followed, they wanted him to pay all the income tax, they wanted two thousand dollars a month alimony. I asked for five hundred dollars a month and it was scheduled to run five years, but at the end of two years I just couldn't stand it any longer. I didn't want his money. I didn't want anything from him. I signed it all back for a lump-sum settlement of six thousand dollars. Besides I didn't need his money. Through my father I was getting money from Grandma Immoor. At least that's what my father told me, but I've often thought that it came from him and my mother. For many years my father claimed me as a dependent and provided quite handsomely for my well-being.

Travis was a singer. He had a good voice, but he too had his problems, and had been in analysis for five years before we started living together. Travis's problems started when his father committed suicide. His father had been a very success- ful builder and was quite wealthy. After the war, he had built thousands of tract homes in the valleys surrounding Los Angeles.

With Travis I began to move in different circles. Many of his friends were wealthy businessmen. Some had winter homes in Palm Springs and we began going there regularly, staying either at the Racquet Club or at the homes of friends like Bob Whittaker who headed a large financial empire. Other good friends included Dick Elwood, who was in electronics, and Marshall Edson, who owned the Little Club in Beverly Hills.

Travis's friends became my friends. I wasn't as withdrawn. For the first time in my adult life, I started communicating with people. Instead of saying, "How do you do?" I'd talk with them. I had a completely different attitude. I learned to enjoy conversations with people. They were not people who sat around talking about themselves, or about their next picture. There were some actors in the group, but they were on a different level.

I had this new found freedom, but I was still shy in given areas and I still couldn't put myself in a position where I knew attention was focused on me. For example, Travis and his mother, Sylvia, were both members of the Beverly Hills Tennis Club. We spent considerable time there and at first I just sat and watched. I avoided taking lessons because I wasn't totally comfortable doing it. The learning process, when you look awkward, is what bothered me. If there was no one around, I enjoyed playing games. That was the ideal situation.

When I was a little girl people would come up to my mother and say, "What a beautiful child. She's going to be a great beauty when she grows up." I never quite believed it. I never was that thrilled with my appearance. Once I grew out of the little girl stage, it took many years before I would wear a bathing suit and then only in fairly private places. There were too many girls who looked so sensational in bikinis. They made me feel like something inside of me was missing. I felt I just couldn't stack up. Slowly, I got over some of these feelings, but not entirely. After a while I even took tennis lessons, and that was a giant step forward.

Falling in love with Travis at that time was the best thing that could have happened to me. For the first time in my life, I was important to a man. He taught me what it was to be made love to and to make love. He was very open in his

46

lovemaking. I learned that when you love someone there is no good and bad, there are no boundaries for those two people. I felt joy in making love. With Billy it had been a biological function, with Travis it was total freedom without guilt.

Also with Travis I was back more or less in my natural element. He enjoyed good food, fine wines, caviar—his whole family loved caviar—and I was back to living the way I had and enjoying the things I had grown up with.

For a long time there wasn't any doubt in my mind that we would be married when my divorce became final. But the insecurity we both felt in ourselves really intensified our jealousy. I think jealousy and a little possessiveness is good when you're in love. It's natural. But when it goes beyond that point then that's a problem you have within yourself. The greater the insecurity, the greater the jealousy.

When I think back on it, I feel that I was the one who caused the breakup. We were having difficulty together and in some ways I think I was growing beyond that way of life. I had kept my apartment because I couldn't live with the idea that Travis was keeping me. I knew so many girls in that situation. My apartment was my shelter. In the event of an argument, I had a place of my own to mend my wounds. After two years with Travis, I felt I needed to be completely on my own. Yet I was afraid to let go.

Finally, in August 1959, I went to New York for two weeks on a trial separation with Alice Wallace, who was a former model for Oleg Cassini, and we stayed at the Plaza. Time goes very fast when you're in New York on a vacation. You sleep late in the morning, you meet friends for lunch, you go shopping, you meet friends for cocktails at four, and by the time you finish with cocktails, it's time to go back and change for dinner engagements. Alice was contacting a number of people she hadn't seen in a while.

Alice Wallace was a lovely woman. She later married Kem Dibbs, who worked for Bob Whittaker as a personal aide. He arranged all the entertaining for Bob. Many of Bob's subsidiaries worked on government contracts, and I remember dinners and parties for generals and government officials.

Kem could always come up with a bevy of pretty girls to decorate the room.

When I came back from New York, Travis and I had dinner and we talked it out. The next day I moved into my sister Jackie's Beverly Hills apartment. It was one of those things: I couldn't live with him and I couldn't live without him. But I knew I had to try. We saw a great deal of each other in the next few months. It wasn't as if I had completely cut that cord. But it was different now. I was completely and totally on my own. Travis eventually became a great friend of mine in succeeding years. I could call and cry on his shoulder. He was that kind of person. At that point in my life, I can't think of anyone who could have been better for me. He was there when I needed him. Contrary to what has been written about me, I am a one-man woman. When I am with someone, I don't see the other men in the room. I'm grateful that Travis was that man at that moment.

IV

The first indication I had that Frank Sinatra was interested in meeting me was when Nick Sevano approached me one night while I was having dinner with friends at Puccini's.

Nick said, "I really would like you to meet Frank."

I had known Nick for a number of years. I think he was connected with Paramount when Jackie was under contract. I said, "Thanks, but I've met Frank at parties."

Nick laughed. "You know what I mean. Would you like to go out with him?"

"Yes," I said, without hestitation. "I'd like to go out with him."

Frank called a couple of days later and invited me to dinner but I already had plans for that evening. A few nights later, again at Puccini's, Frank himself approached our booth. He had been sitting at a large table with a group of friends and I could feel that he was watching me. He sat down and we talked briefly. He was extremely charming. Before going back to his table, he said he'd call me again, and I didn't discourage him. I've never been a game player in any relationship. I have never worked out any kind of strategy that keeps a man guessing. Some women spend all their time playing games.

Frank called me the very next day and he didn't waste any time. He said he was going to Hawaii, and would I like to go with him. We had quite a discussion. I liked the prospect of going to Hawaii and of seeing Frank, getting to know him, but I wasn't giddy about it.

I refused to go on the same plane with him but I promised to meet him there. He didn't sound too happy about it, but I tried to explain that I just didn't like the way that looked. I was sensitive about it. I could see what my getting on a plane with Frank Sinatra would look like to other people, and how it would sound in the gossip columns. I wanted to see him, I wanted to go to Hawaii, but I didn't want to go that way. He came around, but I think he thought I was going to stand him up.

I took the midnight flight on November 9, 1959, and I arrived at 6:45 the next morning—they were still flying propeller planes at that time. I went directly to the Surfrider Hotel. They didn't have a reservation in my name, but they gave me room 1509. I just stretched out on the bed until Frank called later in the morning and asked me to come up to his penthouse suite. There were two suites on the penthouse floor, one at each end, with two rooms in between. Frank had one suite, Pat and Peter Lawford had the other, and Dr. Leone Krohn (they called him Red) and his wife, Ester, occupied one of the rooms. I was given the other.

My nerves were strung pretty tight when I walked into Frank's suite. I hadn't been with him except for that brief moment at Puccini's. We had talked on the phone, but phone conversations are a lot easier if the person I'm talking with takes the initiative. If they wait for me to direct the conversation, then the phone is not easy for me. Frank was an artist on the phone. He had everything under control, and that was just fine with me. The rapport we seemed to have established on the phone left me anticipating the time we would be together. There is no question that I was attracted to him, and I was looking forward to a good time, but I certainly wasn't thinking of falling in love. I was still trying to get over Travis.

Frank, Peter, Pat, Red, Ester, and Al Hart were in the suite when I arrived.

AUTHOR'S NOTE: *A former liquor distributor who had connections with Joseph Fusco, a Chicago gangster who started out in the rackets as a beer-runner for Al Capone, Al Hart later headed the City National Bank of Beverly Hills.*

There were others, as there always were others around Frank, but he never bothered introducing them. They were hangers-on, bodyguards, gofers, flunkies, men who were always there but who never spoke unless spoken to. They moved in and out of the suite, but you hardly noticed them at all. It was almost the same with Al Hart. He was in and out, and I seem to remember him being there that first day, but it could have been the next day. He sticks in my mind because of the comical image he presented when he walked out in swim trunks. They were of a jersey material, jockey style, very tight, and his paunch and saddlebags hung over his waistline like an innertube. None of the parts—legs, arms, torso, head—seemed to go together. He reminded me of a koala bear.

It was a leisurely afternoon. We sat out on the patio, which ran the whole length of the penthouse floor, a tremendous area, and though the drinking was pretty heavy, the conversation was light and airy. There was a lot of hip talk. Frank and Pete—somehow Pete never seemed right for Peter Lawford—communicated in a language of their own. It was a mixture of slang, a vernacular that originated with hip musicians, comics, hoodlums and teenagers. Their favorite words were gas and gasser, clyde, bunter, cool, crazy, harvey, fink, mother, hacked, smashed, pissed, charley, and, of course, ring-a-ding, or ring-a-ding-ding, depending on the enthusiasm of the moment. The meaning of many of these expressions seemed to change daily. This was at a time when Frank was known as The Leader (he was also The General, The Dago, The Pope) of the Rat Pack, which he inherited from the late Humphrey Bogart. The name of the group was later refined to the Clan. Besides Lawford, the membership included Dean Martin, Sammy Davis, Jr., Joey Bishop, Sammy Cahn, Sy Devore, Mike Romanoff, Jimmy Van Heusen, and for a time, Eddie Fisher and Elizabeth Taylor.

Much of their conversation, as I was soon to learn, was inconsequential. They communicated by using only the punch lines, or buffo lines, as they called them, to *in* jokes. If you didn't know the joke, you had no idea what the words meant. They might just as well have been talking Chinese. Much of the time I sat there smiling while they slapped their thighs and guffawed. There was little said worth remembering. When people use words or talk about subjects or people that I'm not familiar with, I have a tendency to daydream.

Pete made the only remark that afternoon that I can recall. It got me off to a bad start with Pat Lawford almost immediately.

Pete turned to his wife and said, "Look how beautiful Judy's hair is. Isn't it marvelous? Pat, why can't your hair look like Judy's?" That's not what you say to your wife, especially a Kennedy wife. Of course, at that time I knew nothing about the Kennedys. I was not a politically oriented person. I knew the names of California senators, but I knew little about senators from other states. Just the same, it didn't take me long to get a bearing on Pat Lawford. There was no question that she was the strong one in that family. She's such a strong woman. Looking back on it now, Pete is all flowery speeches and no guts. The expression I've heard used is that Pete is a steer, not a bull. I think that fits him and perhaps it also fits the other men married to Kennedy women. They marry weaker men. Anytime I see Sargent Shriver and his wife on television, when she talks, I see Pat and hear Pat. There's a certain strength there, and when Shriver talks I get the same feeling that I would get from Lawford. There's something unmistakable about the Kennedy women. They are their father. They've got the same strength as the men in the family. Except perhaps for Teddy. Somehow I feel less strength from Teddy than Pat. That could be because he was the baby of the family. Very often there's a change in personality with the baby.

Prior to Pete's observation about my hair, Pat had just remarked that the humidity in Hawaii was doing terrible things to her hair. It was obvious from looking at her that her problem involved more than humidity. The humidity was terrible, but Pat doesn't have the greatest hair in the world to work with. Besides she doesn't seem to care that much about her appearance. I've known many people like her. Because they are so terribly wealthy, they kind of flaunt it. The attitude is, "I've got so much, why care?" It's a sort of Howard Hughes syndrome.

Pat could be an attractive woman. All it takes is a little pride in yourself. If you can't have pride in yourself, there's something missing somewhere. It's so much nicer to look upon something that's pleasant than something that is deliberately ugly. When a woman is deliberately disheveled or doesn't give a damn about herself, that's very distasteful, and it's just as distasteful with a man. Pat never seemed to care what she wore. Her favorite outfit was blue jeans and a blouse. On the other hand, Pete was a fashion plate.

Speaking about things that are distasteful, Frank's favorite colors are orange and black. It's a color scheme that makes me feel like I'm at a Halloween party. All his swim trunks were a vivid orange or black. His idea of a sharp outfit would consist of black slacks, an orange shirt, and a black alpaca golf sweater. The only flower I ever saw in any of his homes or hotel suites was the bird of paradise. There were at least twenty-five of them in that penthouse suite. You couldn't turn your head an inch without having another one staring at you. The motif of his Palm Springs home was orange and black. And when I say orange, I mean orange orange.

That afternoon I called a record shop, and ordered a copy of every album Frank had made, with instructions that they get them elsewhere if they didn't stock them all. I still have a copy of the bill from the House of Music, $47.87 for nine albums. They were delivered to his suite, and although Frank never said very much about it, they were played constantly.

That first evening there was a barbeque on the patio for about twenty people. The view of the city, the soft night air, the moon, the stars—it was all magnificent. I couldn't get over how beautiful it was. The setting was absolutely entrancing.

It was a perfect evening. I sat next to Frank and he was very attentive and very charming. As always, there was a lot of kidding and laughter. Everybody was smiling, and, as I was soon to learn, whenever Frank was happy, everybody was happy. And grateful. Because when Frank scowled, there were no happy faces around.

After dinner, when everybody had wandered off, Frank and I sat on a couch on the patio. I felt relaxed and contented. We listened to his records and now and then he would hum a few bars. It was very romantic.

Then his mood seemed to change when the song *Here's My Rainy Day* was playing. It's a very touching song and for some reason I had the feeling that he associated it with Ava Gardner. He became quiet, very sad looking, as he listened to it. Later he said the song had a special meaning for him, but I didn't pursue it.

We kissed. He was gentle, and really very sweet. After a while he stood up, took my hand, and said softly, "Let's go inside." He put his arm around my waist and steered me into his bedroom. He was very gentle, romantic, expressive, sensual, and very active when we made love, and very loving afterward. He seemed genuinely concerned that I was happy and just kept his arms around me all night long. We made love again during the night and when we awakened in the morning. It was the most idyllic night I ever spent with Frank.

It was a lazy week. People kept coming in and out of Frank's suite. We sat in the sun—Frank worked hard on his tan—and drank Jack Daniels. One day flowed into the other without any noticeable transition. Much of it was not memorable, but there were moments that remain with me.

Frank and I went shopping one day, just the two of us, and we had great fun. We went to a market and he was like a kid in a candy store. We bought milk, bread, cheese, and piled all kinds of delicacies into a shopping cart. He got such a kick out of it that it was obviously a long time since he had been in a market. For a moment he was able to act like an ordinary shopper. People paid very little attention to him, which was surprising since he was then at the peak of his career. The only damper on the day was when we went into a department store. I bought a purse, hose, a scarf, and a full petticoat, and he wasn't too thrilled when I wouldn't let him pay for them. But it was no major catastrophe. We even walked back to the hotel holding hands.

On the third night we went to a Japanese restaurant. We had a private room and sat on pillows while two Japanese girls cooked the dinner at our table. Pat was getting annoyed at the attention Frank and Pete were paying the girls, and vice versa—Japanese girls know how to stroke a man's ego. Pat whispered a few snide remarks about the girls. She thought the boys were going overboard in their attention, but they were just having a good time; much of it, I think, was designed to pull our leg. Finally, completely exasperated, Pat scribbled on a cocktail napkin and passed it over to me. The first thing I noticed was the strength and boldness of her handwriting. It looked more like a man's writing, with the letters going straight up and down. She wrote: "I still think they're full of shit!" She had shit underlined about seven times. Pat's language is basic. There's nothing flowery about her speech. When she wants to emphasize a point, she has no hesitation about using four-letter words.

One afternoon while everybody was sitting around in the living room, two Japanese girls—pretty, delicate little things—were escorted into Frank's bedroom. Frank and Pete stood up and Frank said something about it being time for their massage. It was so blatantly obvious. You just knew what the score was. Neither one was just getting a massage, there just wasn't a chance. The funny thing is that I don't remember really caring. Pat was furious. To Red Krohn and Ester, who were close to Frank, there was nothing unusual about it.

That evening Frank excused himself and said he was going to lie down a while. He didn't feel too sharp. Pat and the others disappeared and the first thing I knew there was just Pete and me sitting there finishing our drinks. Pete came over and sat next to me on the sofa, and after a little light banter, he just casually suggested that we take a walk on the beach. The way he said it, it was plain he had other things on his mind besides walking. I told him I didn't think so. The British accent got a little more pronounced as he leaned forward to look deep into my eyes. "But darling," he said, touching my hand, "don't worry, Frank will never know." He was a little high and coming on a little too strong. I took my hand away and stood up. "Thank you," I replied, "but I really don't think so." He stood up and gave me his most boyish grin. "Look, I'll call Pat and tell her I'm going to take a walk on the beach. Come on, why not?" I figured the easiest way out of it was to play along. "All right," I said. "Let me go to my room first. I want to freshen up and get a wrap. It may be a little chilly out there. When you get downstairs, call me and I'll meet you on the beach." I felt like adding, "If I'm late, start without me." I went to my room, locked my door, and went to bed. The phone rang a long time but I didn't pick it up.

The next morning, which was Saturday, Frank seemed a little perturbed. "What happened?" he asked. "Why didn't you just come in when you wanted to go to bed?"

"I went to my room," I said. "I thought you weren't feeling well."

He let it go at that but I could tell he was disappointed. Although we had been sleeping together since the first night, I kept my clothes and cosmetics in my own room down the hall. When I wanted to set my hair or do my face, or shower and freshen up, I had a room I could go to. I never would have moved into his room, even if it meant getting a room on a different floor. I still needed that little shelter away from everybody, a place I could call my own, preferably a place I could pay for with my own money. That made me feel independent.

Pete had an even longer face when he came into the suite, but he had the good grace not to mention it. That afternoon the four of us—Frank, Pete, Pat and I—went to play golf. I should say we went to the golf course. I rode in an electric cart with Frank but I certainly didn't play golf.

Something strange began to happen out there. Frank was

getting sullen and I could see that it had nothing to do with his game. He and Pete did a lot of talking as they fooled around the greens, and I had the feeling that they were talking about me. Later, when I looked back on it, I felt that Pete might have said something about me to Frank. I was the new girl in the crowd. Pete was a trusted friend. It occurred to me that Pete might have wanted to protect himself in case I said something to Frank about the night before. I could visualize him saying something like, "Boy, is she something. I don't know how you feel about her, Frank, but be careful." Then he could twist it around and say that I had suggested a walk on the beach, and he being the good trusted friend that he was, had naturally rejected my advances.

That evening we went out to dinner and it was a nightmare. There were about twelve of us seated at a rectangular table, and Frank and I were facing a dark-haired woman and her husband, who was loaded. In fact, everybody was pretty well loaded. The dark-haired woman, in her middle thirties, was completely enthralled with Frank, who was gradually getting vicious with everyone except her. He would stare at her, openly flirting, and had no interest in anyone else. He totally ignored me. A couple of times I asked him what was wrong, and he just looked at me and there was a surly expression on his face as he snapped, "Nothing."

If I had known what he was really like I would have told him to go stuff it. I'd have gone back to the hotel for my bags and would have been on a plane back to the mainland that night. But I was confused. I thought, how can this charming, loving person all of a sudden turn so ugly?"

"What did I do?" I asked again. "If I did something, please tell me."

He looked like he was going to spit on me. "Nothing," he said, and if he could have just turned his back to me, I think he would have. I finally just didn't talk to him.

I've had time to think about Frank Sinatra and his Jekyll and Hyde personality. This will come up again in the book, but for the moment I'd like to say that I was not totally unaware of his reputation as a tough guy. I had read about his bodyguards and his fights in public places. Without trying to analyze him, it's possible that much of it has to do with the fact that he's a tiny man with a big man complex. Frank gets considerably shorter when he takes his shoes off. He's heavyset today but his bone structure is small. His wrists are delicate. In his mind he feels he's a big man, that he has power, and the way he proves it is to push people around.

Everybody around Frank walks on eggs all the time. Everybody is smiling and happy when Frank is smiling and happy, but the minute Frank starts to frown, everybody is quiet and fearful. No one dares talk back to him. He berates everybody mercilessly and they take it and take it. It's a very distasteful atmosphere to be in. I resent seeing people who are recognized for their own accomplishments take his tongue lashing and kow-tow to him in the bargain. Frank knows what he's doing. He was always careful about what he said to Pat, since she was a Kennedy, but he just pulverized Pete at will.

Once he gets someone under his thumb, it's never-ending. He will just mistreat that person whenever it suits him, whenever he gets in one of his black moods and needs to abuse something or someone. He will do it to those who will take it. And he'll try it with some who won't, but not too often. I think when Frank gets into fights or when people are hurt by his bodyguards, it's because he picked the wrong person to give a bad time to. There are people who say, "I don't give a damn whether you're Frank Sinatra or Jesus Christ. Nobody talks to me like that."

When we got to the hotel that night, I went directly to my room. I asked Red Krohn to come in and I said, "What's the matter? What's happening?" He said, "Don't pay any attention to it. He'll be okay." So I left it at that. When I went in the next day and saw that Frank was the same way, I told him I was leaving. I said I had things to take care of at home and he didn't even look at me. I went back to my room, called the airlines and booked a midnight flight.

Red Krohn came to my room and I said, "I'm really very upset about all this. I don't know what's going on and I'm very hurt by it and very insulted by this treatment."

I made an excuse at that point because my ego was hurting.

I told Red, "Well, it worked out for the best, really. It's made me realize that I'm very much in love with someone else." I was referring to Travis, and boy, I was so happy that I could fall back on that. It seemed the perfect lie. All I wanted was for Red to go back and tell that to Frank. It was such a childish thing to do.

That evening they gave me a going away party, like everything was just fine, everything was peaches and cream, but Judy had to leave, you know, and don't we all love Judy. If I had been strong enough, I think I would have taken Frank and thrown him over the balcony. On the other hand, I didn't want to let him know that it bothered me that much.

The party that evening in Frank's suite was just a replay of the night before. The dark-haired woman was there and he was still flirting, still just giving her such a snow job. The vile mood he was in, I think he was daring her husband to do something about it. I didn't even want to sit next to him. It was a long evening. I just couldn't wait to get out of there, but finally it was time for my exit and I didn't even say goodbye to Frank. Everyone at the party gave me their leis and Pete took me to the airport in a limousine. The leis were put in a large box and Pete said he would see that they were checked through with my luggage. I never saw them again. I was furious. I could picture Pete getting them back after I walked away.

I don't have an ounce of respect for Pete Lawford. I think he's an ass. He makes the best flunky in the world because it's important to Pete to be with important people. He'll sacrifice himself, take a tremendous amount of punishment, just to be there with Frank. When Frank gets into one of his black moods and turns on him, Pete just sits there and takes it. And when Pat talked, he listened. If there was a disagreement in their conversation, it was Pat who had the last word. He kept his mouth shut. Later, I would learn from Sam Giancana that he too had no respect for Pete. More on that later.

Anyone would think that after that week in Hawaii I would have had my fill of Frank Sinatra. Not so. I arrived home the morning of November 16, and that evening when I returned from a dinner date with Travis and his mother, there was a message from Frank which my sister Jackie had left for me on about twenty feet of toilet paper.

The message started out with, "Hawaii called twice, Aloha, I told him you were out on your surfboard," and it went on in that vein across the room, the paper draped over chairs, lamps, sofa—wall-to-wall Western Union. The last line was something like, "Can I borrow ten bucks till Thursday?"

I was very excited, very thrilled, that he had called, because at that point I was more confused, more hurt than angry. I was sorry it had gone wrong and I was disappointed because I would have loved to have it continue the way it had been the first few days. It had been a frustrating experience. There was something about Frank that I really liked, and I was questioning myself, wondering whether I had been too quiet, not interesting enough, and I didn't like that thought. Perhaps he was just too worldly and I was too naive. I had agonized over it until I was kicking quite a hole in my ego, which was not that resilient to begin with.

Frank called at two the next afternoon. He was very concerned about whether I was all right. The thought that struck me was, "What did you think I was going to do? Go jump off a bridge because I was treated badly by Frank Sinatra?" Yet I sensed that he was uncomfortable, that perhaps he suffered a little when he mistreated someone that really didn't deserve it. He sort of apologized but he didn't offer any explanation and I didn't ask for one. He promised to call again and I said that would be fine. I had a peculiar reaction after he hung up. Instead of feeling giddy and girlish, I thought, "Well, you big shot, you feel guilty don't you?" It restored my ego somewhat.

Now that I was free of Travis, and had moved in with Jackie, the phone never stopped ringing. I don't mean to sound immodest, but I had met a lot of people when I was with Billy and Travis who were just waiting for the day I became unattached. It was the first time Judy Campbell was available. I could have had dates morning, noon and night. As I said earlier, for the first time in my life I began dating the way most girls date when they're in high school.

Life became so good. I slept until nine, sometimes ten if I was up very late, and tried to paint at least two hours every morning. I lunched with friends or went to the studio and had lunch with Jackie. I painted some more in the afternoon, or went shopping. I didn't have dinner at home one night a month. And I never went out to dinner in a restaurant alone or with just other women. To this day I don't like the picture it presents. When I travel alone on a train, I never leave my compartment. The same applies to hotels. When I'm alone, I live on room service.

I traded in my Olds 98 for a new Pontiac convertible. It was marvelous riding to Palm Springs with the top down. I visited the Whittakers, the Elwoods, Sam and Marilyn Sontag, all the people I had met through Travis. I became a regular weekend guest at the Racquet Club.

It took a few calls before I agreed to meet Frank in Palm Springs. I wanted to see him but I didn't want to just go rushing in. Our date was for the evening of December 7, and I drove up in the morning and checked in at the Racquet Club. I had an early dinner with the Sontags and at nine-thirty that evening I arrived at Frank's Palm Desert home, which is a few miles beyond Palm Springs.

I was surprised at the size of Frank's house. It was nice and comfortable, but compared to the opulent homes I had lived in and the homes of others I knew, it was a modest, quite ordinary house. It certainly was not the home of a famous movie star.

Even the living room was small. There was a wall bar and a piano at one end. Two beige couches faced each other in front of the fireplace, with a large coffee table between them. There were sliding glass doors leading out to a patio and pool, and the motif was orange and black Oriental.

The only impressive thing about Frank's bedroom, as I was to discover later that evening, were twin beds and a glass shower in the room itself. Luckily, there was another bathroom connecting with the bedroom which had a shower and tub. There was no way I would have used the bedroom shower.

Frank's houseboy, George, opened the door and Frank was right behind him. He seemed very relaxed and in fine spirits. He bussed me on the cheek and gave me a big wink. "I'm glad you could make it," he said, taking my elbow and guiding me into the living room. Besides Pat and Pete Lawford, there were three others in the room. Jack Entratter, who was president of the Sands hotel in Las Vegas, Jimmy Van Heusen, a song writer, and Johnny Formosa, who, as best as I could make out, had some connection with the Chicago underworld. Frank walked very carefully around him.

Before I arrived, Frank and Jimmy Van Heusen had been working on a song for a picture called *Oceans 11* that Frank was going to start shooting in Las Vegas. After the introductions they went back to work. Jimmy was at the piano and Frank was singing but moving around the room, and quite often he would come to the sofa and put his hand on my shoulder as he sang, all the while giving me that twinkle of his, flirting with me, but in a gentle way. It was the same kind of attentiveness he had first given me in Hawaii.

We had a spaghetti dinner, which I hate when I'm eating out because it's always such a messy thing to eat. But Frank, like most Italians, just loves it. After dinner we went back into the living room and Frank sat next to me, keeping his arm around my shoulders the whole time we sat there. From time to time he would give me a little squeeze, lean over to kiss my cheek, and say softly, "Are you all right? You want anything?" There was a lot of joking and laughter, but again I was very quiet and had very little to say.

Frank was particularly pleased that Formosa was there. He liked being with him, having him around. Frank always seemed partial to underworld types. You could tell when he was around someone like that. He enjoyed them more than anyone else. Sometimes I think he was just a frustrated hoodlum. It was an element that he thrived in.

But Frank made sharp distinctions between a genuine

hoodlum like Formosa and a man like Jack Entratter. Frank could be brutal with Entratter, who, like Pete Lawford, took it without a word of protest.

As the evening came to an end and people began leaving or disappearing into bedrooms, Frank leaned over and said, "You'll stay, won't you." I knew what he meant and I said, "Yes."

We made love and it was the same as it had been before. He was very gentle, very attentive, very loving, and very active. He did not expect to be made love to. We slept in each other's arms.

For breakfast the next morning, Frank had a scrambled egg and bacon sandwich on toasted sourdough bread. I never had that before and it was quite good. I've had it many times since then. It's a much tastier way of having scrambled eggs, if you're just having plain scrambled eggs. I'm a garbage scrambled egg eater—I empty the refrigerator and dump it all in.

Everyone just stretched out on chaise lounges around the pool and took the sun. Frank had a tap beer dispenser out on the patio and there was a lot of beer drinking. Jack Entratter and I hit tennis balls on Frank's court. Jack was about six foot four and three hundred pounds, but there was something wrong with his feet or his legs. He had difficulty moving around. I had to hit the ball right to him because he just stood there without moving. Nobody paid any attention to us and so it was fun.

That evening Frank and I and the Lawfords went to Romanoff's for dinner—his restaurant in Palm Springs wasn't open too many seasons. This was the first time I remember the name of Jack Kennedy coming up in the conversation. The whole evening was a political discussion, and Pat had the floor. I remember how amazed I was at the thought that her brother was making a bid for the presidency. Slowly it dawned on me who Jack Kennedy really was and then I could see the striking resemblance to his sister.

Frank was all ears as Pat analyzed Jack's chances in the coming primaries. He seemed so subdued and respectful.

Even Pete commanded his attention when he talked about Jack. The more Pete talked the more British he became until it was downright ridiculous.

After we made love that night Frank still had Jack Kennedy on his mind. "You know," he said, "I'll bet even money Jack gets the nomination."

"It sounds like something you really want," I said, struggling to keep my eyes open.

"Why not," he said. "Jack's a great guy. And don't forget, he's my friend. I know how to help my friends." He gave me a hug and I was soon sound asleep.

The next morning Frank was very quiet, not sullen yet, but slowly on his way there. I decided it was time for me to leave. I just couldn't figure him out. He seemed so complex. I think he wants to be so many different people that he doesn't know who he is. The one thing I knew was that I wasn't going to take any of his abuse. But I kept coming back to Frank because there is something compellingly attractive about him that draws you like a magnet. I think that's why so many stick to him even when he grinds his heel into their very soul.

Though Travis and I were no longer lovers we still saw a lot of each other and became, as I said, very close friends. That was before he married Carolyn Taper, Mark Taper's daughter, and I became that other woman. We went to Palm Springs on December 12, which was Frank's birthday, but I didn't see Frank. The week before I had ordered leather album covers as a gift for Frank. A day or two before his birthday I took them to his office in Beverly Hills and gave them to Gloria, his personal secretary. I later saw them on a shelf at his Beverly Hills home, but he never mentioned them to me.

That whole month of December, Travis and I spent more time in Palm Springs than in Beverly Hills. I was extremely fond of the Springs, but as I look back on it now, I can see that it wasn't exactly the paradise that I thought it was. We went to a different party every night. I say different, but actually all these parties were exactly alike. There were cocktails and hors d'oeuvres, and no matter what time the party started, whether it was six-thirty or nine-thirty, dinner was always served, and it was almost always buffet, between eleven and midnight. There was a tremendous variety of food, but it was always the same variety, really not very imaginative. They were fun because a great many of the people we knew came to these parties in a very pleasant frame of mind.

Bob Whittaker had the most interesting parties. He often entertained important people from Washington. I remember dancing with Senator Ribicoff at one of Bob's parties. Bob doesn't believe in doing anything unless he can do it the very best way possible. If he served caviar, it was *Baluga*. If he served vodka, it was Russian. When Bob had a formal dinner, he would serve authentic dishes from the country he was favoring that evening. Bob's homes were designed for entertaining. Besides his Palm Springs home, he had a beautiful place at Lake Arrowhead and a grand old mansion on June Street in Los Angeles. Bob was the quietest, the gentlest, the most unassuming man I had ever met.

Scotty Rubin also threw some of the parties I attended. Scotty was typical of the rich, older man with the big house, the big car, and the big blond on his arm. There are certain men who always have a flashy girl on their arm. If straight skirts are in fashion, the flashy girl's skirt is cut so that it completely shows the contours of her body, with the slit just a little higher in the back. Her décolletage is a little lower, her hair is more lacquered, her false eyelashes a little longer, her mascara a little heavier—everything is a little flashier. The walk is a little different too. The stride is longer, the hips move a little more, and dignity hasn't a great deal to do with it.

Escorting this type of woman seems to work miracles for the ego of some men. The other men sit around saying, "Wow, see what Scotty's got tonight!" It lends itself to a certain type of men's humor. You see them whispering together, "Whoa, whoa, whoa!" and giving it that limp-wrist shake of the hand. Like the food at the party, flashy girls come in a variety of shades and sizes, but it's always the same variety. They are presented as "actresses," that's the standard line whether they are starlets or hookers. In New York, the term is model.

I used to get so irritated when my name would appear in the newspaper and they would call me an actress. It upset me because I wasn't an actress and I wasn't passing myself off as one. I didn't like the association. If you are an actress, that's fine, but if you're not, it creates a different picture. I never liked publicity, but you couldn't move in those circles without getting into the gossip columns. For example, when I came back from Hawaii, Harrison Carroll, who wrote a truly gossipy column for the old *Herald Express,* carried an item about it. He wrote, "Judy Campbell says she wasn't dating Frank Sinatra as such but that they did get around together in Hawaii since they were in a group and saw a lot of each other. Frankie was enjoying a couple of weeks over there with Peter Lawford and his wife and kids." Harrison called me often but most of the time I was able to dissuade him from using my name.

Life in Palm Springs moves at a slower pace than in Los Angeles or New York. The weather in winter is ideal, warm and dry, and you can get your tan, all of which is conducive to feeling good. People go there to have a good time, to play tennis and golf, to swim, to sit out in the sun, to party, but it's not a racing kind of party life. There is a cocktail hour in New York that never seems to end. Lunch is a cocktail hour, four o'clock is a cocktail hour and so is seven o'clock. Much has been written about the loose life in California, and some of it is true, but New York doesn't take a back seat to any other place. Successful businessmen in New York stick their wives in the suburbs and stay in the city all week. New York wives probably do the same thing at their suburban country clubs that California wives do in Palm Springs or Beverly Hills. Or, for that matter, wives at some cheaper country club in the midwest. Men are men and women are women, whether they have a dime or a million. Both the poor and the rich get bored. They either play around or they don't. Geography has nothing to do with it. Perhaps it's a little more available in some areas, but if sex is what you really want, you can find it.

I liked the atmosphere at the Springs. The whole town was clean and compact and expensive enough to be exclusive. I thought it was sophisticated. I loved the Racquet Club and its ambience then, although I couldn't stand it today. Now I can see a certain phoniness. Even then I couldn't mix with the wives who spent all day in their little tennis skirts, flirting with the glamour boys (the young bit players who try to make it in the movies by pleasing the wives of successful Hollywood men), playing gin, discussing their affairs and gossiping about the affairs of others. They are players, hard as nails, and if you don't like the games they play, you're out.

Perhaps because my marriage to Billy had been so disastrous, it seemed to me that the married men were worse than the single ones. They were always looking, always hunting. You'd see them at parties with different girls and every once in a while you'd see them at a party with their wives. As far as I was concerned, I had made up my mind that if I got married again, I'd have to accept the fact that my husband would cheat.

No matter how long I live, I'll never forget January 5, 1960. That's the day I had dinner with Richard Ney, the actor who played the son of Greer Garson in *Mrs. Miniver* and who is now a stockbroker.

He picked me up in his Rolls, and when I say he drives slowly, I mean he crawls along the street. You get the feeling that he's living in another world; that he is not with us. He drives that car the way the car looks. I don't know quite how to express it, but I was really awestruck. His manner was so proper and precise. There was never a lull in his conversation. He always thought of something else to say. As the car slowly inched its way through the streets, I felt like he and the car had an agreement. He wasn't going to hurt the car and the car wasn't going to hurt him; he was going to take care of it and it was going to take care of him.

When we arrived at his house in the hills above Sunset, he

took my elbow gently and guided me into the house. There wasn't a chair that wasn't placed just properly for two people to spend an evening together. The dining room table, which I could see partly when I came into the living room, was already set. The lights were just right—they weren't too bright or too low. The hors d'oeuvres were already out. If he had someone in that house preparing things, you never felt it, you never knew it.

I felt I was being swept out of this world and almost as if, "My God, I wonder if I'm ever going to get back." And not only out of this world, but out of this time—I was going back in time to when Hollywood was something else.

He put on some romantic music, fixed the drinks, and sat for a few minutes, talking all the time. Then he took a gentle sip from his perfectly chilled martini, turned to me and said, "Would you like to dance?" I couldn't believe it. I didn't know what to say. I know that the movies have done this scene so that it looks very romantic. There is a fireplace and candlelight and the couple dances beautifully together. You may even feel envious as you watch the movie. But it just doesn't fit in real life. Nevertheless there we were dancing all alone in this room and I felt that pretty soon someone was going to say, "Cut! That's a print." I wasn't entirely sure that it was really happening. The dance was torture because I didn't know whether I was going to burst out laughing or run out of the place and yell "Help!"

When we sat down, and again I didn't even have to think of anything to say because he would not allow a lull in the conversation, I had a terrible urge to cross my legs. But I didn't dare because I was afraid that my hose would make a noise or my foot might accidently touch the coffee table. That noise would not have belonged in that scene. I was happy that I hadn't worn taffeta.

He put his arm up around my shoulder but it was as if he had looked at the clock and said, "Well, now it's time to put the arm around the shoulder." It was just exactly the right time before dinner was served.

When we entered the dining room, the candles were lit and the dinner was in serving dishes. He served and by now I was really getting nervous. What would I do if my knife clanked on my plate? Throughout dinner he sat very erect and he always had the proper thing to say.

After dinner he escorted me back to the living room. I had the feeling that instead of walking I was on rollers and he was just steering me around, with never a halt, to the right place. I floated down on the sofa. The liqueurs were on the coffee table and by now I was convinced that there was someone else in the house, perhaps an Oriental houseboy tiptoeing in his stocking feet. But I never heard a sound or saw a soul.

It was survival now. He offered me a liqueur and I took it. I was afraid not to have something in front of me. I had to be busy because strange as the evening had been, I didn't know what was coming up next. I wouldn't have been surprised to see him turn into a werewolf. There had to be some kind of drastic change. This couldn't continue.

So we sat for a couple of minutes, and I began to get the feeling that he was talking slower. Something was coming. This was the time to be more romantic—the clock said so, or the book said that after dinner you do such and such. Again this studied way of putting his arm around my shoulder and when he leaned over to kiss me I had the feeling that someone said, "Camera! Action!" because everything was perfect. His arms went around me and one hand reached the back of my head gently; his head lowered toward me and stopped when his face was in front of mine.

I was trying to be very quiet and nice, and I let him kiss me, but very gently. I'm surprised that I didn't stare at him wide-eyed. He kissed me again very gently and whatever his words were I just don't know because my head was going a mile a minute. My biggest fear was that I would start laughing. Finally, when he began to get a little more amorous, I made some outrageous excuse that I had to leave— something like I think I'm coming down with the plague— anything to get me out of there. He was surprised, but in a way that a person might be when he doesn't want you to know he's surprised. His eyes seemed to say, "But my performance was so great, why is this review so bad."

You could almost feel what was going on inside of him. I

sensed a little extra effort then in maintaining the conversation without a lull. But he did and he was very nice when he escorted me out to the Rolls. It took forever for him to back up. He let the motor run for ages, checked and rechecked the instruments, and checked and rechecked the rear-view mirror. Again it was, "Don't worry, I'm going to take care of you." We crawled down the hill and now I had the feeling that the wheels were not touching the road, that we were floating down the hill.

Even on Sunset Boulevard, with cars whizzing by and people crossing the street and lights flashing on and off, this car was just going slowly down the street and nobody touched it. To tell the truth, I don't think anybody else could see it.

When we arrived at my place, he just came around, opened the door, and escorted me to the front door. He held my shoulders gently as he leaned forward to kiss me and I turned my face and he gave me a light kiss on the cheek. I said, "Good night," thanked him for the lovely dinner and lovely evening, and apologized for having had to end it so early, all the time thinking, "God, if I don't get in that door soon I'm going to explode." He said he would definitely call me the next day and that he wanted to have dinner with me again soon, and perhaps I had a favorite restaurant we could go to. He waited until I was safely in the building before turning and walking very slowly back to his Rolls. I barely made it to my apartment before getting completely hysterical. I laughed and laughed until it hurt. He did call me the next day, and he called several times before he finally gave up. I think of him at times and wonder if he's real. There's an old expression that says a man, whether he's a king or a peasant, puts his pants on one leg at a time. That's not possible with Richard Ney: I have the feeling that he wishes his clothes on and off, he's that different from the rest of us.

Although I was dating a great deal during this period, I was more interested in having men as friends than as lovers. I've always preferred the company of men to that of women.

Marty Tamambaum and Sy Devore were two such friends. Sy was the most fashionable tailor in Beverly Hills and a member of Frank's Rat Pack. I think Marty was involved in horseracing and had all kinds of irons in the fire, none of which he ever talked about. Sy and Marty were the best of friends. Marty was also a close friend of Jerry Lewis, who comes up later in this story.

To this day I haven't been able to figure out Mort Viner. I don't know whether he was a talent agent, a business manager, or a hanger-on. All I know is that he seemed involved with the entertainment industry. Mort was Mr. Average—average height, average build, average age, average intelligence, average looks.

I had met Dean Martin about ten years earlier, but through Mort I became reacquainted with Dean. Early in January 1960, Mort and I had dinner at LaScala with Dean and his wife Jeanne. Jeanne was a good friend of Gloria Cahn (Sammy's wife). They were typical Hollywood wives. They were not very nice to a single attractive woman and tended to band together against outside threats. Yet they didn't feel threatened by starlets who would sleep with anybody's husband to get a part. There's such an overabundance of them that it's become just another facet of the business.

I was an unknown factor. They couldn't quite place me. Although I was more comfortable talking to men, I never paid much attention to their husbands simply because I didn't want them to reciprocate with their wives sitting there. I wasn't completely comfortable with the wives because I could feel them withdrawing, being cautious, and then I would have to try to prove myself. Very often I felt like saying, "Look, I don't care about your husband. I'm not the least interested. Now, do you want to be friends?" Of course I'd never say it, but it was a feeling I had whenever I was around Hollywood wives.

I was about seventeen and dating Billy the first time I met Dean Martin. Jackie was part of The Golden Circle at Paramount, which was a group of young people they were grooming for stardom. Barbara Rush was in the group. Paramount changed Jackie's name to Susan Morrow. Two of her early costarring roles were in *The Savage* with Charlton Heston and *Burning Forest* with John Payne.

71

One day while I was visiting her at Paramount, we went over to the set of a picture that I think was called *Sailor Beware,* and it starred Dean Martin and Jerry Lewis. To say that the boys were exuberant is to put it mildly. The next thing we knew the studio wanted Jackie to go to San Diego with Dean and Jerry to do a layout for a movie magazine. I was to accompany her. We were told the studio was sending a limousine to drive us to San Diego, but Jackie got suspicious and checked with the studio. The boys were pulling a fast one. It was their limousine and the picture layout was just part of their little scheme. Jackie was furious, but not as furious as Billy, who swore up and down that he was going to kill Dean. Danny Arnold had told him that Dean was trying to date me.

If Dean remembered the incident that evening at La Scala he gave no indication of it. His secret preoccupation that evening, as it was many of the evenings I was to spend with him, was with Mort Viner. Dean thought that Mort and Jeanne were seeing each other. I saw a lot of Dean in the next few months. He would call me at all hours of the day or night, and much of the time he just wanted to talk about Jeanne and Mort.

Even so, Dean and I had a pleasant relationship. I know that Dean is a player, but he never made a serious play for me. He would kid about it from time to time, but I don't think that Dean is a very virile man. He's a slow-moving, relaxed kind of human being; there's nothing pretentious about him. He likes to sit up and drink all night. I think he enjoyed our relationship because I wasn't after anything, and he didn't have to give a great deal of himself. He could be great fun to be with when he was in a good mood. He has a tremendous sense of humor. People around Dean always laughed a lot.

My next date with Frank was a total disaster. It made Hawaii really look like paradise. The evening started with dinner at Romanoff's in Beverly Hills. It was a long dinner, followed by some heavy drinking in the bar. By the time we got to Frank's house, my stomach was feeling a little queasy.

Sometimes when I dined out I wouldn't eat enough of my dinner and the liquor would hit me harder.

Frank was sympathetic. He said, "Go in the bedroom and go to bed. I've got to make a phone call and I'll be with you in a few minutes."

I remember I undressed in the bathroom and went to bed. I dozed off and the next thing I knew Frank was getting into bed beside me. He put his arms around me and as I turned to look at him I saw the bedroom door open and this tall black girl came in without a stitch of clothing on.

I blinked my eyes, trying to clear my vision, not really wanting to believe what I was seeing. She was smiling as she crawled in beside Frank.

I just absolutely froze. I went rigid: no one could have moved my arms or legs. You would have had to pry them loose with a steel bar, that's how stiff I was.

She immediately pulled down the covers and began to make love to him, orally, while I remained absolutely rigid. Frank realized what was happening when I started to shake. I was trying to keep from crying—I could feel it welling up inside of me, choking me, until I thought I was going to lose control. I wanted to run out but I knew I couldn't move a muscle.

Frank waited until she had completed the sex act before he eased her out of the bed and followed her into the bathroom. I could hear him whispering to her, and then they came out and he opened the bedroom door and she left. He got back into bed, put his arms around me and began apologizing. By then I was sobbing out of control. He said he was sorry, but he hadn't realized I would be so affected by it. He said he should have known better, or at least he should have first discussed it with me. When that didn't work, he tried to calm me down with reassurances that she was gone and wouldn't be coming back. I just crumpled. The last thing I remember before falling asleep was Frank cooing to me like one does to a baby that won't stop crying.

Frank was still sleeping when I got up the next morning and went into the next room to dress. A few minutes later he came into the room and put his arms around me. He was wearing a robe and there was a sheepish look on his face. "Are you all right?" he said. I nodded and he said, "I'm sorry about last night."

"It's okay," I said, "but I don't really want to talk about it."

"I don't blame you," he said. "It was a mistake. But how was I to know you'd take it so hard."

"Have I ever given you any indication that I would take it lightly?"

Frank laughed and pulled away from me. "Judy," he said, shaking his head. "You're so square I can't believe it."

I could feel anger rising inside of me. "Frank," I said, and my voice was shaking, "you may think I'm a prude, but it's just not my cup of tea." I could hear how stupid that sounded but I forged ahead anyway. "It's not something I'm interested in. But I'm not criticizing you. I don't care what your tastes are. That's your business. When someone closes the bedroom door, whatever goes on in there is their business, but it's got to be something the two people consent to. If they want to add a third, fourth, fifth or sixth, that's fine as long as it's what they all want. I have no objection to any of it as long as you don't try to include me in it against my will."

My voice was really off key by the time I got that mouthful out. I was looking down at the floor because I could feel myself—my insides—just shaking. I knew if I looked at him I would break down and cry. I wanted to make my point and yet I didn't want to talk about it. Several times I said, "I don't want to talk about it," and then I'd go off on a tangent. I could see that he was very uncomfortable, but instead of caring, I was pleased. I wanted him to be miserable.

When I finished dressing, he took my arm and guided me into the breakfast room. "Come on," he said, "I want you to have something to eat with me. I don't want you to leave feeling the way you do right now."

I sat at the table and had coffee, but I wanted to get out of there. I wasn't going to really calm down, if even then, but I knew the first thing I had to do was get out of there. I was on the edge of hysteria, and the last thing I wanted was to get

74

hysterical in front of Frank. Nor did I want to leave in anger. I knew he was genuinely sorry for what had happened. That's probably why we remained friends.

My problem was that I knew how Frank could be. His physical contacts with me had been most pleasant. After making love, he was loving. He was understanding when I was upset. He could be a very thoughtful, very attentive, very gentle person. He just was not consistent. You couldn't spend too much time with him and expect him to be that way all the time. I had seen his black moods and I would see them again. I knew how he treated the people around him. His attitude reminded me of someone kicking a poor defenseless mutt in the ribs. He was venting whatever ugliness was inside of him, taking it out on whoever was handiest, whoever was closest. People around Frank were always trying to explain him. They all had a different explanation or reason for the way he behaved. He was something different to everyone because they each had to find an excuse for taking his abuse. Whatever was lacking in them showed up in Frank.

Now I had seen still another side of Frank and I was terribly disappointed. There was something about him at given times that I just adored. It was so frustrating to think, "My God, why does this man have to change so at times?" Although I was blaming him, I still had the feeling that there was something wrong with me. I was too quiet, not outgoing enough, and I just couldn't adjust to Frank and the people around him.

Perhaps if I had been in love with Frank, I would have tried harder to please him. I was infatuated with him. I just adored him when he was being nice. He knows how to make you feel like a complete woman.

Frank sent me home in a limousine and later in the day called me. He was still being apologetic. "I just wanted to check and see how you are doing," he said.

I said I was fine and he said, "Good to hear." Then he started telling me that he was going to start filming *Oceans 11* in Las Vegas with the Clan. They were going to shoot in the daytime and put on a show at the Sands at night.

"Why don't you come up and see the show? We're going

to be there for quite a while, and I thought maybe you'd enjoy a little change. Come on, say yes, it'll be a gas.''

I remember saying something like, ''No more antics, no more rabbits out of the hat?'' I said it lightheartedly and he laughed, and I could sense that he was relieved. It was as if I had pardoned him.

Another good friend who liked to talk about his wife was Ray Anthony. Ray was an orchestra leader and married to Mamie Van Doren. He carried a torch for her all his life. But he was fun to be with. Back in January 1960, Ray was enjoying another of his many comebacks.

On January 12, we went to a party at the home of Joe Perrin, whom I had known for many years. There was a story Joe loved to tell about the Saturday morning he took Aly Kahn to my home to meet Jackie. That was after Aly and Rita Hayworth had separated, and Jackie was a beautiful girl with flaming red hair that looked very much like Rita's.

It was the old story. If you can't have the original, get a good copy. The only problem was that Jackie was a very independent headstrong girl who was not impressed by celebrities. Just minutes before Joe and Aly were to arrive at our home, Jackie said to my mother, ''Tell Joe I had to go somewhere,'' and off she went. My father was working in the garden, all grubby, and my mother was making out her shopping list because Saturday was the day they did their weekly shopping—by then the cupboards were bare.

When Joe arrived with Aly Kahn—Jackie had neglected to mention him—my mother invited them in and asked if they would like something to eat, not thinking for a minute that they would accept. All she had left was a Coke and a couple of hot dogs. They said they'd be delighted. So Aly, one of the world's richest men, sat in our kitchen and shared a Coke with my mom and dad and had half a hot dog. Joe has told the story a thousand times, exaggerating it a little more each time, about how embarrassed and yet how dignified my mother was through it all. Of course, what Joe never realized was that my mother would have been just as embarrassed and just as dignified if it had happened with one of our neighbors.

76

Frank called again and insisted that I come to Las Vegas to see the show, which according to the reviews was a blockbuster—it starred Frank, Dean, Peter Lawford, Sammy Davis, and Joey Bishop. Frank wouldn't take no for an answer. We made a date for dinner after the late show on January 23, which was a Saturday, and that morning I flew to Las Vegas with Dick and Marilyn Elwood.

After checking into our rooms we met in the lounge for a drink, and within minutes Dean Martin was at our table, smiling at us in that soft way of his, and saying, "Hi, there, how are you today. Are you going to be here long?"

I introduced him to the Elwoods and he sat down. "Hey, it's good to see you again," he said. "Going to see the show tonight?"

I said yes and before I could say another word, he said, "Okay, I want you folks to sit at my table, you hear? No arguments, now."

I hated to tell him. "Frank has already invited us," I said. Dean didn't bat an eye. "That's fine," he said. "Maybe I'll see you after the show. You staying here at the hotel?"

This was before he had confided his suspicions about Jeanne and Mort Viner. When he stood up to leave, he very casually said, "Have you seen Mort lately?"

It was one of the funniest, one of the best shows I've ever seen. There was a barrel of talent up on that stage. They were all great ad-libbers. The only weak link was Lawford, the one with the least talent, and the least amount of respect from anybody. Pete was the butt of all the jokes. He was there because he was in *Oceans 11*, and I think he was in that picture because he was married to Pat Kennedy. Sammy Davis was one of the most versatile performers in the business, an unbelievable talent. Dean was on the same level as Frank, and Frank always treated Dean as an equal. Dean was a star in his own right and Frank showed his respect. Frank knew better than to berate Dean. He knew that Dean wouldn't have put up with it for a second.

Sammy Davis was another story. He idolized Frank. Whenever Sammy was around Frank, I often had the feeling that Sammy would have crawled on his knees for Frank.

Joey Bishop's star was at its peak then; he was very quick witted and worked well with the group. But as far as Joey was concerned Frank was the boss. I always had great admiration for Joey's talent as a comic. Years before I had been in New York with Jackie when she was married to Gary Morton, and the three of us had run into Joey at the Stage Delicatessen. He walked us back to our hotel and on the way did a very funny, very clever routine. He mimicked a boy trying to walk me home after school. He imitated all the antics of a young boy showing off. He jumped over fire hydrants, walked the curb, walked backwards, ran up stairs into an apartment house, jumped off the stairs, faked a somersault, pretended he was carrying my books. It was hysterical. Gary was laughing so hard he could barely walk.

I never asked Joey if he remembered that evening. When I was first married to Billy I used to be amazed sometimes when an actor that we had spent a whole evening with did not remember me. Then I realized that a lot of performers are not aware of anyone but themselves. They just don't know that anybody else is around. This is particularly true when that someone doesn't sit there and talk about them all night long, which I never was prone to do. I never enter a conversation or feed a conversation in which someone is talking about himself all the time. I will listen politely but I won't encourage it. I won't keep asking questions to keep it going because I think it's a bore to watch people flex their egos.

After the show Dean was the first one to join us in the lounge. He had a drink with us while we waited for Frank, who came in about a half hour later with a huge group of people. We sat around drinking for a couple of hours before going to an Italian restaurant for dinner, and then back to the lounge for more drinks. Frank and his friends knew how to drink. The details of that evening, like the details of so many other evenings with Frank and Dean, are locked in limbo. They are all the same. You drink, you make jokes, you eat spaghetti, you drink some more and make more jokes, and pretty soon the sun starts coming up and it's time to go to bed.

When people started drifting off, I excused myself and

went to my room. The phone woke me up around noon. Frank wanted to know what had happened to me.

"Nothing," I said. "I just got tired and went to bed."

"Well, that's great," he said, and I could tell he was a little peeved. "I thought you came here to see me."

"Yes, I did, Frank," I said. "I came to see you and the show."

"Okay, so why didn't you wait?"

I knew I had to tell him in plain language. "Look, Frank, I came here at your invitation to see the show." I paused, not sure if I should go on, then said to myself, "the hell with him." Then I said: "But not to sleep with you. I'm not ready for that yet, Frank."

"Oh, Christ," he said, "haven't you gotten over that yet?"

"No," I said, and I just let the word hang there.

There was a long pause and I could hear his breathing. "All right, goddamnit, but promise me you're going to stay a couple more days. I want a chance to talk to you. You and I have got to talk this thing out."

"I told you, Frank. I don't want to talk about it."

"Will you stay a couple more days, goddamnit? That's all I'm asking. Now, promise me."

"All right, Frank. I'll stay."

"Go back to bed," he said, and the warmth was back in his voice. "Sleep warm, baby."

Dick Elwood left that afternoon and Marilyn moved into my room with me. That evening we had dinner with Ray Anthony, who was appearing in one of the lounges. After dinner we had a drink with Frank and then we went to see his late show. Then we had more drinks in the lounge with the whole group. When Frank went to gamble, Dean asked me to go see the Mary Kay Trio. It was then that Dean started asking me questions about Mort and Jeanne. Although I told him I didn't know anything about it, and I didn't (even if I *had* known something I certainly wouldn't have told him), it made no difference at all. Once he had caught my ear, there was just no letting go. I had drinks with Dean in the afternoon, in the evening before and after each show, we had breakfast together, and the times we weren't together he would telephone from whatever movie location they were shooting in that day. When I went back to Beverly Hills on Wednesday, without having been alone with Frank for a single minute, Dean called me at least twice a day. He created endless convolutions to this ''affair'' which could have been a figment of his imagination. What is ironic about it, and this is probably par for the course, is that throughout this period the movie magazines were writing about poor Jeanne sitting at home with the kids while her wayward husband was playing the field.

Gossip moves like prairie fire in Hollywood. This reminds me of the night I went with Sy Devore to an opening at the Coconut Grove. Sy went to the men's room and came back shaking his head.

''You're not going to believe what I just heard,'' Sy said. ''I just ran into newspapermen and they wanted to know what I was doing with Dean's girl. I told them, 'You guys are out of your mind. She's not Dean's girl.' I don't think they believed me.''

From then on, whenever I saw Sy, he would say, ''Oh, I know whose girl you are,'' and would just laugh his head off.

As I said, I preferred the company of men to that of women. Sy is a good example of what I mean. Sy was no romantic hero, and he wasn't all that interesting, but he was a good person and very pleasant company. It's nice when you're single to have people to spend time with that you don't have to fight off. That's why I had a tendency to hang onto friends who were not all that exciting but who were enjoyable and safe. I could go out and have dinner, see a play, a concert, a nightclub show, or just have a few drinks and laughs. I certainly didn't want to have an affair with every man I went out with.

If to enjoy sex a woman has to go to bed with a great many men, or with every man she goes out with, then I think she has a serious problem. I know that the newspapers have painted me as a scarlet woman, and I suppose I am to some people, for it is, after all, a question of individual morals. As strange as it may sound to some people, I really am a prude. I attribute that to my strict upbringing and Catholic teachings. They are appendages that I can't shake loose. The mistakes that I have made have troubled me far beyond their importance. Once society paints that scarlet letter on you, all distinction is lost. But there is a vast difference between a hooker, a nymphomaniac and someone who has had some affairs in her lifetime.

There is a certain quirk in some men that makes it perfectly fine for them to run around, but they just can't live with the thought that their wife might be cheating. Dean was becoming obsessive, or so it seemed in our conversations. For example, he called one night from Las Vegas and asked me to check if Mort was at home. Then he said, "Is there any way you can find out if Jeanne's with him?"

"My God, Dean," I said, shocked at the prospect of what his request entailed, "you can't be serious."

He chuckled. "I'm going to make you my private eye."

"Oh, no, you're not."

"Come on, be a pal."

"Dean, I don't like any of this. I will call Mort to see if he's at home, but I can't—"

"It's okay," he interrupted, giving me another friendly chuckle. "I understand. But you know I'm really very worried about this."

"I know you are."

"Thanks, Judy, I'll call back in a few minutes."

I called Mort and he wasn't home. When Dean called back I took the opportunity to ask him for a favor. Marilyn had left a gold bracelet at the hotel and I asked him to inquire about it.

He called from Los Angeles the very next day and told me he was on his way to my place to deliver the bracelet. Jackie's apartment was on the second floor and when he arrived I met him at the door. Jackie was washing her hair, I think, or there were some other reasons, but I couldn't invite him in. He laughed and said, "That's okay, let's sit outside and talk awhile. I have a little time before my flight back to Vegas."

So we sat on the brick steps and talked for an hour about the perils of married life in Hollywood. I told him what I thought about Hollywood wives and he told me what he thought about Hollywood husbands. Then we switched sides. It was one of our most interesting conversations.

I had a special feeling about Dean as an individual. He was not like the rest of the Clan. He was the kind of person who wandered around by himself. He didn't need a retinue walking with him when he walked from one room to another. Dean walked alone, which is a rarity for a man in his position. But Dean was a loner in many ways. I don't think he could stand haivng a lot of people around him all the time the way Frank did. I was only in Dean's suite once and there wasn't another soul around. He didn't have that need for constant attention, for having people at his beck and call. All he had was Mack Gray to run his errands. He was around Dean sometimes, but he wasn't everpresent.

As I said, Dean enjoyed my company because he could sit and talk and not have to worry about being the romantic, glamorous movie star. I wasn't after a screen test, or money, or sex. I was just a friend. And a good listener. Some men like the idea of having a woman friend. I think that's why he sought my company. That along with the need to have a woman's viewpoint on his problem. So contrary to all rumors, there never was any romance involved.

Not long after Dean left Frank called again and within hours I was back in Las Vegas for another long weekend. To avoid the possibility that Frank would "comp" my bill, I checked into the Flamingo. My mind was made up that our relationship would be platonic.

I was supposed to spend the evening with Frank in his room, but I got tied up in the Garden Room with Dean, who really was moaning and groaning. To be truthful, I just didn't feel like going over and holding Frank's hand. Finally around three in the morning he paged me, and when I got on the phone greeted me with, "What the hell happened?"

"I'm having something to eat," I said, "and I got caught up in conversation."

"Well, for Christ's sake, I thought you were coming over."

There was more surprise than anger in his voice. It was as if he couldn't believe that anybody would stand him up. He was so used to people jumping when he snapped his fingers. "It's getting pretty late and I'm a little tired," I said. "It's been a long day. How about a rain check."

Two things were going to happen. Either the phone was going to melt in my hand or my eardrum would be shattered beyond repair. Frank surprised me. "Yeah, okay, I'm tired too. In fact, I'm taking the day off tomorrow. I'm just going to lay around here and take it easy. Come on over and spend the day with me."

"The whole day?"

"Yeah," and he mocked a growl. "I expect you here at eight sharp."

"In the morning?"

"You're damn right. We're shaping up around here."

"Good night, Frank. I'll see you tomorrow; in the afternoon."

The next day was remarkably tranquil. There is no way anyone can ever spend a day alone with Frank Sinatra. His quarters are a crossroads, with traffic moving in all directions, day and night. I think he would dry up and blow away if he were left totally alone.

Everything considered, it was a peaceful, pleasant day. I brought a book and sat out in the sun on his patio and read while Frank talked on the phone, glanced through a pile of scripts, dictated a few letters, acknowledged the comings and goings of an endless string of visitors, growled at flunkies, drank martinis, ate lunch, drank Jack Daniels, ate hors d'oeuvres, drank Jack Daniels, ate dinner, and drank more Jack Daniels. Frank was not feeling well that day. That was his way of recuperating from a grueling schedule of shooting a movie in the daytime and sometimes at night, and doing a couple of shows a night, plus a lot of drinking, gambling, talking, not to mention doing a few unmentionables. As for me, for the first time since I had met Frank I felt comfortable around him. The sex part was behind us. Although he kidded about it during the day, asking me to bring a little happiness to a tired man, I had been able to kid right back and hold my ground. I wasn't too sure he liked it, if only because he likes women to want him, but now I thought I knew how to handle him.

I left for Beverly Hills on Monday, February 1, and Frank called on Tuesday in the afternoon, to chide me for not having registered at the Sands.

"I had a good room for you," he said. "What's the matter with you anyway? What makes you so goddamn independent? I don't understand it. Afraid to get compromised, for a lousy room, why don't you grow up."

"Frank, I'm not going to listen to you if you keep going on."

"Okay, have it your way."

"Thanks."

"On one condition. Come over this weekend. I still want to talk to you."

I had already agreed to go with Mort Viner and a group that included Jeanne Martin, Gloria Cahn and Pat Newcombe, who was Marilyn Monroe's secretary and confidant.

I told Frank I would be there and he had no sooner hung up than Dean was on the phone wanting to know if I would be up over the weekend.

We took the eight o'clock flight on Friday evening. I sat with Mort, but Jeanne, Gloria and Pat acted like I wasn't even there. I realized they must have been listening to the gossip about Dean and me, but there was nothing I could do except weather the storm. Protestations were pointless. As I said, Hollywood wives are really bitchy. They completely ignored me the whole weekend. Sometimes when I found myself almost alone at a table with them, they acted as if I wasn't sitting there. If I hadn't been the kind of person that I am, there would have been a very bad scene. Instead I would act interested in anything they were saying and then would go back to my room and kick the furniture. I tried to avoid them whenever it could possibly be arranged.

Again I registered at the Flamingo. A half hour later, Mort and I went to a cocktail party in Dean's suite. An hour later the whole group had dinner in the Garden Room, then sat at Frank's table for the midnight show. I was happy to see that a new member had been added to Frank's retinue: Juliet Prowse was now Frank's number one girl. That made me feel even more liberated.

V

Although it began as a typical Las Vegas weekend it ended, for me at least, quite differently, for this was the weekend I met Jack Kennedy. The first time I saw him was at ten o'clock Sunday evening (February 7, 1960). He and Teddy were at Frank's table in the Sands lounge. He looked so handsome in his pin-striped suit. Those strong white teeth and smiling Irish eyes. The introduction, as all introductions in that group, was so perfunctory that it took me a moment to realize this was actually Pat Lawford's brother. But of course the moment he opened his mouth there was no mistaking the Kennedy voice.

I had a drink and someone said, "Who wants to have dinner?" Five of us (Peter Lawford, Gloria Cahn, Jack, Teddy, and I) had dinner in the Garden Room. There was nothing memorable about the dinner. Pete and Gloria competed in monopolizing the conversation. Every time Jack or Teddy tried to talk to me, Gloria butted right in with some inane political comment. Anything to keep the attention away from me and on herself. Pete expounded at interminable lengths on the filming and merits of *Oceans 11*.

From dinner we joined the others in the Copa Room for the late show. I sat next to Teddy and Jack sat across from me. The show was so fast moving and riotous that it allowed little time for conversation. It was one long uninterrupted laugh from beginning to end. But I had seen it often and this made it possible for me to concentrate a little more attention on Jack. I could observe him without creating attention, and I must say I was tremendously impressed by his poise and wit and charm. He talked to all the women at the table, and when he listened, it was as if every nerve and muscle in his whole body was poised at attention. As I was to learn, Jack Kennedy was the world's greatest listener. I have never known anyone like him. When you talked to Jack there was total concentration and absorption. He really wanted to hear what you had to say. He had a habit when he listened of tilting his head slightly toward you, as if to facilitate the process, guarding against the possibility that a word might mischievously try to slip by him.

After the show we returned to the lounge for the ritual drinking session. Teddy was sitting next to me and after the first drink and a few pleasantries, he leaned over to ask if I would show him the town. Having spent three weekends in Las Vegas, I felt eminently qualified to give him the full tourist treatment. After all, the Las Vegas Strip in 1960 was one mile of wall-to-wall casinos and hotels. The rest was tumbleweeds and sand.

Casino hopping was and still is great sport in Las Vegas. We saw various lounge shows, played a little blackjack, had some drinks and lots of conversation. It was my first experience with the Kennedy interrogation, their need to know everything about your life, not only who you are but what you are. It was flattering and most enjoyable. What woman doesn't like to talk about herself when she has a truly devoted listener?

Our last stop was at the Flamingo Lounge. By now, with the drinks and conversation, we were both very relaxed with each other. As I look back on it, Teddy was such a rosy-cheeked little boy, very good looking, full of the Old Nick, a great teaser with a ready laugh, and eyes that never stopped flirting. But he had nowhere near the charm and sophistication or just plain likability of Jack. He was the baby brother walking in his older brother's shadow.

When it came time to say goodnight—it was closer to good morning—he insisted on escorting me to my room. He asked for my key, unlocked the door, and waved me into the room, bowing as I went in. He was right behind me, but I stopped abruptly at the end of a little alcove that led into the room and we nearly collided. He laughed and put his hands on my shoulders.

"Wait a minute," he said, quickly moving around me and into the room. There was a copy of *Time* on my bed that I had bought earlier in the day but had not yet looked at. He flipped it over, turned and pointed a finger at me. "All right," he said, grinning. "Let's test your memory. Describe the cover?" That was another Kennedy trait. They like to test you, just to see how observant you are, how quick or perceptive you are, how large a vocabulary you have, anything that will give them information about you. Generally, that smacks a little too pedagogic for my comfort, but this evening I was more amused than anything else. It seemed more like a clever ploy to get into my room.

I remained in the alcove, with the door open, and beckoned him with the crook of a finger. I felt like I could handle the situation in a pleasant way. Compared to the people I had been associating with, he was a baby. I had no idea then that he was already married.

"I thought you lived here," he said.

"Oh, I do."

"Well, then, come right in. Make yourself at home. If you feel like going to bed, don't mind me, just crawl right in and go to sleep. I'll sit here and read *Time*. I want to know what they have to say about Jack this week."

"Oh, very funny," I said, "but I'm getting a little tired standing out here and I know you wouldn't want me to lose my patience."

"Oh God, no," he said, laughing, "that's the last thing I want you to lose."

"Then be a good boy and say goodnight."

"All right," he said, stepping over to the alcove, "but you can't blame a guy for trying."

He put his hands on my shoulders again and looked at me very seriously. "I have to leave for Denver in an hour," he said. "Why don't you fly up with me. It will be great fun."

He looked so eager and sweet that I hated to disappoint

him. I tried to let him down gently. I told him I had come with friends and besides I couldn't just go flying off with someone I had met only a few hours earlier. He persisted and I tried to keep it light and airy.

"All right," he said, "I'm going to the airport and I'm going to call you. I'm going to wait until you agree to come with me."

"I'm afraid you're going to have a long wait. You better bring your sleeping bag."

"We'll see," he said, and leaned forward to give me a kiss just as I turned my head. He quickly pulled back to avoid an awkward situation.

He left and it seemed like I had just gotten into bed when the phone rang and it was Teddy calling from the airport. "Everything is all taken care of," he said. "The pilot has promised to wait for you. So please hurry over. Remember, the success or failure of the campaign rests on your beautiful shoulders."

I started laughing and he said, "It's not funny. This is a serious matter."

Although I was amused and flattered by his persistence, I tried hard to convince him that he was wasting precious time. Finally he hung up, but an hour later he was back on the phone to say that he had not taken his plane and he was waiting for me. I couldn't believe it. It seemed so incredible that he would do that when the campaign was obviously so important to so many people.

Jack called later to ask if I would have lunch with him and I said I would love to. He was having a press conference in the covered section between the casino and the pool area and he suggested that I meet him there around twelve-thirty.

I wore a burgundy Kimberley knit suit, with a soft black leather belt, black leather shoes and matching bag. My hair style was pretty much the way I wear it today, perhaps a couple of inches shorter. When I arrived he was addressing a group of newspapermen. I tried to be as quiet as a little mouse as I moved over to a bench across the way. Jack immediately saw me and called out: "Judy, I'll be right with you, we're just finishing up." I could have fallen off the bench in a dead faint. "Fine, take your time," I managed to vocalize to my complete surprise, my face turning every shade of red. All the newspapermen had turned around to look at me. Jack didn't seem to mind at all. He didn't even flinch.

When the press conference broke up, Jack came right over, and again I was struck by his good looks. He seemed so young and virile, so dashing, not at all the image I had of a politician.

"Do you mind having lunch on the patio of Frank's suite instead of going inside?" he said, his eyes looking directly into mine. "I want a chance to talk with you without the interruptions we would get in the restaurant."

That was absolutely fine with me. I was not anxious to be the center of attention. God knows, that was the last thing I ever wanted in life. "Yes," I said, "it's too beautiful a day to be inside."

It was lovely on Frank's patio. There was not another soul around. I don't have the faintest recollection of what we had for lunch. My memory works in peculiar ways. Sometimes I can remember every detail of a room that I saw only once twenty or thirty years ago and can't remember a word that was said by anybody. Other times it's just the opposite. On this day, I do remember a great deal of what we discussed because of his attentiveness and what seemed an almost insatiable interest in *what* and *who* I was. He asked about my parents, my brothers and sisters, and we discussed the merits of coming from a large family. He was one of nine children. He thought it was much more fun to come from a large family, and he compared it to what it would be like being an only child. I didn't realize it then, but he was feeling me out, trying to see how I felt about things. At one point, he asked me if I was a Democrat or a Republican, and I honestly confessed that I didn't know. He said, "Well, we'll change that." At that moment, I am sure he had every intention of converting me from nothing to something. His job was to convert people. He wanted to convert the world.

The main topic of conversation, once I had given him my

family history, was religion. He was surprised, I think, that I had stopped going to church after my divorce from Billy. Until then, as a devout Catholic, I had gone to mass every Sunday. I explained that I knew I would one day remarry, and for me to continue going to church knowing that I would then be excommunicated was just pure sham. I lost faith in the church because I knew I could buy my way back into it. All I had to do was tell a few lies, find someone to swear to them, and pay the required fee to have my marriage annulled. How hypocritical that seemed to me.

When I was growing up, the teachings of the Catholic Church were based on fear. Going to confession used to terrify me, even when confessing the simple things a child does. As I kneeled in the darkness of the confessional, waiting for the priest to slide open the little panel behind the mesh screen, I would start to tremble as I tried to remember the sins I would have to confess to God so that the priest could punish me and cleanse my soul before I could receive Him at communion the next morning. If I had to confess a lie, then I was panic-stricken at the thought that he might want me to explain that lie. What if I forgot to confess everything and then received communion while still in a state of sin? There were times when I thought a bolt of lightning would strike me dead just as the priest opened the panel—he either was going to have horns and fangs or a halo and a toothless grin. It's terrible what the Catholic Church does to children—the fear it instills remains hidden inside you all your life.

When Jack asked if I had any objection to a Catholic president, I said that if he had the same feeling inside him that I had as a child, or that my mother had all her life, then I was concerned about it. "So much of it is so unrealistic," I said. "So much of it is controlled by the Pope. It has to affect you as President."

He smiled. "That's interesting and it's precisely what I have to find out," he said. "That's why I have to expose myself to as many people as possible as soon as possible. I want them to see me and hear my views. I want them to believe in me, as a free thinking individual, and not to worry about the influence of the Pope. The issues I'm interested in have nothing to do with religion. As I see it, it's basically a question of educating non-Catholics.''

"I don't agree," I said, now completely engrossed in the subject. "Some non-Catholics may resent you at first, but I think you can win them over for the very reason that they don't really know all that much about the Church's method. The resistance, I think, will be with people who had a strict Catholic upbringing and later walked away from it. I'm sure there must be millions who have left or are on the borderline of leaving. You will get more opposition from them than from non-Catholics.''

He was smiling, no doubt amused by the intensity of my feelings when I talked about the Church. Jack's attitude was more sophisticated. Like so many educated Catholics, he was more interested in the philosophy of religion than in the methods by which it was implemented. Paradoxes did not trouble him. Most of them, he felt, were problems created at the teaching level by nuns and priests, not by scholars and philosophers. I have heard this argument before, and it never fails to confuse me. It was the last thing I wanted to pursue with Jack Kennedy on that beautiful day.

As I was to learn time and again during the entire presidential campaign, the Catholic issue was constantly on his mind. We talked about it often. Another important concern was his age. He was only forty-two on the day we sat out on Frank's patio—he was born May 29, 1917. If elected, he would be forty-three, just a few months older than Teddy Roosevelt, the youngest president.

Although he was concerned about his age, he felt that he could overcome it during the campaign. He thought people would forget about his age, but no matter how much he tried, for some people the religious issue would be irreconcilable. He thought it was terribly unfair to mix religion with politics. It was his feeling that if he had been good enough for the navy during the war, he was good enough to be president.

Jack was very proud of being Irish and Catholic, in that order. He was exceptionally proud of his family, particularly of his father. As the world was to learn, the Kennedys were

92

close. You took on one Kennedy, you had to take on the whole family. They never made derogatory remarks about one another. The most I ever heard Jack say about a member of his family was his response when I told him about my evening with Teddy. He had asked whether I had a good time the night before, and I said, "Your brother Teddy is really something." Then I recounted Teddy's antics about my going to Denver with him. After my experience with Pete and Frank in Hawaii, I thought it best to speak out first.

Jack thought it was hilarious. "That little rascal," he said, shaking his head as if it were too funny to be true. "You'll have to excuse his youthful exuberance. He's still quite a kid in many ways, but his heart is in the right place. He's a little immature, but time will cure that. Right now he thinks politics is a game, and that's all right too. I'm glad he's having fun. The point is that he's carrying his share of the load. Teddy is working out just fine."

We sat over lunch nearly three hours. The time went by so quickly that I couldn't believe how late it was until I realized that I had about an hour to get ready for a five o'clock reception being held in Jack's honor in one of the banquet rooms at the Sands. I can take an hour just soaking in the tub. Ideally I like three hours to get ready for an evening out. Putting on my face takes no time at all. The only makeup I use is mascara and powder. What takes time is my bath, my hair, my nails, and selecting the proper attire for each occasion. Everything from top to bottom must be coordinated.

Our whole crowd was at the reception and I was never more talkative and friendly with them than I was that day. I would have done anything to keep a respectable distance from Jack. I felt terribly conspicuous every time he came near me. I had such mixed feelings about him; would always have mixed feelings where he was concerned. The fact that he was married, that he was a public figure, with all the dangers that implied; the fear that I might fall in love and be hurt again, or that perhaps it was just a passing fancy; the fear that we would have an affair and it would become serious, or that it would not be serious; the fear that I was heading for a hard fall, and could not stop any of it from happening. I knew something was going on inside me that I could not fully comprehend. I was becoming restless, anxious in ways I could not satisfy. I saw myself as a rudderless ship in a storm, being tossed in all directions, without the slightest bearing on where I was headed. Self-examination has always left me with an empty feeling, a sadness I can't explain even to myself.

There was no avoiding Jack at the reception—I don't mean to suggest that I was trying to avoid him, but I was so afraid that others would get ideas. Frankly, I don't really know what I wanted. I think I felt like a schoolgirl infatuated with the new boy from out of state that no one knows anything about. The mysterious stranger. Every time he made his way over to me in the crowd and I saw that big smile on his handsome face, my heart skipped a beat. It made me lightheaded. I had this wonderful happy feeling and yet I was uneasy and uncomfortable. I thought that every time he came over and touched my hand, all eyes were focused on us.

Once when he came over, he said, "We have a date at eight o'clock. Don't forget."

"Oh," I said, and I know I must have had a big smile on my face.

"Jack Entratter offered us his table and I'd like for just the two of us to see the show. I have to go to Oregon later tonight, so this may be our last chance to be together for a while."

I must have looked disappointed because he said, "Don't worry, I plan to see a lot of you, campaign or no campaign, we can arrange it somehow if you're willing."

"I'm willing," I said. "Don't worry about that."

"Good. Now don't go away. We'll go directly from here to the Copa Room."

Entratter's booth was in the back, but elevated, with an unobstructed view of the stage. It was as private as one could be in a room with hundreds of people. It was dark enough to create a feeling of privacy. I don't think either one of us had the slightest notion of what was happening on the stage. By this time it was plain to both of us that we were deeply interested in each other. I was terribly impressed with him, and, as the saying goes, my heart was on my sleeve. But I could tell that the feeling was mutual. He wanted to be alone with me. He didn't want other people intruding on our conversation. It was the feeling that you get when someone just wants to talk to you. That was the way we both felt. Every time he reached for his drink, he gave my hand a little love pat or squeeze. Nothing more. He wasn't all over me. It made that furtive touch in the dark all the more thrilling.

After the show, as we were walking out of the Copa Room, we were overtaken by Gloria Cahn and Pat Newcombe who very skillfully formed a wedge between us and swept him off. I could hear Gloria frantically saying, "Come on, Senator, we're going to such and such for dinner. Everybody is going to be there." By then they had succeeded in separating us. They had him surrounded and were literally pulling him away with them. I watched him being propelled across the casino, with the crowd around him getting larger, and I remember Gloria turning to give me a last smug look just before they disappeared in the lobby.

I took a cab to the Flamingo and went directly to my room to kick away at the furniture before I exploded into a million little pieces. Yet I was more unhappy than angry. I felt terribly disappointed, particularly since he was leaving to campaign later that night and I might not see him ever again.

I don't remember what I did for the next two hours, but when the phone rang a little before twelve I just knew it was Jack.

"What happened to you?" he said. "What are you doing in your room?"

"Well, you were swept away," I said. "I thought you had plans that didn't include me."

"I almost died when we got to the restaurant and I realized you weren't with us. I asked a couple of people but they didn't know. Then Gloria said you had other plans for the evening."

"That doesn't surprise me in the least," I said, wondering why she was working so hard to do me in.

"Did I offend you in some way?" he asked, and he sounded so puzzled by it all. "Was it me?"

"Oh, no," I said. "Nothing like that. It's just that I had the feeling I wasn't wanted. Also I didn't know when you had to leave for Oregon."

"All right, then. Come on back over. We're going to see the late show and I would very much like for you to be with me."

I didn't know what to say. Again that dilemma. I wanted to see him, but I was hurt, and I would rather have had the others believe I had missed dinner because I had something else planned, than for them to think that I was sitting in my room waiting for his call.

While I was debating with myself, he said, "Please come over. There's no sense in my sitting through the show again unless you're with me. I'm going to wait for you at the entrance to the Copa Room and I won't go in until you get here."

He was waiting for me, but so were Gloria and Pat. The only consolation was that they didn't know he was waiting for me until I arrived. Gloria looked daggers at me and it gave me all the satisfaction in the world. Not only that, but Jack didn't say a word to them during the entire show. We sat in Entratter's booth again, and I was on Jack's left and they were on his right, and we acted like we were completely alone. You could feel it from head to toe how happy he was that I was with him. We exchanged telephone numbers and there was no question that this was the beginning of what would be a long and intimate relationship. He was so different from anyone I had known up to then that I just didn't know how to evaluate my emotions. Getting to know Jack Kennedy was going to be not just an experience, but an adventure.

After the show, we sat in the lounge a few minutes until he had to leave for the airport. He didn't say anything in front of the others, but from the way he looked at me I knew that everything was fine.

I went to my room and a few minutes later Dean called.

"How come you left?" he asked. Jeanne had already left for Beverly Hills.

"I was getting tired," I said.

"Come on back down, will you? Come have something to eat with me."

It was always hard saying no to Dean. I went down and we talked for a while, and then I went to bed and thought about Jack. I was anxious to be alone with my thoughts. I wanted to try and sort them out. The fact that he was married was bothering me, and yet it wasn't bothering me. The thought that he liked me was the most important of all.

Something wonderful was happening to me. I was lying in bed and smiling at the ceiling. I was almost giddy. It was a feeling that I had when I was young and had a crush on someone—that first meeting when you realize that he's someone special. It's all anticipation, hoping and wondering and feeling good. Then doubt creeps in: "I wonder if I'll ever see him again?" There was not much doubt that night. I slept well and woke up feeling like Scarlet O'Hara the morning after Rhett Butler carried her up the stairs.

I returned to Beverly Hills the next day and the first thing I did was to buy Jack's two books: *Why England Slept* and *Profiles in Courage*. I couldn't get him off my mind and I wanted to know everything about him I could possibly learn. I bought every book I could find concerning the Kennedys.

Jack called me from Fresno on February 12. Earlier in the day I had received a dozen red roses from him. He sounded pumped up and raring to go. There would be calls when he was completely exhausted and my heart would go out to him. I never have understood how a man can survive a presidential campaign. It boggles my mind to think about it. Going to all those places, meeting all those people, shaking all those hands, making all those speeches, eating all those cold dinners, attending all those meetings, not to mention the smoke-filled-room ones. If there is such a talent in homo sapiens classifiable as a natural born politician, Jack Kennedy had a genius amount of it. Politics wasn't something he learned in school or from his father. There was something about him that made people feel happy and safe in his presence. I think people felt his interest in them. Whoever he talked to, that person knew Jack Kennedy was talking to him, and to no one else, that he was interested in him, and wanted to hear his views exclusive of any other. When he shook your hand, you felt that he was really shaking your hand, that it was not just another hand along the way. He had a quality that touched people. They believed him when he told them what was good for them. He had a good face, an honest face, and the people liked and trusted what they saw.

We talked a long time that evening. He told me how much he missed me, how pleased he was we had met, and most important of all, he wanted to arrange another meeting. From that moment on, the phone calls never stopped. He called almost every day—no matter where he was, or how tired, he found the time and the energy to call me. Sometimes I called him, routing the calls through his secretary, Evelyn Lincoln, at her office in the Old Senate Office Building. She always knew where Jack could be reached. Most of the times I called her with a request to speak to Jack, it would be only a question of minutes before he returned my call.

I became an avid Kennedy follower. I read newspaper accounts, watched television, read magazines. My need to know more about him was insatiable. I read that while in Madison, Wisconsin, Jack began his day in darkness at the gate of a sausage works and ended it in Kenosha with a coffee hour for two hundred women. Jack trekked through snow in sheepskin-lined shoes but hatless as usual. With that marvelous head of hair, he didn't need a hat. He visited places like Beaver Dam, Waupun, Oshkosh, Appleton, West Bend, Mayville—sixteen cities in three days. Children were excused from school to see him, for the first time since William Jennings Bryan's campaign. I thought, "My God, a sausage works in freezing darkness in Wisconsin. Just to shake the frozen hands of a few workers." I truly felt for him. What a tortuous road candidates travel and so much of it in vain.

On the afternoon of February 24, I went to Warner

Brothers to have lunch with my sister Jackie. Afterwards we went to see Frank on the set of *Oceans 11*. He was extremely solicitous and gallant, making sure that chairs were provided for us so that we could watch the shooting of a scene. Later, over drinks in his dressing room, I asked what he was going to do next. He said he had an engagement at the Fontaine-bleau in Miami and that the Clan was planning on joining him for some of the shows. Their show had been a huge success at the Sands and Frank thought it would be "a gas" to repeat it in Miami. "Hey, why don't you come down for the opening. Always great to have a pretty girl up front."

I didn't accept, nor did I refuse. I said I would think about it. I wasn't about to make any plans that might later conflict with my seeing Jack. As luck would have it, we decided on the place and time for our next meeting that very evening when Jack called from Wisconsin. Throughout this period, we both had been anxious to see each other, but it was a question of finding a suitable time and place. I didn't feel comfortable just flying to a rendezvous point in some obscure part of the country. Because of the way I felt about his situation, being married and a candidate for the presidency, I didn't want to compromise him or myself. We discussed this at great lengths on the phone, at times for an hour or more. I didn't know how or where he found the time that he spent with me on the phone, and I didn't care really, as long as I could hear his voice—I read newspapers and magazines not because I cared all that much about politics, but just to see his name in print.

When he mentioned that he would be in New York on the evening of March 7, I told him I would be at the Plaza. He offered to get my airline ticket and to make my reservation at the Plaza, but I said I would take care of it myself.

"Are you sure that you're really coming?" he asked.

"Of course," I said. "My God, why do you ask?"

"Then why won't you let me make the necessary arrangements?"

"Because I feel more comfortable doing it myself."

"Well, for a moment I thought you might have changed your mind."

"I have every intention of being there. I want to see you, Jack, as much as you want to see me."

"I don't think that's possible, Judy, not the way I've missed you these past two weeks. I wish I had taken Teddy's idea and brought you along with me. I wish you were here tonight."

"I wish I were with you, Jack, I really do."

We talked in this vein for a while, and then before saying goodnight, he said, "I would be terribly disappointed if you weren't at the Plaza on March 7."

It wasn't until the next day that I realized that March 7 was the eve of the New Hampshire primary. What a man, I thought, to find time for me on a day when he would be campaigning all over the state in a last effort to gain votes.

When I arrived in New York, I remember seeing a headline in one of the newspapers to the effect that the stop-Kennedy drive had failed. Jack was the favorite Democratic candidate. It was exciting news. I called room service and ordered a drink to celebrate.

It was a long evening. It's one thing to get comfortable with someone on the phone, but a whole month had gone by since we had met and spent that brief moment together in Las Vegas. Talking and kidding with him on the phone was one thing, but in a little while he was going to be right here in this room with me. The longer I waited, the more nervous I became. I must have gotten up to look in the mirror a hundred times. Then I thought that perhaps I should have worn something else.

It's terrible waiting for a knock on the door. I could hear footsteps coming down the hall and my heart would stop until they went by. Finally there was a light tap on the door. He was all smiles and out of breath. I remember thinking that perhaps he had run up the stairs. My room was 1651—that would be some hike.

We looked at each other and at first he was a little hesitant.

I said, "Hi, Jack. How are you?" I didn't know what else to say.

He looked at me, still smiling, and said, "I'm sorry I'm late."

"That's all right," I said. "I understand. I know how busy you've been lately."

He closed the door and put his arms around me. "God," he said, "it's good to see you."

It takes me a long time to be at ease with people, and I think he felt it because he pulled back and held me at arm's length. "Let me take a good look at you. You look sensational." He kept his arm on my shoulder as we walked into the room. The bed just seemed to zoom in size. It·looked to me like I had the smallest room and the biggest bed in the Plaza. There were two chairs and a small table at the other end of the room. There was a bottle of Jack Daniels, ice and two glasses on the table. As we walked toward the chairs, I offered him a drink, and he asked if I would prefer to go out for something to eat. I could tell that he wasn't too keen about it. I said, "Sit down and let's just talk. I would rather not be seen with you right now."

He was visibly relieved. I made drinks and we sat facing each other, drinks in hand, and began to make conversation. I asked if he would like to remove his jacket and he promptly stood up, removed it, draped it over the back of his chair and loosened his tie. Now it looked like I was planning to spend the evening in bed. My head was going in different directions. I wanted to be with him and I didn't want to be with him. It was easy to talk on the phone, but once something else started, I just knew how difficult it would be for both of us. I was afraid of getting hurt. I was just getting over Travis, and I wasn't sure I wanted to become deeply involved with anyone. Still it was happening to me and I was letting it happen.

That damn bed was getting bigger by the minute. Finally, after interminable small talk, Jack took the initiative. He stood me up and kissed me. It was all well and good, but I knew what was coming and something inside me was beginning to resist. He was amorous and just very loving. I realize today that I was overly sensitive about it. All of a sudden, I was discounting every phone call, every flower, everything. I just didn't want what was happening to happen.

By this time, he had maneuvered me over to the bed, and had gently pushed me on my back. His kisses were more passionate now and my head was beginning to reel. Suddenly, I pushed at him and said, "No, Jack."

He couldn't believe it. "What do you mean, no?"

"I just can't do this right now," I said. "I haven't seen you for a month."

"But we've talked on the phone every day. What's the matter?"

"Yes, we've talked on the phone, but I just can't say, 'Hello, there, how are you, have a drink, let's go to bed.' I feel so uncomfortable."

"But, Judy, don't you want to be close to me?"

"I do, Jack. I really do, but not this way. I need time to think it out."

I could see he was getting impatient. "I've waited so long to see you," he said. "I tried to see you before now, in other places, and it was your choice to see me in New York."

"I know that, Jack."

"And time-wise, you knew what you were getting into."

"I know, I know . . ."

He was getting more annoyed as the discussion went on. Finally, he stood up and walked over to the chair for his jacket. I sat there just feeling dreadful. I thought frantically: "What do I do now?" I knew that if he walked out that door, I was going to be just miserable. I had gotten myself into a situation I couldn't resolve. I wanted to be with him, but it was so abrupt, so cold and calculated. Somewhere, also, hidden in this jumble of thoughts was the question of what he would think of me, how it would look to him.

I knew he had been anticipating our meeting the way a man anticipates when two people start getting close. A woman anticipates in another way. Most women—I know I am—are incurable romantics. Love should be the way it used to be presented in the movies. You're romanced and the hero is gentle and charming and ever so considerate. Of course, it's not realistic. A woman can't be brought a rose, a single rose, and have dinner by candlelight every night. If only violins had played outside the door to create a romantic mood. Anything to soften it.

I was absolutely desolate as he walked to the door. I sat there, a hurt soul, hoping he'd turn around and say he was sorry, that everything was all right. But he was leaving, there was no doubt about it.

He turned around and looked at me: "I'm really sorry," he said, his hand on the doorknob.

I said, "Jack, come here."

He came back to the bed and sat down, putting his arms around me. "Don't misunderstand this," he said. "I don't mean to be impatient. I know it probably looks that way, but I have been anticipating this moment for a long time. This has been the longest month."

I nodded. "It has for me, too, Jack."

"I could have walked in this room and picked you up and put you down on the bed." He stopped to kiss me. "I have so looked forward to being close to you, to making love to you, and then to just lie in bed and talk the way two people can talk after making love."

We kissed and after a while I went to the bathroom to disrobe. When I came back, Jack was already in bed. He was smiling as he reached out for me. I snuggled close to him under the covers. "I didn't mean to act badly," he said. "I was so disappointed. I hope you understand how much I've anticipated this moment." I placed a finger against his lips and he kissed it. Then we made love.

Once I had made up my mind, there was no hesitation. I am very emotional and very demonstrative with my love and in lovemaking. That is my nature. I am very active, but the man has to take the initiative. When people make love, they should make love to each other. I mention this because, as I was to learn in my relationship with Jack, his attitude was that he was there to be serviced. Partly this was due to his back problem, and partly I think he had been spoiled by women. There is a world of difference between a man who expects to be made love to and two people making love to each other.

This attitude, or inclination, was not apparent that first night. He couldn't have been more loving, more concerned about my feelings, more considerate, more gentle. There was no question that he cared deeply about me. I was happy that I had called him back. Yet I was concerned about where the affair was leading me. He was married and perhaps someday he would be the President of the United States. How does the President of the United States carry on an affair without arousing suspicion? At the same time, I was busy rationalizing, trying to convince myself that everything was fine because he truly cared about me. I couldn't picture anyone working that hard just to go to bed for one night. Anyone who put in that much time and effort and energy for a so-called conquest had to have a serious problem. Jack was the last man in the world to have that kind of problem.

After we had made love, we lay in each other's arms for a long time. Mostly we talked about ourselves, but he did relate anecdotes from the hustings. I loved the way he pronounced hustings. The tempo of the campaign seemed so hectic—frantic, really. I remember his reciting the wording of a sign made up by one of his aides: "As soon as the rush is over, I'm going to have a nervous breakdown. I worked for it. I owe it to myself, and nobody is going to deprive me of it."

Jack was a great teaser and had a marvelous sense of humor. And he could take it when you teased back, but there were areas where he was sensitive. One was the money his family was spending on his campaign. Other candidates had criticized him for this. Hubert Humphrey had charged that Jack was on a "spending spree." One of the sore points was the twin-engined Convair airplane Jack's father had purchased for him. I personally loved that airplane. It had made our evening possible. Jack hated that "little rich boy" image his opponents were trying to create.

What fascinated me about Jack was that he was the same in person as he was on the television screen. His mannerisms were natural. I don't think he ever sat down and tried to create an image. He wasn't two different people. Some politicians deliberately use their hands in certain ways. They have been told that this is the way to be effective before an audience. Jack used his hands the same whether he was talking to millions on television or sitting up in bed after making love.

"I told Hubert that I will be happy to sit down and agree on a maximum spending figure," Jack said, his right hand sawing the air the way I had seen him do so often on television.

We were propped up on pillows drinking Jack Daniels. "Poor Hubert," I said. "There are so few Humphreys and so many Kennedys. Anybody could become President if they had a family as big and as hard working as yours. How can one country stomach so many Kennedys."

He laughed. "Don't forget the grandkids. Wait till they come along. We'll take over the whole country—maybe the world."

I loved the wonderful airy, light side of him. It was amazing to me that he could be so relaxed on the eve of the first important primary. Not once did he mention New Hampshire. He had an air of confidence that was unshakeable. Come hell or high water he was going to win. He was a winner. He came from a family of winners. They would do anything to win. They never thought of losing. His attitude with me was always on the up-side. If he was worried about anything, he never let me know it.

After he left in the wee hours of the morning, my emotions were still mixed. I was happy and I was sad, and that pretty much explains my relationship with Jack Kennedy. As time went on, I would vacillate between these two emotions, with the emphasis first on one and then the other, which kept me in a state of continuous anxiety.

What a delight it was to be awakened by a bellman with a dozen red roses. The card said, "Thinking of you—J." And then to hear that he had won in New Hampshire made it complete. He was on his way and I was so proud of him.

When he called later that day, he didn't even mention the primary. All he seemed interested in was us. He wanted to know if I had slept well, and did I get enough rest? He was sorry he couldn't have stayed longer; he was anxious to see me again, and he would call and try to set something definite in the next few days, perhaps in Washington, if that met with my approval. I, in turn, was saying the same things to him. Don't worry about it, I'm happy I was able to see you, and, yes, I would love to see you again, and Washington was a fine place.

It was then that I congratulated him on his victory in New Hampshire. "I guess we showed them we're going *All The Way,*" Jack said. "That and *High Hopes* are our theme songs. Frank recorded two parodies. One of the lines goes, 'Oops, there goes the opposition—Kerplop!' " He laughed and it was such a hearty laugh. We laughed a lot on the telephone. We teased each other all the time. Jack went on to explain that he had a station wagon equipped with loudspeakers following him whenever he went out on the street to shake hands. "Frank's voice gets them out of the barbershop and general store. All I have to do is grab them and convince them that they've just shaken the hand of the next President of the United States."

Every time we talked on the phone, and I am referring to before and after our meeting at the Plaza, he invariably would ask, "Have you seen Frank lately?" I would answer, "No," or "Yes, I saw him on the set," or "He called last night and I wasn't home," or whatever was the circumstance at the moment. Jack would say, "Ohhh, you still want to see Frank?" I would say, "We're just friends, Jack." Then he'd say, "Okay, okay," in almost a little boy's "See if I care" voice. Then the very next day, "See Frank? Where did you go last night? I called and you weren't home." I would tell him I had been out to dinner with Travis, or Dick Elwood, or Jeff Chandler, or Dewey Martin, or Sy Devore, or whoever, and he would respond, "Is he a good friend, is he someone you're interested in." He wanted to be the star of the show. He was married and yet he was jealous. I was always reassuring him that they were only friends and that there was no personal involvement with any of them.''

On this day, however, I told Jack that I was leaving for Miami in two days to see Frank's opening at the Fontainebleau. He wanted to know how long I would stay and I said only a few days. "Have a good time," he said, "and I'll try to call you every day. Don't forget we have a date in Washington very soon."

Toni Carroll flew to Miami with me. She had long since been divorced from David Wolper and had resumed her career as a nightclub singer. She was living in a small apartment off Central Park South. She was between engagements at the time and just leaped at the chance to get away from the snow. I had planned on staying only two days, but as it turned out I ended up staying much longer.

We got in late and both went straight to bed. The next day I left word for Frank that I was there with a friend and Tony, his valet, called to say that Frank was tied up that night but he wanted to know if we wanted to see the show. I said we would like to see the late show. "Fine," he said, "Frank wants to take care of the table and everything for the show. Do you want to have dinner late in there?" It was Frank's way of smoothing things out when he wasn't available.

When Frank called to invite me to dinner the next day I had already made plans to see my uncle, Armand Cerami, that evening. I said I would stay on a few more days, and he said, "Okay, I'll call you tomorrow." Toni left that afternoon.

I call Armand Cerami my uncle but he is my uncle's brother. Uncle Armand owns part of two Miami restaurants called Tony's Fishmarket and Tony Sweets.

The next night Frank called and invited me up to his suite. "We'll have cocktails while I finish getting ready for the show," he said.

It was absolutely amazing. There were only two others in the room with Frank when I arrived. Tony, his valet, who let me in, and a man Frank introduced as Joe Fish.

AUTHOR'S NOTE: *Joe Fish was an alias for Joseph Fischetti, a cousin of Al Capone, and a brother of Charles and Rocco Fischetti, now deceased, but once high ranking mafiosi in the Chicago Syndicate.*

Frank was in a good mood. As I came into the room, he held out his arms and crooned, "A pretty girl is like a melody." Then he went, "boom, boom, boom," rotating his hips like a stripper. "Come on, baby, let's have a little kiss and hug, a little rock and roll," he sang, "it's been a long dry spell in Campbell land."

I walked across the room and sat down. "That's a likely story," I said.

"You have a cruel heart, Campbell. That's your German blood. *Achtung!*" He clicked his heels and slapped Joe Fish on the back. "Hey, Joe, what about this little Campbell chick?"

"Beautiful, Frank. Very beautiful."

"What would you say, Joe, if I told you that this little broad, with the cold German blood, has broken my heart. Not just once, Joe, but many times. You might even say often."

"That wouldn't surprise me, Frank. It breaks my heart just looking at her."

"Come on, you guys, cut it out, will you," I said, trying to suppress a giggle.

While Frank talked, Tony was all over him, first with a whisk broom, then a shoe brush, and finally straightening his tie and pocket handkerchief.

When Frank was ready, all four of us went down to the lower level and went through a door that brought us backstage. I watched the show from the wings. In those days Frank was magnificent. There is no other way to describe what he did on that stage. He would snap his fingers, sing a couple of bars, and the whole audience would fall under his spell. It was like watching mass hypnotism. Women would stare glassy-eyed while their burly husbands furtively brushed away tears as Frank took them on a sentimental journey.

Frank could evoke any mood he wished almost at will. He was a magician and a hypnotist. He stole hearts and made the old feel young again.

While Frank was onstage, people backstage were falling all over themselves trying to be nice to me. For days afterward, whenever I encountered any of them in the hotel, they would whisper, "That's the girl that was with Frank!" People can be so silly. I could just imagine what would have happened if they had seen me with Jack.

After the show, we went to Ricco's for dinner. It was the first time I tasted Italian baked clams and they were delicious. For some reason, my liking them delighted Joe Fish. Then we went to a burlesque place to see Hank Henry, an X-rated comic who was a friend of Frank. As we parted that evening, after I had gently deflected Frank's advances, he invited me to come to his penthouse suite for brunch the moment I was up.

Something happened the next day that I have often wondered about. We were out on Frank's patio, and Frank, I remember, was wearing his favorite orange trunks, and I had on slacks and a blouse, instead of the bikini he always wished I wore. I was standing looking over the balcony when Frank said, "You know, Campbell, you're really stupid."

I turned to look at him and he wasn't smiling. "Well, thanks a bunch," I said.

"I mean it. You're so beautiful, and you're bright, but you're so square. I've told you that before and I mean it. You don't know how to take advantage of the opportunities open to you. You don't walk through any of those open doors. Goddamnit, the things you could have if you weren't so fucking stupid."

"You have a strange way of complimenting someone."

"It's not a compliment," he said, his mouth twisting in disgust. "Do me a favor, will you? Don't be a sucker all your life. Wake up and realize what you've got in the palm of your hand. Sometimes you remind me of some silly schoolgirl. Get with it. Swing a little. You only live once, baby."

That was the first and only time Frank Sinatra offered me personal advice. I considered his evaluation a compliment. I was glad I was not the kind of person he wanted me to be. I wasn't as stupid as he imagined. I knew what he meant. I knew all about people going through open doors, or busting through them, and grabbing everything in sight. That had no interest for me. All I ever wanted in my life was love and peace of mind, to be *comfortable* with myself. I know this word comes up often in my story. It has a special meaning for me. I cannot function unless I am comfortable. I mean comfortable inside, with my thoughts, with my code of conduct, which may seem cockeyed to some people but it's what I'm stuck with, and what I must live with if I want to survive as a rational human being.

After deciding to stay on in Florida, I had changed the departure day for my flight back to New York to March 16. The day before I was to leave, Frank asked if I would mind dropping off one of his watches at Cartier's for repairs. I had scheduled an early flight, but it was cancelled because of a bomb scare. This was when the bombing of airplanes first started. I think Eastern Airlines had had one of its planes blown up a few days before. I made a reservation for later that night but I got cold feet and cancelled it.

The next day I called Frank to have Tony pick up the watch. I didn't want to be responsible for it. Frank asked if I wanted to see the show. I said that I was going to spend the day in the sun, relaxing, and was planning on going to bed early.

I found a fairly secluded spot above the cabanas near the pool, and was lying there, enjoying the sun in a Jax swimsuit, which was a modified bikini, when all of a sudden I heard, "Hey, Campbell, what are you doing down there!"

It was Frank from the balcony of his patio. He knew it would embarrass me and he was laughing like a loon. "Hey, where did you get the bikini, Campbell? Hey, I can see you!"

When I refused to acknowledge him, he shouted. "I mean you, there, Campbell, in the orange bikini. Come on up here!"

I must admit I was wearing an orange swimsuit, but it was

110

a very pale orange. By now, of course, everybody was either staring at me or laughing with Frank.

I clenched my teeth, turned over on my stomach, and buried my face in my arms. I wanted to get some color. I knew I would be going back to see Jack. He called almost daily, from places like West Virginia, Pennsylvania, Indiana, Wisconsin, Washington. Evelyn Lincoln and I became old telephone friends, or at least co-conspirators. She never failed to give Jack my messages and Jack never failed to return my calls. Every time I would mention that I had seen him on television, Jack would invariably ask, "How did I look? Did I come across?" Sometimes he even asked me if I liked his suit. He was always concerned about his appearance. I was complimentary when he asked, but I never paid gratuitous compliments. I just felt that people in the limelight received too many compliments as it was.

There may be a whole lot of things historians will take away from Jack, but no one can say that he wasn't attractive, or that he couldn't charm a crowd. He had a little boy charm for some and for others he was so sophisticated. God, some women would have done anything to get near him. He had sex appeal. And he knew it.

One night when he called I told him that Uncle Armand had contributed to his campaign—I may be wrong, but I think it was $20,000. I said, "See we have Democrats in the family." I was only kidding, but many months later when I was visiting him in the White House, he acknowledged that Uncle Armand was a good Democrat and even named the amount he had contributed. When it came to politics, there was very little that slipped by Jack Kennedy.

One night after Jack had asked me who I was seeing in Miami, he said something I have never forgotten. "You don't seem to care who I see," he said, and he actually sounded a little petulant.

"What do you mean?" I asked, really taken aback by the remark.

"You never ask who I'm seeing. Don't you care?"

"My God, Jack," I said, now even more incredulous. "I can read about you every day in the newspapers. You're on television every night. If I want to know where you are or who you're seeing, all I have to do is pick up a paper or switch on the dial.''

Years later, when I began to hear rumors about Jack's various extramarital relationships, I often wondered about that conversation.

As the song goes, the ''days dwindle down'' fairly rapidly in Miami. Some of my escorts there were Bill Orr and Hugh Benson, who were producers at Warner Brothers and were in Florida scouting locations for a television series. Another was Bob Neal, a young Texas oilman, who has been described by Pete Lawford as a ''real ladies man.'' According to a recent (1976) interview Pete gave to a tabloid, Jack once greeted Neal with, ''Ah, Bob, the man who lives the life we all want to lead.'' If Bob Neal is a ''real ladies man,'' then Don Knotts is Casanova. That comment by Pete makes about as much sense as the one he made in the same story concerning me: ''This lady [me], to my knowledge, I have never met. I never saw her in the company of the President, never saw her in the company of Frank Sinatra and never saw her in the company of Sam Giancana.''

Bob Neal was as docile an escort as I ever had. Not as interesting as some, perhaps, but certainly as safe. Bob's family was in oil and he lived accordingly. On March 23, I took Bob to one of Frank's parties. We had dined on Bob's yacht and had gone to see the late show, sitting at Frank's table. After the show, Tony had invited us to a party in Frank's suite.

The next evening I went with Bill Orr and Hugh Benson to see a Cuban show in one of the hotels. We sat at a long table with at least fifteen people, including Desi Arnaz, who couldn't take his eyes off me. Bill told me that everybody was going to Desi's suite after the show for a party—Desi had even invited the Cuban performers. Afterward in the parking lot, everybody was going every which way and I found myself in the car with two friends of Bill and Hugh, who had sat next to me at the table and who were connected with the Miss Universe Pageant.

112

Since it was getting chilly, on the way to Desi's hotel I asked them to stop at the Fontainebleau so I could get a wrap. I ran into the lobby and Tony, Frank's valet, was standing there watching me. There was a message from Dean under my door, which meant he had arrived, but I didn't have time to answer it. When I came back, Tony was standing beside the car talking to the two men. Upon arriving at Desi's hotel, which I think was the Diplomat, the man driving the car said, "You two go up and I'll be right with you." I didn't think anything of it.

The light went on quickly enough when I walked into Desi's suite. There were only three of us in there—my escort, Desi, and me. The next time I looked around there were only two—my escort had vanished. By now Desi was talking a mile a minute, but I wasn't listening. I was frantically thinking of a way out. Finally I just said, "Excuse me a moment," turned around and walked out the door without looking back once. I went down the elevator and took a cab to my hotel.

I spent most of my time with Dean the next couple of days. The whole Clan was now in for the show. Others included Sammy and Gloria Cahn, Jack Entratter, and Juliet Prowse. Each girl in Frank's life has a certain amount of time allotted to her. Jeanne Martin had not come and if Pat Lawford was there, I just don't remember. She became the kind of person that I didn't see even when she was sitting at the same table.

On March 26, Dean and Jack Entratter took me to a party in the Poodle Bar at the Fontainebleau. We came in about two in the morning and Frank was sitting at the head of the table with Juliet on his right. I said, "Hi, Frank—" but the rest of the words stuck in my throat as he turned to look at me, his eyes narrowed and cold as ice. I thought, "Oh God, not again," and hurried away from him. The moment I sat down, Frank stood up, and I knew I was in for it. He was quite drunk, leaning forward, with a finger pointing right at me. He proceeded to dress me down for what he thought had occurred the night before at the so-called Arnaz party.

It was like instant fire. My head was exploding and my legs were shaking so badly that I was afraid to stand up. I looked at Jack Entratter, who was sitting on my right, and I said, "Jack, I have to get out of here. Will you help me?"

"Boy," Jack said, also struggling to stand up, "I'll tell you, the mood he's in, that's a good idea."

So Jack, who had trouble walking, helped me walk out of that room in front of all those people. I think if I had had a weapon in my hand, I would have killed Frank. I was that blood-curdling furious with him.

The next night was the big farewell party—the last night of the show. I had already made plans to go with Bob Neal and I was angry enough to keep the date regardless of Frank's ugliness. I slept late that morning and when I got up I decided to spend the day in my room, relaxing, reading magazines and *The New York Times* which I had delivered to my room every day. Through the pages of the *Times,* I could keep track of Jack and of the campaign on a day-to-day basis.

I read in that Sunday's *Times* that the Missouri state committee was urging that the state's slate be pledged to Stuart Symington. I laughed because former President Truman was for Symington, and I remembered Jack telling me that "the old bastard will come around." Jack, as always, was convinced that his rivals would be unable to form a coalition against him. He was the front runner, the man to beat, and opponents were coming out of the woodwork every day. Now Sam Rayburn was promoting Lyndon Johnson. Even Rose Kennedy was out in Wisconsin campaigning for her son. In Eau Claire, she had met with three Protestant clergymen who were opposing Jack on religious grounds. The Catholic issue remained unresolved.

Around four o'clock that afternoon there was a knock on my door and when I asked who it was, Jack Entratter said, "I'd like to see you for a minute, Judy."

I was wearing a caftan-style robe, which was perfectly proper for the occasion. I opened the door and said, "Hi, Jack, what's going on?" Instead of answering, he pushed me aside and barged right into the room, closing the door behind him. All he had on was a robe and slippers.

"What the devil are you doing here dressed like that?" I

asked, backing away as he tried to grab me. "Get the hell out of here," I shouted, "and don't ever come back." He got hold of me and began pulling me toward the bed, all the while saying, "Come on, Judy, what's the matter with you?" He was a big hulk of a man but his legs were weak. I shoved as hard as I could and he stumbled, letting go of me as he reached for something to steady himself. I ran to the door, opened it, and shouted, "Out!"

He was crouching on one knee in the middle of the room, his face contorted with anger, and I knew that if he had had good legs he would have leaped at me. Instead he struggled to his feet and as he went out the door, he said, "Who the hell do you think you are?"

I closed the door and leaned against it, my own legs barely able to support me. I felt sick to my stomach. I thought to myself: "What is wrong with me? What could have made him think that he could barge into my room like that?" This coming on top of the incidents with Desi Arnaz and Frank was more than I could cope with. I just sat on my bed and cried.

By the time Bob Neal picked me up that evening I had forced myself to stop thinking about what had happened. I was determined to go to Frank's party and not let anyone know how upset and unhappy they had made me. I wore an ice blue *peau de soie* cocktail dress with matching shoes and bag, which I had worn only once before, for the party at Dean's house. I had a necklace made for the dress, strands of matching ice blue beads. There is nothing like clothing to lift a woman's spirits.

VI

The party was in the French Room. There was a reception area and beyond it a large dining room and dance floor. We arrived at the cocktail hour and it was jammed with people. As we walked around greeting friends, Bob spotted Joe Fish and Skinny D'Amato and started toward them. At first I didn't see Frank, and by the time we got there it was too late. He was behind Skinny and caught up in conversation with a man I had never seen before. Joe Fish said, "Hey, Frank, look who's here."

Frank turned and actually smiled. I couldn't believe my eyes. "Come here, Judy," he said. "I want you to meet a good friend of mine, Sam Flood."

I offered my hand, but instead of shaking it, Sam Flood held it in his two hands. "It's a pleasure, Judy," he said, giving my hand a little squeeze but still holding on. He was middle-aged, of medium build and ruddy complexion, but with penetrating dark eyes. "Do you mind if I say something, Judy?"

"Not at all—I think."

He laughed, and it was a hearty laugh, the kind you hear from people who laugh a lot. "You're far too beautiful to be wearing junk—excuse me—I mean costume jewelry. A beautiful girl like you should be wearing real pearls and diamonds and rubies."

"A girl like me does sometimes."

"No offense, please," he said. "Real pleasure meeting you. Hope to see you again soon."

He released my hand and Bob and I continued to circulate.

AUTHOR'S NOTE: *Sam Flood was one of at least sixteen aliases used by Sam Giancana, whose real name was Momo Salvatore Giangono. As the author of* Captive City, *a book about crime and corruption in Chicago, I learned a great deal about Giancana, the criminal, as viewed by various records, but next to nothing about his personal life. Consequently, getting to know Giancana through Judy's reminiscences was a new experience for me.*

Born on May 24, 1908, his rap sheet dated back to 1925 and listed more than seventy arrests for crimes including contributing to delinquency, vagrancy, burglary, assault and battery, larceny, fugitive, assault to kill, damage by violence, conspiracy to operate a "book," possession of burglar tools and concealed weapons, bombing suspect, gambling, fictitious driver's license, murder—prime suspect in countless murder investigations, three before the age of twenty. In one murder indictment at the age of eighteen, in which he was released on bail, the sole prosecution witness was murdered before the trial. With all that, he was convicted only twice: thirty days for auto theft and four years for operating a still.

His first important job was as chauffeur and bodyguard for "Machine Gun" Jack McGurn (nee Jack Demore), a syndicate killer and a prime suspect along with Tony Accardo in the St. Valentine's Day Massacre. By 1932 Giancana was known as one of the fastest "wheelmen" on the West Side. And by 1948 he was described in police records as "in charge of the rough stuff department for Tony Accardo." In 1950 he was one of the principal Chicago area hoodlums and was considered a "general overseer" of illegal gambling in Chicago. In 1951 he was spending "considerable time in Florida but never at the same time as Tony Accardo as one or the other is always around the local area to make sure that business is conducted as usual." In 1952 he had "gambling interests in Cuba" and was a "big man in the shrimp industry." Also in 1952, he was attending a "meeting between Sheriff Kelly of Miami and Murray (the Camel) Humphreys, Jake (Greasy Thumb) Guzik, Gus (Shotgun) Alex, and Tony (Big Tuna) Accardo in Miami." In 1953 Giancana and Accardo and Guzik were "holding conferences in Reno and Las Vegas with other kingpins of the national syndicate." In 1954 "Judges John A. Sbarbaro and Joseph A. Pine attended the wake of Giancana's wife, Angeline, along with politicians and hoodlums." In 1956 he was "proclaimed 'Enforcer' during a dinner party at the Tam O'Shanter Country Club." The coronation ceremony was deceptively simple. Accardo merely placed a hand on Giancana's shoulder and said, "I want you to meet my good friend, Sam Giancana." He was forty-eight when he became the boss of all bosses of the Chicago Syndicate. Although he was not as precocious in gaining the leadership as his predecessors—Al Capone, Frank Nitti and Tony Accardo—he ruled longer than any of them.

Once described by a police official as "a snarling, sarcastic, ill-mannered, ill-tempered, sadistic psychopath," Giancana was a sixth-grade dropout at the age of fourteen. His lack of education was reflected in a psychological evaluation performed in 1940 at Terre Haute prison. The tests indicated he was still the equivalent of a sixth grader in knowledge, with a general IQ of 71 verbal and 93 nonverbal, with poor accuracy and good speed. Drafted by the U.S. Army in 1943, he was rejected as "a constitutional psychopath" with an "inadequate personality and strong anti-social trends." Actually, when they asked what he did for a living he said he was a thief. It is possible that he knew what he was doing.

As the chief executive officer, the president, so to

speak, of this vast criminal enterprise, this "constitutional psychopath" was responsible for its day-to-day success. Under him were vice presidents, department heads, district supervisors and straw bosses. This executive staff of approximately a thousand men commanded a force conservatively estimated at over fifty-thousand—about one percent of the population of Cook County—consisting of burglars, hijackers, fences, counterfeiters, extortioners, narcotics peddlers, loansharks, collectors, torturers, assassins, crooked cops, venal judges and politicians, union and business fronts, plus an array of gamblers including bookies, steerers, and policy runners. The annual "revenue" in Cook County was estimated at more than $2 billion, a figure arrived at by local authorities and newspapers—federal sources placed the gambling take alone at more than $1 billion.

In terms of leadership, this made Giancana the most powerful archcriminal in the world. Where New York rackets were divided among four or five separate organizations, Giancana was the ostensible ruler of a single syndicate with interests extending as far west as Hawaii. His immediate perimeter stretched from Cleveland to Kansas City, from Hot Springs to New Orleans. Trusted lieutenants operated lucrative rackets in Florida, the West Indies, Arizona, Nevada and California. The Chicago branch of the international crime conglomerate has always been the most politically insulated and police-pampered "family" this side of Sicily.

This, then, was Sam Giancana on paper. What follows are the impressions of someone who knew him in a far different way.

Dean joined us and as we wandered around I noticed that Sam Flood's eyes never left me. I was used to people watching me or doing double takes, calling attention to someone else: "Look at her!" I seldom paid any attention to it. But this evening I was very much aware of his eyes on me. There was a little smile on his face whenever I looked at him. Although he wasn't what I would call handsome, he was a pleasant enough looking man, who seemed very sure of himself. I noticed another man, a big bruiser, standing a short distance away. He never took his eyes off Sam Flood. Later I would learn that he was John Matassa, who was one of his bodyguards, chauffeurs, and trusted emissaries. His devotion to Sam was remarkable. I have no doubt that he would have sacrificed his life for him without a second thought.

Once we went into the dining room I forgot about Sam Flood. He got lost in the shuffle. There were two main tables. Frank and Juliet with their group had one; Dean, Bob Neal, and I with our group had the other. It was a long evening. I danced with Dean and with Bob, drank a little too much, and got a terrible headache. Everyone was having a good time. It was noisy, lots of laughter as always, and I think also the pressure of Frank being at the next table got to me. It was like sitting near a time bomb. Finally, I told Bob and Dean I was tired and asked them to excuse me. As I walked by Frank's table I said, "Good night, Frank. Thanks!" There was more sarcasm than gratitude in my voice. I walked away before he could think of anything to say.

I talked to Jack the next day and agreed to see him in Washington on April 6, the day after the Wisconsin primary. I was supposed to have flown to Washington on March 24 but I missed my flight—I missed many planes and trains in those days—and when I called Jack, he said he was returning to Wisconsin the next day and would not be back in Washington until April 6.

It was time to leave Florida. I had been there two weeks and my bill, because of a lot of shopping, was close to two thousand dollars. To avoid any problem with the desk when checking out, I tried to reach Joe Fish to see if he would OK my check. Although no one had said anything to me about him, I was under the impression that he either owned the hotel or was one of its top executives.

In between calls while trying to track down Joe Fish, I received one from Betty Winikus, whom I had known for several years. She went with Brad Dexter, a bit actor who a few years later saved Frank's life when he got caught in a riptide in Hawaii. From then on, Brad and Betty were around Frank every chance they had. Brad even got a couple of small parts in Frank's movies. Betty knew everybody in Hollywood. When she walked into a restaurant there wasn't anybody important in there she didn't know. She was invited to all the parties; she obviously had good connections, but I never really knew her story.

Betty was calling to see if I would have dinner with her and a friend. I explained about my interest in finding Joe Fish, and she said, "Don't worry about it. I'll talk to somebody."

I said, "Thanks, Betty."

"Don't mention it. Look, I'll meet you in your room about seven-thirty and we'll go up to his suite."

"You mean have dinner in his suite?"

"No, Judy, we'll have dinner at the Eden Roc."

"Okay, Betty, but I have to catch a plane at ten."

"Don't worry, we'll have you there in plenty of time."

The gentleman was Sam Flood—it would be months before I knew his real name. When we arrived in his suite, he invited us in for a drink. There was not another soul there. Betty did most of the talking. It seemed as if she felt compelled to keep things moving right along all by herself. Sam—he had corrected me when I called him Mr. Flood—sat there with that little smile on his face. His eyes were friendly, but again he never took them off me.

Dinner at Eden Roc was hasty, but the conversation was pleasant and surprisingly easy. I talked about my family and he told me that he was a widower. He asked me what I did and I said I was an artist, that I worked in charcoal and oils. At the time I was mainly doing children's faces. He expressed a desire to see some of my work, and whenever anyone said that, I used to kid about it, doing a switch on the old line: "Ah, you want to come see my etchings?"

"You bet," he said. "I'd like that very much."

"If I ever have a show, which I hope to have very soon, I'll send you a special invitation."

He asked where I would be staying in New York, and wanted to know if he could call me, and I said, "Yes, that's fine." The answer even surprised me. There were very few people I would say that to on a first meeting. The fact was that I enjoyed his company. He was a calm, low key person—so much more mature than the younger people I knew. It was partly what impressed me about Jack. They had a different way of handling themselves.

From the way people behaved around him, Sam was obviously a man of "position." I was used to seeing the help jump whenever Frank walked into a restaurant, but with Sam they fell all over each other trying to please him. And he, on the other hand, acted like royalty, completely ignoring their existence, which seemed to spur them to even greater effort. The more I watched the various performances, including Betty's, the more intrigued I became with Sam. But I wasn't about to ask him what he did for a living. For all I knew, he could have been president of General Motors. Because of my shyness, I have always avoided asking questions that could make me look foolish. Besides what difference did it make at the moment? Later, when I began to suspect, I found that I didn't want to know anything.

I paid a terrible price for my association with Sam, but I have never been one to judge people because of what others have said about them. I believe in finding out for myself. This is not a conscious effort—it's just the way I am constituted. If I like a person, I like that person until I find out that person is not a friend. Then, and only then, do I say, "Go away."

After dinner we went back to the Fontainebleau to pick up my luggage. As we walked into the lobby, I asked Betty if she had talked to anyone about clearing my check, and Sam said, "Just a minute." He walked over to the cashier and was back in two minutes flat. He handed me my bill and it was marked "Paid."

I looked at him. "What are you doing?"

"Don't worry about it," he said. "It's all taken care of."

"No, I can't have you do that. I'll give you a check."

"No, Judy, please, I want to do it." He had a big grin on

his face, proud as a peacock for what he had done, no doubt expecting me to be all giddy about it and say, "Oh, goodness, thank you so much."

I said, "It's ridiculous. There's no way I can accept this. I'm either going to give the cashier my check, or I'll give it to you, but only if you promise to cash it."

"Okay, okay," he said, "give me the check."

I wrote out a check and gave it to him. Betty was getting a big kick out of it. She later told the story over and over again, embellishing it as she went along, until finally Sam had not only paid my hotel bill but had also paid for my trip to Miami. She never mentioned that I had given Sam a check, which he did cash.

I stayed at Toni Carroll's place in New York, and was awakened around noon by the delivery of five dozen yellow roses from Sam. Whenever I received flowers from Sam, it was always five dozen yellow roses. I know that yellow roses mean jealousy, but I never understood the significance of five dozen. Sam called shortly after the flowers arrived and again later that day.

That evening I went to dinner with Morris Levy. I had met him through a friend of Travis, Frank Satinstein, whose family, I think, owned American Bookbinding in New York. He also either produced or directed the original Jackie Gleason shows. I had a rather peculiar experience with Frank Satinstein. He had a girlfriend, Jennifer, who was really gorgeous, and he wanted me to do a portrait of her. Then it came out that he wanted a nude portrait, and it further came about that he wanted to be there when I painted the nude portrait of Jennifer. Then I started getting calls from Jennifer in the morning and she wanted to come over to see me. Then I severed my relationship with Frank Satinstein and his Jennifer.

Morris Levy would probably be considered unattractive by most people. He looked very much like Telly Savalas, and had a certain charm that you find with some very unattractive men. He talked with "dese, dem and dose" but in a light, kind of charming way. He was a character, but he was also a friend I could call and say, "Morris, I'm bored, want to go out to dinner?" I have never understood Morris's connections. As far as I knew, he owned Roulette Records, Birdland, and the Round Table restaurant. Later I discovered that one of Sam's sons-in-law worked for Roulette Records.

Sometimes when I called Morris would say, "Not tonight, Judy. I'm having certain people over." He was another one who enjoyed the company of hoods and hookers. He once gave a party for a hoodlum by the name of Johnny Dio when Dio was either coming out of jail or going in. He would not have me around when those people were there.

I could call him at midnight and he would whiz over to take me out to the Stage Delicatessen for a cup of coffee. There never was any romance between us. I doubt that I was the kind of woman he would have been sexually interested in. His leanings, I suspected, were more exotic. I don't know how to explain my relationship with some of these men. Without meaning to sound immodest, perhaps I flattered their egos. I was a beautiful girl, always impeccably groomed and with an elegant wardrobe, and they liked being seen with me. Once we got beyond that stage, I think they enjoyed having a woman as a friend or drinking buddy, someone to whom they could tell their troubles and find a sympathetic ear. In some ways, Morris wanted less from me and gave me more of himself, and more fun, too, than anyone I knew in those days.

Although he was tough and had rough friends, he was always a gentleman with me. And extremely protective. He had a magnificent apartment on Central Park South, and one night when he was entertaining friends, someone brought out a small vial and poured a white powder-like substance into a tiny spoon and sniffed it. Then he passed it around and others sniffed it.

"What is that?" I asked.

"It's nothing for you," Morris said.

"Well, thanks a lot."

"You better thank me," he said, "because that's nothing for you, *ever*."

They all laughed and later, after his friends had left,

Morris told me it was cocaine.

One of Morris's friends was Sarah Vaughan. I stood in awe of her, and that hasn't happened too often in my life. She has such an incredible talent. I went with Morris to her home in New Jersey. She had some music in her hand and she transposed it to another key, all up in her head, never went near the piano. I was enthralled. I just couldn't believe what I was hearing. For a moment I had a glimpse into her world, the world of great musicians, people with gut-level genius, who live and breathe a music that's in their very soul. Frank was talented, but there was no comparison. They lived in different worlds.

By now, between Jack and Sam, I was spending a great deal of time on the telephone. Sam was calling from Chicago two and three times a day, trying to suggest a time when we could see each other. My response at that point was, "Have you deposited that check?" And he would say, "Now what makes you think I wouldn't deposit that check?" I would say, "If you don't deposit it, I'm not going to see you." "Well," he would say, "it looks like I'm going to have to deposit that check, because I sure do want to see you."

Not only was he bombarding me with telephone calls, but every single day I would get five dozen yellow roses. I had to throw them out even before they started to wilt. And always in a green glass vase. I collected them when I was back in California. Everyone in my family has a collection of those green glass vases.

As the days went by, I discovered that Sam had a good sense of humor and just loved to tease. He loved to get my goat. He just thought that was the funniest thing on earth. I couldn't stay mad at him because his laugh was so hearty. His sense of humor wasn't like Jack's, who was so bright and really so quick and so witty. It was more elemental, a little more mundane, but very pleasant just the same. Everything with Sam was lollipops and roses. If I'd accepted it, I think he would have sent me the Hope Diamond. Instead he was sending me what he thought I couldn't refuse—every woman loves to receive flowers. I adored getting flowers and he could tell that I was getting a big kick out of it. He was winning me over right where I lived.

He wanted to visit me in New York but I told him I was going to Washington. Then he wanted us to meet in Florida, or in Chicago where he could show me his town. He would say, "What time did you say you were arriving?" I would laugh. "I didn't tell you I was arriving at all, Sam." "Oh, I must have misunderstood." He would laugh, thinking he was being quite clever. "If you ever get me there at all, you're not going to get me there by tricking me." He would say, "Okay, straight forward, will you come?" I would say, "No." "Well, then I've got to try another way."

He would ask who I was seeing in New York, and when I told him he would say, "You can find time to go out with that jerk, why can't you let me come and see you or come see me?" His tone was always light, always very friendly, never heavy.

On April 4, the day before I left for Washington, Sam called four times. During his last call, he said, "How long will you be in Washington?"

"Probably about a day."

"Why don't you fly to Chicago from there. Give me a chance to show you a good time in my home town. I promise you that everything is going to be on the up and up. You'll be as safe here as in your mother's arms."

"Maybe I'll take you up on it," I said. "Let me think about it."

His persistence was making me a little nervous. It's not easy to put someone off two and three times a day, especially when you're sitting in a room full of his flowers. By the end of the week, he had pretty well broken through my defenses.

When he called the next afternoon—I was to leave for Washington at nine-thirty that evening—I told him that it looked promising, but I would call him from Washington with the final decision. It was then that he gave me the telephone number of the Armory Lounge in Forest Park. I was to ask for Butch or Joe Pignatello, and they would put me in touch with Sam Flood. The Armory was operated by Carmine and Doris Fanelli.

126

Meanwhile, of course, Jack was also calling every day, wanting to make sure that I would be in Washington at the appointed time. Since I had missed that plane in Miami, he wasn't too sure whether he could depend on me. He would say, "You better be here Wednesday or I'm coming up there to get you."

"Don't worry, I'll be there," I would assure him.

"That's what you said the last time." Jack was kidding and yet it had something to do with an attitude men in certain positions have toward women. They are used to snapping their fingers and having women run to them. It has to do with wealth and power and fame. With Jack it was all of that plus great charm, erudition and sex appeal—an irresistible combination.

I missed my flight that evening. I met Uncle Armand and some of his friends for cocktails at the Pierre and dinner in the Plaza's Persian Room. Then it was the Village Vanguard and on to Birdland for Count Basie and Joe Williams.

I flew to Washington the next morning. Before boarding the plane I bought several newspapers. I had thought about the Wisconsin primary the night before, wondering how Jack had fared, but it had been too late when I returned to the hotel to get any news report on television. I pored over the newspapers, happy at what the headlines proclaimed, but very unhappy when I realized that Jack's margin of fifty-six percent of the popular vote came entirely from heavily Catholic districts. He was badly defeated in the four Protestant districts. He barely squeaked by in the one unclassified district. The meaning was crystal clear. It was a Catholic-Protestant contest. Jack was still the *Catholic* candidate for President. The columnists were bursting with dire predictions about the upcoming West Virginia primary, where the population was ninety-five percent Protestant.

If Jack had been a Protestant, his vote margin would have been considered a landslide. Yet it was Hubert Humphrey who was acting like the winner. "I'm encouraged and exhilarated and sorry it's all over," he told newsmen. He was going directly to Washington and on to West Virginia the next day. "I was going to try and get a ride with Jack on his plane, but he thought I ought to catch the next bus. Why don't you fellows come along? We're selling popcorn concessions down there.'' Humphrey was described as laughing and joking, very jubilant about what he called his ''moral victory.'' "I always told you fellows politics could be fun, didn't I?''

I stopped reading. Poor Jack, I thought, his religion would destroy him. By the time I arrived at the Sheraton Park in Washington, I had a terrible empty feeling gnawing at me. But when I came into the room and found a dozen red roses from Jack, I felt better. I ordered a drink and took a long hot bath. That always works miracles for whatever ails me.

Then I stretched out on the bed and called Evelyn Lincoln, who had made my reservation, to see what instructions Jack had for me. She was extremely cordial as always, and told me how happy Jack would be that I was in Washington. I was to go to Jack's Georgetown house at seven-thirty that evening. The address was 3307 N Street, Northwest.

Since Evelyn Lincoln has now chosen to deny any knowledge of our relationship, I have decided to list some of the addresses and telephone numbers given to me by her and Jack during the time we saw each other.

When I first knew Jack, Evelyn lived at 3132 Sixteenth Street, Northwest, apartment 507, telephone AD 4-5745. Other numbers were MA 4-1011, MA 4-9335, HO 2-5632. Her number at the Old Senate Office building, room 362, was CA 4-3121, extension 3341. The private number was RE 7-0064. After the election, Evelyn moved to 1440 Rock Creek Ford Road, Northwest, apartment 402, and the number was TA 9-5552.

Jack's Georgetown home number was FE 8-2325; in New York it was PL 5-7600 and EL 5-4878, and his apartment was at 277 Park Avenue. The White House was NA 8-1414. At Hyannis, I could reach Evelyn at the Yachtman Hotel, Spring 5-4600. In Palm Beach, numbers for Jack were TE 2-7117 and TE 3-4622; Evelyn's, at the Palm Beach Towers, was TE 3-5761.

Later in the day, Jack called to welcome me to

Washington. "I wish I could show you the city," he said, "but—" I said, "Jack, please, you don't have to apologize. You know how I feel about being seen in public with you. All I want is to be with you."

I listened closely to his tone, trying to detect his mood, but it was impossible. He seemed very cheerful, as he always did to me in those days. He wanted to know if I liked my room. Did I need anything at all? When he offered to send a car to pick me up, I told him I preferred taking a cab.

His call helped lift my spirits, but now I had butterflies. I didn't relish the idea of going to his home. That was Jackie's home. As much as I was beginning to care for him, I had serious misgivings about the evening.

I wore a black knit suit and a brand new black diamond mink coat with horizontal fur that I had bought in New York that week. Jack answered the door and his eyebrows went up when he saw me.

"You look fantastic," he said, as he helped me out of the coat. He leaned over and gave me a kiss on the cheek. He was grinning from ear to ear and from head to toe. It was that kind of genuine welcome. That's saying a lot for Jack, because he was naturally reserved. He was affectionate, but he never gushed. We were similar in that respect, and that was probably the attraction between us. We weren't all over each other, and I think he liked that—I know I did.

As we came into the living room, a large man stood up and Jack introduced us, but I have never remembered his name. He was very tall, large in stature, and from what was said, I gathered he was a railroad lobbyist. I was almost relieved to see him. It is hard to describe the feeling, but, as I said, I was sensitive about seeing Jack in his wife's home. I couldn't even think of it as being his home. I had come to Jackie's house to see her husband. I was thinking how I had suffered through Billy's affairs, and now I was doing the same thing to another woman. Unfortunately, my interest in Jack, my need to be with him, was stronger than my conscience.

We had a drink, and while we made small talk, I looked around the room and tried to figure out the style or period of the furnishings. The living room was small—all the rooms were small—and the house was long, skinny and tall. It was typical Eastern architecture, designed to provide all the living space a narrow lot allows.

The couch and chairs were soft, very billowy. The colors were light, with soft floral prints, to create a feeling of comfort, and there were a lot of delicate-looking pieces from various French periods. Since I had read that Jackie had magnificent taste, the room was a disappointment. There was too much around, too much clutter for a small room.

Dinner started with a cold soup, which is something I avoid like the plague—too many hidden calories. Jackie loved French cuisine, but Jack, as I was to learn, had an Irish palate. Finger bowls were brought out after the soup, and then it was down to basics: meat and potatoes.

Meanwhile, Jack and the lobbyist were analyzing the Wisconsin primary. From what I gathered, Humphrey's optimism was ill-founded. Jack thought that regardless of the religious vote, Hubert's defeat in Wisconsin, a neighboring state of his native Minnesota, meant that he couldn't deliver anywhere else in the Midwest. If a politician couldn't deliver his base, he was finished, Jack said. Both Jack and the lobbyist felt that Humphrey's decision to campaign in West Virginia would prove fatal to him. A victory would only deadlock the convention, opening the way for some of the peripheral candidates, but his defeat in West Virginia would make Jack's nomination a certainty. There was no question in Jack's mind that he would win in West Virginia, regardless of the religious issue. The Kennedy spirit was indomitable. I was so proud of him.

Once he had disposed of Hubert, Jack began discussing the kind of staff he wanted as President. He seemed particularly troubled about Evelyn Lincoln. He wondered whether she was capable of handling the broader responsibilities of the White House. When he asked for my opinion, I said she seemed extremely efficient and loyal, putting as much emphasis on the word loyal as I could without making it an issue.

We had an after dinner drink in the living room and then the lobbyist left. Jack escorted him to the door and when he came back into the room, he sat next to me on the sofa.

"This has been a long evening," he said. "It was very hard sitting away from you when all I wanted to do was to come over and put my arms around you like this."

We kissed and he said, "Let me show you the rest of the house." We wandered through various rooms until we came to the master bedroom, which was upstairs at the front of the house. There were twin beds with pale green spreads, very filmy and delicate.

He put his arms around me and we sat on one of the beds. We kissed and he was almost immediately amorous. I went to the bathroom to undress, and when I came back into the room, the lights were very low and Jack was already in bed.

"I've missed you so much," I said, as I went into his arms.

We kissed passionately, and he said, with his lips still on mine, "Do you think you could love me?"

"I'm afraid I could," I whispered, and it was so true. I was so afraid that it was happening to me. I was really mixed up. The thought of loving him made me happy one moment and unhappy the next. I wanted to be with him, but I hated being in his bedroom, having that close a contact with his wife. And I worried about the servants, of what they thought of my being there, and I couldn't quite understand how he could do that with the servants in the house. Yet every time I really started to think about it, whether it was in his home in Georgetown or later in the White House, I would whitewash it with excuses—the servants probably knew they weren't happily married. To be perfectly honest about it, I think I was caught up a little with the intrigue of it. The sneaking around, a mild form of cloak-and-dagger, the anticipation, and "Boy, we didn't get caught!"

I adored Jack's possessiveness after we made love. He

didn't want to let go. He would lie with his arms around me and I would rest my head on his chest and listen to the beat of his heart as we talked for hours. Much of it was pillow talk, light and teasing, nothing ever too serious, but this evening he said something that really took me aback.

"If I don't get the nomination—"

I said, "What?" without waiting for him to finish. It was the first negative thought I had heard him express. "I didn't really hear you say 'if'!"

"Let me finish," he laughed.

"I can't believe my ears. Jack Kennedy, the erstwhile candidate for the Presidency of the United States, has just said, 'If I don't get the nomination.' "

He squeezed me. "Will you shut up. This is important."

"Important? I have a good mind to call your mother. I can only hope she doesn't tell your father. He'll take your little plane away from you."

"All right, you had your fun, now it's my turn. If—now don't say anything, I know it's a big if—but if I don't get the nomination, we're going off and sit on a deserted beach somewhere for a whole month, maybe longer, just the two of us. We're going to hide from the world."

I knew how much he loved the water and the beach. "Oh, tell me another one."

"What's wrong with this one? Think of some romantic, faraway place you'd like to go to."

All right, I thought, two can play this game. "You mean where it's warm and we can make love in the sunlight and moonlight."

"Yes, and never wear clothes."

"That's going too far," I said.

"Do you mean you wouldn't give up your wardrobe for me?"

"I'd give up anything for you, Jack, anything but that."

It was all in fun, or so I thought.

It was very late when I reluctantly decided that it was time for me to leave. As I sat up, Jack said, "Is it possible for you to be in Miami on the twelfth?"

"Yes, if we can see each other."

He explained that he was going to Indiana, Arizona, and West Virginia, covering some twenty or thirty towns and cities in a campaign swing, and it would be extremely difficult for him to call me. He would be in Miami for just that one day and I promised that I would be waiting for him at the Fontainebleau, at whatever time was convenient for him.

While I dressed Jack called for a cab, and then put on his robe and went downstairs to get my coat. We watched for the cab out the bedroom window.

As he helped me into the coat, he said, "What a beautiful coat."

"I'm very proud of it," I said. "I just bought it this past week."

"You shouldn't be spending that kind of money on a coat."

"Well, I wanted it. I'm not married. If I want something, I have to buy it for myself."

"I don't see why," he said. "Plenty of people would love to buy this coat for you."

"I don't want plenty of people to buy my coat for me. I'm very happy buying my own coat for me. Then no one can come and take it off my back."

We laughed and he said, "How about my buying it for you. I'd never take it off your back."

"Oh, no," I said. "This coat is bought and paid for and I don't really want to discuss it."

"Judy, be reasonable. There's so little I can do for you. Please, let me buy the coat."

"I've told you, Jack. It's already bought and paid for."

"Let me do something, please."

He wasn't kidding anymore. It was obvious that he wanted to do something for me, and though I knew he could well afford it, I had a rule about men giving me expensive gifts. I had seen too many gals running around with mink coats and diamonds and living in apartments paid for by married men. That was not my style. It was important to me that I paid my own way.

In a way, I told Jack, the coat was a gift from Billy. The

month before I had signed away my alimony payments for a cash settlement. But that did not satisfy him. He wanted me to understand that if things were different, he wouldn't want to buy me a mink coat. "That just isn't my way," he said. "But the situation being what it is, you won't let me pay for your room or your plane tickets, and you're the one coming to see me. Let me do something for you. This is something you love, so let me be a part of it."

The discussion went on until the cab arrived. Then he said, "We'll talk about it later. I haven't given up."

What Jack couldn't understand was that I was hanging onto myself for the first time in my life. I was taking care of me and paying my own way. I was doing for myself, and I was living my own life on my own terms, coming and going as I pleased. I was my own keeper, and I loved that freedom.

We walked downstairs and he said, "Call me at my office in the morning. Do you know what time you're leaving?"

I said, "No." I had told him I was going to Chicago to visit friends, for I had already made up my mind to go see Sam.

"Well, make sure you call me before you go."

He waited at the front door until I reached the cab. I looked up and smiled at him, and he nodded and closed the door.

The phone rang almost the moment I walked into my room. It was Jack wanting to know if everything was all right. I said I was fine and he gave me his home number. "Now, you call me if you need anything during the night." That surprised me. It made me think that I was more concerned about his wife than he was.

I was tired but I lay in bed a long time and thought about Jack. I was happy that he wanted to buy the mink coat for me, that he thought that much of me, that he truly wanted to do something for me. I was on the edge of falling in love, but I was fighting it because he was married and deep down I knew the relationship was doomed to failure. In some ways, I was an emotional cripple. I was so afraid of getting hurt. I was instinctively holding back.

The fact that he might be President one day was not what attracted me. And I was not bowled over by the fact that he was interested in me, or that Sam was interested, or Frank, or Dean, or anybody. I expected it. I have often wondered about myself. As insecure as I was in given areas, I was never surprised by the attention showered on me. I think a psychiatrist would say I had a problem.

When I called his office the next day, Evelyn said he had already left for Indiana. I took the train for Chicago at five-thirty that evening. I love trains, especially the old Eastern trains. I used to take a bedroom, drawing room, living room suite and it was tremendous—it could accommodate a family of three. I ordered drinks and dinner, and sat back in the splendor of my privacy, and thought about Jack and Sam. Although it may sound strange to the reader, this was a time in my life when I was exploring. I was infatuated with Jack, not really in love yet, but I couldn't just sit home and wait for his calls which came at all hours of the day or night. He was on the go constantly. He had something else to occupy his time. It was exciting for me to be going to Chicago instead of just going back to New York and moping about Jack. It was a new adventure. I didn't feel any pressure from Sam and I was looking forward to seeing new places and meeting new people. In my mind, I was not going to Chicago to see another man, to become emotionally involved with anyone. I was in a happy frame of mind. I liked the idea of being with someone that really wanted to be with me.

It never occurred to me that I wouldn't be able to control the situation. I may have been a little naive but I was a big girl. No one ever talked me into the bedroom. I felt myself getting stronger all the time. But I had my insecurities. I wasn't alone, however; I don't care who you are, or how strong you are, we are all vulnerable in some ways.

Jack Kennedy was insecure in certain areas. He was insecure as to how he looked when he dressed. He always needed to be reassured that he looked just right. He used to ask me all the time, especially after he was in the White

House, "Do you like this suit? How does it look?" He would ask it over and over again. He needed the confidence that comes from reassurance.

If you look at the women in that family, I think they dressed because the law says you have to wear clothes. But once the public eye zeroed in on them, they took a little more care. Their mother was probably a very elegant woman, but I think all the children took after the father.

I don't think Jack realized just how great he looked. But that's not unusual. Very often you'll find the most attractive people will look in the mirror the most because they are told so often—I think it's part of my insecurity—that they are so beautiful. And you think, "Am I really?" Then you get used to people looking at you and you become very conscious of always looking right. That's a very fine line. You can become overly conscious of how you look and constantly worry about it, like some actors and actresses, who often go off the deep end worrying about their looks. They never think they look quite right, or perfect enough.

Jack was used to dressing a certain way because it was required of a young man going places. Now, suddenly, he knew he had to make sure that he looked elegant. His natural inclination was to be sloppy—that is, Palm Beach and Hyannisport sloppy chic: old trousers, sweatshirt, and scuffed loafers without socks. That was fine for weekends but not for the limelight, not for the President of the United States, not for the most powerful leader in the free world. Everything had to be perfect. If he walked the wrong way, someone was going to put it in the newspaper. If he got a cinder in his eye, someone was going to have him going blind. The same applied to the way he dressed. He was a conservative dresser, and sometimes a conservative dresser is just a safe dresser. A very conservative dresser is someone who wants to feel safe in what they wear, and I think that was Jack's basic insecurity.

136

VII

We pulled into Chicago at eight-thirty the next morning. I looked out the window and there was Sam smiling at me. I was thrilled. Finally I knew someone who cared enough to meet me. I slipped into my mink and hurried to meet him. Sam was there to take my hand as I stepped off the train.

"Ah, I finally got you here," he said.

"Don't get too cocky," I said. "I may get back on the train and go home."

"Boy, you're really hard on a guy."

The porter started bringing out my matched luggage and I said, "How strong are you?"

Sam started to laugh after three large suitcases were brought out—by the time it got to number seven he was hysterical. Joseph Pignatello, a short, stocky man with black hair, who was another of Sam's many chauffeurs, was scratching his head and looking frantically for a redcap.

As I stood there in the grime of that railroad depot, I was truly happy. Because I didn't have a romantic attachment, I felt free and comfortable. Sometimes the more you care about someone, the uneasier you are, because you anticipate every move you make, you want to be right in everything you say or do. Sam was just somebody who was amusing and was just showering me with attention. There was no emotional tie and therefore no anxiety. I could just relax and have a good time.

I don't know how Joe ever got all that luggage in that little black Ford. It was in the trunk, the front seat, the floor in back.

"My God, Sam," I said, as I sat with my feet on a suitcase, "why are we riding in this terrible little car?"

"Well, what did you expect?" he said, laughing. "Isn't this good enough for you?"

Sam thought that my distaste for little cars was the funniest thing in the world. That was the one thing about him that used to drive me crazy. He always traveled in a little black Ford or a taxicab.

"Besides, what were you doing on the train?"

"I love trains."

"Ah, go on, you're afraid to fly?"

"Are you kidding? I fly all the time."

"Then you must have been stalling."

"What do you mean?"

"The train takes longer. You just hated coming to Chicago."

"I tell you, I really love trains."

"Tell me another story."

That's the way it went with Sam. We kidded a lot, but his attitude was one of being flattered that I had come to see him. I think he was getting a big kick out of the fact that I didn't know who he was. That he could fool me, that I would come to visit him because I liked him, and not because of what he could do for me. As I was to learn in time, Sam could do a lot for people, particularly people in the entertainment business, or he could do a lot to them.

My reservation was at the Ambassador East. I think it was the John Barrymore Suite, which was the one I stayed in most of the times I came to Chicago. Lo and behold, there were five dozen yellow roses in a green glass vase. I thanked him and after he was sure I liked the suite, he said he would be back around noon.

I suppose the reader is wondering at this point what I could see in Sam. Besides what I have already said about his sense of humor and his attentiveness, he was always well dressed,

138

very neat, and always conducted himself, at least in my presence, like a gentleman. He created a nice impression. He wasn't handsome, but everything was where it should be. His whole attitude, his personality, the way he treated me was very appealing, not physically or emotionally attractive, but as a friend, someone who was enjoyable.

Now, as I read about Sam, I find another whole side of him of which I was never a part. Perhaps he always looked like a hoodlum to the police or to the public at large. All I can say is that he was different when he was with me. At that time, it was all that mattered to me.

When he picked me up that afternoon, he said, "Come on, I'm going to drive you out to a place. I have to see some people. Then I'll show you around."

The place turned out to be the Armory, and it wasn't much of a place—perhaps I should say it wouldn't be much of a place in California, but in the Midwest or East, it was perfectly respectable. Typical Eastern saloon-type place. There was a jukebox and the bar was the length of one side of the room. There was a pay phone on the wall near the kitchen entrance that Sam kept pretty busy. There was a dining room and behind it was a back room, kind of a storeroom, with a table and chairs. We sat there one night to watch television returns of a local election. Sam would often have a "meet"—I learned to use that expression after hearing so often "we've got a meet"—in the back room with important people. However, he conducted a lot of business at our booth in the bar right in front of me. As he did on that first day. But it was in Sicilian.

Sometimes in the middle of one of those rapid fire discussions, he would turn to me and say, "Bet you can't understand that?" The smile on his face was as if, "I'm really putting one over on you."

I would reply, "You don't know. One of these days I'm going to understand every word you're saying."

"Honey," he would say, "there is no way on earth that will ever happen. We're Sicilians and we talk our own dialect. We know how to do it."

"I'll go to Berlitz."

He just about fell over laughing. "You can go anywhere you want, but nobody will ever teach you our dialect. When I don't want you to understand, believe me, you won't understand."

Months later he would say, "You don't want to hear what I've got to say to these people."

When I finally realized who he was, I appreciated the fact that whatever he was doing, he was making sure that I was not a part of it. I was particularly appreciative when I saw some of the characters who came to see him. They may have been comical in their appearance and speech, but I am sure there was nothing very humorous about their business. It occurred to me that the ones who looked the most comical were perhaps the most dangerous. The strange ones—but I didn't think about it that way then. I had no fear of Sam. No fear that anything would ever happen to me because of Sam or with Sam or by Sam. That, I know, was terribly naive. There are times when I wonder who or what I was in those days.

Sam used to disappear for a month or more at a time, and I wouldn't hear a word from him. I would say to him upon his return, "My God, why couldn't you call? Why couldn't you let me know you were all right? I was afraid something had happened to you."

"It was a time when I shouldn't be in touch with you," he would reply, or "It's better for you that I wasn't in touch." That is all he would say about it. It always gave me the feeling that he was protecting me.

I was seeing a different environment and it was exciting. I was watching Sam and really wondering about him. But I wasn't about to ask him what was going on. On that first day or any other day. I felt that if he wanted me to know anything he would tell me. Or maybe he assumed I knew and that would be terribly embarrassing if all of a sudden I would say, "What do you do for a living?" And he would look at me and say, "Where have you been anyway, hiding in a closet all your life?"

Doris and Carmine Fanelli ran the Armory. She did all the

cooking and baking, and Carmine tended bar and managed the business. Sam loved to tease Carmine. When I was introduced to Carmine, Sam said, "Turn around Carmine—now, doesn't he look like a taxicab with the back doors swung open." Poor Carmine. His ears did stick out like opened doors.

For dinner that evening we went to Whitehall, which in those days was a private club. Sam liked their steak Diane—they cooked it at your table and the aroma was sheer ambrosia. And again as I had observed in Florida, the owner, the *maître d'*, the wine steward, the waiter, everybody was just showering him with slavish attention. Their performance was so obsequious that it was distasteful. Every other word was punctuated with "sir" and bows—I had the feeling that mentally they were walking on their knees.

What bothered me even more was Sam's aloofness. I don't believe in getting chummy with your waiter or *maître d'* but I do believe in common decency. When you're asked a question—"How is your steak?" or "Is everything all right?"—I think some kind of comment is deserved. When someone is trying very hard to make things right for you, the least you can do is acknowledge it with a yea or nay.

There were times when Sam ignored everybody except me. He did a little of it that night, and the more he got to know me, the more imperious he became with others. I got the impression that unless he made a conscious effort, those people didn't exist for him. I didn't know it then, but he was the *Padrone,* the Godfather, if you will, and how well they knew it. One word from Sam and that restaurant would be closed. The unions would strike, the city would revoke its various licenses, its trash wouldn't be collected, a bomb might go off, fire might break out—in other words, instant and complete disaster.

To be fair about it, I don't have any evidence that any of the above ever happened, but I do know that because of their respect—and anxiety—for him, and their need to endlessly express it with words and deeds, it was impossible for Sam to respond to everybody hovering around him. He held a position of highest "honor" in his world and his cool demeanor was no less than expected. This did not only apply to the help, but to anybody who made contact with him. For example, nobody ever approached Sam's table unless he wished them to approach. There was no buddy-buddy back-slapping good-time-Charlie stuff around Sam. On occasion, Sam would embrace other Italian men of respect, but there was a distinct protocol that was rigorously followed at all times.

Sam was a martini drinker and he drank his fair share. Later in our relationship, I began to notice that when Sam got a little in his cups, he became more abrupt with people—not with me— and this caused great consternation for whoever was at the receiving end. I could well imagine the poor fellow spending hours agonizing over it, no doubt wondering where he had gone wrong in the past and what dire fate awaited him in the future.

As for our own relationship, it was one of gradual attraction for me. It was almost a year and a half before we became intimate. Being a normal male, Sam tried to change that situation, but after I told him about my feelings for Jack, he didn't push it beyond the teasing stage for at least a year. His patience so impressed me at the time that I actually felt guilty.

I told him, "I'm sorry, I just can't carry on two affairs. I love being with you, but if you want more than friendship, then I'm going to have to stop seeing you." I knew that if I had an affair with Sam, if I went to bed with him, it wasn't going to be something that happened because I drank too much one night and made a mistake.

His response was, "It's okay, don't worry about it. Everything is fine the way it is."

As I look back, it's possible that Sam got exactly what he wanted from our relationship. Now that I know of his involvement with the Central Intelligence Agency, it is possible that I was used almost from the beginning. I don't exactly know how it was done, but perhaps it will become more evident as my story unfolds. Except for occasional observations, I think, it would be a mistake at this point for me to indulge in theories. I will continue to tell my story, as honestly and clearly as I remember it happening, or the way it seemed to be happening at that time.

It never occurred to me that Sam's interest in me was simply because of my association with Jack Kennedy. Of course there were people who wanted to be my friend because of my relationship with Jack, backslappers who wanted "little favors," but Sam never asked me for anything, and so I never connected Sam with any of that. Whatever may have been Sam's motivation in the beginning, I do know that he later fell deeply in love with me, and what he did then violates a lot of the theories that certain people find so much pleasure in expounding.

When I told Sam I was going to see Jack in Florida on the twelfth he said, "Well, why don't you fly down with me on the ninth. I have some business down there."

"That's fine, Sam, as long as I pay my way."

He shook his head. "Now, wait a minute, honey. Fair is fair, but you're overdoing it. I've cashed your check—I didn't want to, but I did. And you've paid the freight coming up here to see me. Now it's my turn to do a little something for you."

"You have done plenty. You've shown me a wonderful time."

"I want to do this, honey. And I want to take care of your reservation down there too. Wait! I swear, it's not costing me a dime. It's on the house. Let them pick up the tab. Hell, they comp people right and left all the time."

"You're not pulling my leg?"

"Now, would I pull your leg?" And he laughed. "But don't give me ideas like that. You know how I feel."

Later, when Joe Pignatello handed me my ticket, I saw that it was made out to a Miss Moore—my first alias. We took Delta on the morning of the ninth and we played gin all the way to Florida. Playing gin with Sam was not the world's greatest pastime. I don't know whether he cheated, but there was just no way I could play cards with him. He would knock so fast I barely had time to arrange my cards. He thought that was hilarious.

Joe Fish met us at the airport with a limousine and Sam just looked at me and shrugged his shoulders. At the Fontainebleau I had a large corner suite, and I think Sam had his suite on the same floor.

That evening we went with Joe Fish to the Eden Roc to see Sammy Davis, Jr. Our table was directly center front and Sammy just about played the whole show to our table. This nightclub custom has a lot in common with bullfighting, when the matador dedicates his kill to a pretty lady. In this case, the attraction was Sam. At first I thought that Sam was in one of his aloof moods, for he completely ignored Sammy, but as I soon learned Sam hated blacks, a trait that annoyed and embarrassed me no end.

As far as Sam was concerned, all blacks were stupid, lazy, and not to be trusted. He would refer to them as niggers, a term I have always loathed, and I would nudge him and say, "Don't use that word." I would be indignant, and he would just laugh. The more I objected, the more he did it. Finally I decided that it was best for all concerned if I just ignored it. His hatred was so ingrained that it was hopeless for me to try to change him. He was particularly offensive with cab drivers. He would tease them in a derogatory way, call them "boy," and mimic them with expressions like "Sho'nuff, now."

We went to Palm Beach the next day and this time instead of riding in an old Ford, we rode in an old white and blue Buick, a hideously cumbersome piece of junk.

"What is this car we're riding in?" I saw that little smile on his face and instantly realized that I had taken the bait.

"Why, don't you like it? Look at this man," he said, pointing to the heavyset Italian driving it, "you've got a chauffeur and everything. What are you complaining about? You're going out in style."

"You're impossible," I said. "This car is embarrassing."

"I disagree. I think it's very nice. Don't you pick on my car."

As I look back on the conversation, it sounds kind of inane, but to me it was just lighthearted banter on a beautiful day. This was my first visit to Palm Beach and I was looking forward to seeing the city and Sam's home. Although he never mentioned it, I have since read somewhere that his wife died of a stroke in that house.

The strange thing about Sam's house was that I confuse it in my mind with the house that Jack used the times we met in Palm Beach. Both houses were near the water and typical of what might be typed as Florida subdivision architecture, long and low, with large lawns, large swimming pools, and glassed-in breakfast rooms—both had glass-topped wrought iron tables and wrought iron chairs. The only difference I can remember between the two houses was that Sam's pool was on the left side of the house and Jack's was on the right. Sam's color scheme was muted rose and green, Jack's was more of a grass green.

Sam's proudest possession was a collection of original china figurines, German or Dutch, which he proudly displayed in a lighted glass case in the living room. While he gave me the grand tour of the house and the grounds, his caretaker cooked spaghetti, that eternal Italian sustenance for all occasions. I hate to eat the messy stuff when I'm out, but this was really sensational.

For the rest of the day we basked in the sun and talked about traveling in Europe and South America, two continents Sam had traveled in extensively. Since I had never been abroad, he was more than willing to show me the world if only I said the word. Jewelry was another subject on which Sam could talk for hours. He knew more about jewelry and owned more of it than anyone I have ever known.

The very next day we just had to go look at pearl necklaces at a jeweler Sam knew on Worth Avenue, who also had a store in the Fontainebleau. Shopping on this street is a unique experience. You see all the famous names of stores you find on Fifth Avenue and in Beverly Hills, but here everything has been drastically scaled down in size. Worth Avenue is a miniature street with miniature stores, something out of a child's toyland. The only things of normal size are the prices.

When it came to shopping, Sam was just like me—we both were natural born shoppers. He enjoyed it more than any man I had ever known. That, in my book, was a huge plus in his favor. In those days, shopping was my opiate. I had the world's strongest shopping legs and the most tireless eye. I would hate to calculate the hours I have spent looking at lovely things in lovely stores. If I didn't shop every day, even for a few minutes, I felt like there was something missing when I went to bed that night. That may be a slight exaggeration, but I hope it conveys my passion for this great female sport. I still love it, but the passion has cooled somewhat.

That day in Palm Beach, I bought a pearl necklace with a one-and-a-half carat marquis diamond in the clasp, ringed with small diamonds. Naturally Sam wanted to pay for it, but I declined so firmly that he threw his arms up in disgust. It cost me three thousand dollars, but I now suspect it was worth far more. To me it was a necklace of perfectly matched cultured pearls, but months later Sam wanted to know if I had had it x-rayed. When I replied I had not, he said, "Do me a favor and have it x-rayed." I never did and I have since wondered if perhaps the pearls were not real. The fate of this necklace, along with the rest of my jewelry, will be explained later on.

On our way back to Miami in the old Buick, Sam handed me a small package and said, "Don't give me any trouble." It was a turquoise and diamond earring and ring set. I thanked him and he said, "You were standing right there and you didn't even see me buy this." It always delighted him to put something over on me.

Sam left the next day, which was the twelfth, and I waited for Jack in my room. It was a long wait, and when he finally did arrive, he looked so tired I felt sorry for him. I should clarify this by saying that Jack always looked good to me. He could look vivacious when he was dead tired. Even so the strain would show. This was especially evident when he took cortisone. His face would puff up until his features were distorted.

He closed the door and we embraced. Then we walked over to the sofa and sat down. I had an assortment of finger sandwiches and Jack asked for a soft drink.

"God," he said, stretching his feet out on the coffee table, "it's great to see you, and it's great to sit down."

"You look tired."

"I believe it. This is the world's fastest and longest marathon."

"Why do you do it? You're killing yourself. I don't understand it."

"Welcome to the club. Sometimes I wonder if I understand it myself."

I knew he didn't mean it. It was his way of curtailing that line of conversation. "I missed not receiving your calls," I said. We had talked on the phone only three times since I had seen him in Washington.

He leaned over and kissed me. "I can't tell you how much I missed you," he said. "Even in the heat of this campaign I think of you so often. We couldn't have met at a worse time. I'm the busiest I've ever been in my life."

"I wish we could do something about it."

"Judy, I do too. Fortunately, the campaign won't last forever."

"It seems like forever to me."

He smiled. "Don't forget your promise. We may go sit on that island sooner than you think."

"Don't be silly. You're going to get the nomination."

"You never know. We may be lucky."

"Be serious for a minute. Even if you did lose it, God forbid, you have personal commitments. You couldn't just take off like that in a million years."

"I am being serious. I can't go into it right now, but there will be some changes in my life if I don't get the nomination."

That's all he would say at that time and I didn't press it. Later, through various conversations, I got the impression that it was Jackie who was planning to leave him if he didn't become President. In recent years, of course, there has been considerable speculation to the effect that Joe Kennedy had promised Jackie a certain sum of money to preserve the marriage in the event of Jack's election. I have no idea how much credence to give this gossip. All I know is that I was sticking my head in the sand. I was playing the game according to his rules. I didn't want to discuss his wife and from all indications the feeling was mutual. I find it amusing now when I read accounts by women claiming affairs with Jack who say he criticized Jackie or discussed the other women in his life. I can't imagine him doing that. It's completely out of character. The whole time I knew Jack Kennedy, he never once mentioned another woman in my presence. Nor did he criticize Jackie. The most he ever said was that their marriage was not a happy one. It hadn't worked out as they had hoped. Good or bad, I didn't want to hear anything about her. Nor would I have respected him if he had talked about her in my presence. Besides he had too much respect for her to bring it down to that level. Because their marriage wasn't working didn't mean he had any less respect for her.

Oh, but he loved gossip. He adored it. That was something he was always asking me about on the telephone and in person. He would say, "Who's Frank seeing now?" or "I heard Frank is seeing so-and-so and isn't she married?" I would say, "I don't know any gossip." He would say, "Come on, let me in on a little of it. You're around those people, you see things going on." "If you want gossip, pick up a movie magazine." He would act shocked. "I don't want that phony stuff. I want the real inside dope." I think he wanted to know a little dirt about everybody. He wanted to be one step ahead. He never wanted to be the last one to know anything.

I was always fascinated by the way Jack's mind worked. Although he would ask me if I had seen Frank, and tease me a little about it, he would never ask me specific questions about the people I was seeing. If I told him I went to visit friends in Chicago, he would never ask for their names. He would say, "Did you have a good time?" If I said, "Yes," he would reply, "Oh, that's great."

For example, I told him I had gone with friends to shop in Palm Beach, and he said, "Did you find something nice?" If he had asked me outright for the names of the friends, I would have told him the truth. It wasn't that I was hiding anything from him. He either was not a prying individual, or he believed in the old adage of what you don't know won't hurt you.

He stayed not more than an hour that day. He relaxed, he had something to eat, we talked, and he left. There was no lovemaking. He apologized profusely for not staying longer, but he felt that even a little time together was better than no time at all, a sentiment with which I fully concurred.

As he was leaving he handed me an envelope. "Don't open it until after I leave," he said.

"What is this? What did you do?"

"It's a personal note for you," he said. "Just this once, will you listen to me and not question it."

"Okay," I said, "don't give me a bad time."

He laughed and hugged me. "I promise you, Judy, our next meeting will be longer."

"I'll second that motion," I said.

He must have been clear out of the hotel before I opened the envelope. I found two one-thousand-dollar bills and a note on a plain sheet of paper to the effect that he still wanted to pay for my mink coat. If I wouldn't let him do that, then he wanted me to use the money for something special. What could I do now? When is it time to stop arguing and accept a gift gracefully?

I don't quite understand it, but there was something about accepting gifts that chipped away at my freedom. On the other hand, I was always giving expensive gifts to those I loved. Sometimes I think compulsive givers make poor receivers. That was true with Sam and Jack, which I will talk about later, and Frank, of course, as far as I know, never even acknowledges gifts. As I grew older, I became more understanding, more receptive, but for a while my stubborn pride irritated people who were only trying to show me their love.

I sat with the note and the two bills in my hand a long time, thinking about Jack. I was happy I had come to Florida to see him. I was particularly thrilled at the fact that we had sat and talked instead of making love. This told me far more about his love for me than if he had rushed in with just sex on his mind. It made me feel that his plans for me concerned the future. In other words, I could tell myself that it was not just a fling. I badly needed that kind of reassurance. I think Jack knew it. He was so sensitive to people, and by now, with all that chatter on the telephone, he knew me inside out. He probably knew me better than I knew myself.

Later in the day I called Morris Levy in New York. I was undecided on what to do next, but Morris solved that problem for me. Unfortunately it was bad news. Our good friend, Marty Tannenbaum, had suffered a serious heart attack and was hospitalized in Great Neck, Long Island. I flew to New York the next day and again stayed in Toni's apartment. I called Marty's sister—Marty was divorced and his sister took care of his two children—and she arranged with the hospital for me to visit Marty at a time when he was not allowed any visitors.

I stayed two days, flew to California for a quick visit, and came right back to New York. Sam was at the Hampshire House, Jack was all over the place charming voters, God was in his heaven, and all was well with American Tel & Tel—just keep those calls coming.

On the afternoon of April 22, Sam called to ask if I would mind coming over to his suite for a few minutes around six o'clock. He had something he wanted to show me. Ordinarily I would have rejected the invitation out of hand. However, by now I thought I knew Sam well enough to believe him when he said it was important.

I knew that was a mistake the moment Sam opened the door. He had that little mischievous grin on his face as he gave me a quick peck on the cheek and turned to introduce me to his guests. Sitting on the sofa big as life, with drinks in hand, were Bob Wagner and Natalie Wood. We just stared at one another with eyes like saucers. It seemed hours before Bob stood up and said, "Hey, it's good to see you, Judy. How are you?" Natalie murmured her greeting and at that point I could have kicked Sam. I may not have known his real name, but by now I was reasonably convinced that his line of business had nothing to do with General Motors. If it did, it wasn't something that GM was reporting to its stockholders in its annual report. Yet what difference did it make that his name was Giancana instead of Flood? Both names meant absolutely nothing to me. Unless you're a celebrity, what's in a name? Outside of Chicago, in 1960 how many people had ever heard his name?

As we sat down and continued staring in confused embarrassment, I realized that Sam had planned it exactly that way. It was his idea of fun. A good joke. He had pulled a fast one on somebody—but who? For reasons I couldn't fully grasp, I felt compromised, as I'm sure did Bob and Natalie.

Sam was talking about nothing, happy as a lark, but I wasn't listening. I was frantically trying to unravel the puzzle. Then it hit me. While in Chicago, I had mentioned to Sam that it was Bob who introduced me to Billy when I was only sixteen. And that I knew Natalie in the days when she dated Nick Adams, who was part of the group of young actors I knew in the years I was married to Billy. Nick afterwards fell victim to that lethal combination of sleeping pills and booze that has taken such a tragic toll in Hollywood.

While I sat there wondering what they must be thinking of my visiting a man's hotel room, they probably were equally busy wondering about what I thought of their having a social drink with the Godfather of the Chicago mafia—I assume he wasn't Sam Flood to them.

There were long embarrassing lulls in the conversation. Sam was the only one not visibly confused. In an effort to fill one of the lulls—the three of us were desperately searching for something to say—I mentioned that Toni's birthday was coming up and I had to think of a gift before she left for a singing engagement at the Statler in San Antonio.

Sam jumped up and hurried to the bedroom. A moment later I heard him calling, "Hey, Judy, come in here a minute. I want to show you something." I couldn't even smile when I stood up. Bob and Natalie tried to smile, but they weren't doing too well either.

When I walked into the bedroom, Sam closed the door and said, "Take your pick." His top dresser drawer was open and it was full of jewelry—rings, bracelets, necklaces, but mostly watches—all the finest makes like Movados and Corums, all diamond-studded, and all terribly expensive.

There were three watches lined up on the dresser. "Take these for yourself," he said, "they're the best, and pick one out of the drawer for Toni."

I felt like stamping my foot. "Don't you ever give up?"

"Okay, okay, but pick one for Toni, but don't tell her it's from me."

Not being in any mood for an argument, I picked the plainest one I could find. "I'll give this one to Toni, but I don't want a watch. Now can we go back in the other room? I don't like being in here like this."

This nearly doubled him over with laughter. He had a sharp laugh, and at this point I was sure they could hear him throughout the whole damn hotel.

I dropped Toni's watch into my purse and walked out of the room. I sat for only a few minutes before I excused myself. Sam said he would call me later and I just couldn't get out of there fast enough. By the time I got back to Toni's apartment, I was so upset I didn't want to be there when Sam called. Toni was out on a date and that seemed like a perfect idea at the time. I knew just the man who could cheer me up—I had dinner with Morris Levy.

Sam said he was disappointed when he called the next day. He was under the impression that we had a date the night before. I wasn't upset anymore, but I wasn't about to let him dictate to me. It was time for an understanding. "I've never considered 'I'll call you later' a definite date," I said. "Lots of friends say they will call me later, and if I stayed home waiting for their calls, I would never be free to have a date."

"You're absolutely right," he said. "So how about lunch? *Today*."

"I'm having lunch with Toni."

"Okay, bring her along."

Toni was delighted—but delighted is hardly the word to express her enthusiasm. First I had made the mistake of telling her the truth about the watch when I gave it to her that morning. Now Sam had invited her to lunch. You could see

152

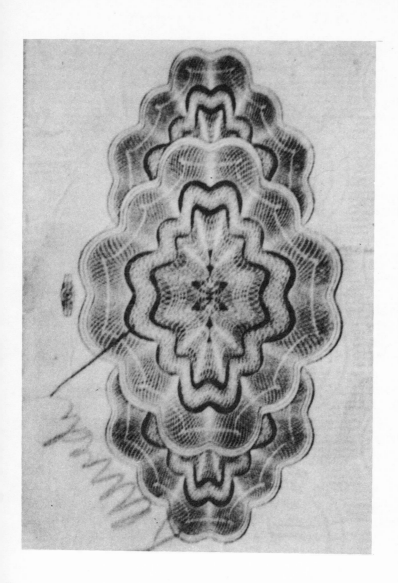

The program Ted Kennedy autographed for Judith's mother at
the 1960 Democratic National Convention in Los Angeles.

WESTERN UNION
TELEGRAM
W. P. MARSHALL, PRESIDENT

LA112 A109 SSA096 L

P WHY229 PD=FAX WASHINGON DC 15 NFT=

MISS JUDY CAMPBELL=

1200 NORTH FLORES LOSA=

BECAUSE OF DISTANCE AND TIME INVOLVED YOUR INVITATIONS
AND TICKETS THAT ARE SET ASIDE FOR YOU MAY BE PICKED UP
AT THE INAUGURAL TICKET OFFICE 921 SEVENTEENTH STREET
NW WASHINGTON DC FROM 9 AM TO 9 PM STARTING MONDAY
JANUARY 16 PLEASE BRING THIS TELEGRAM WITH YOU TO
PROPERLY IDENTIFY YOURSELF WHEN PICKING UP YOUR (
CREDENTIALS IF YOU ARE NOT PLANNING TO ATTEND PLEASE
END 1

WESTERN UNION
TELEGRAM
W. P. MARSHALL, PRESIDENT

P WHY229   LONG 2

ADVISE ME WARM REGARDS=

ROBERT J BURKHARDT EXECUTIVE DIRECTOR
INAUGURAL COMMITTEE 1961 LIBERTY LOAN BLDG
14TH AND D STREETS SW WASHINGTON DC=

=921 NW 9 AM 9 PM 16 1961 14 D SW=

The telegram from the Inaugural Committee.

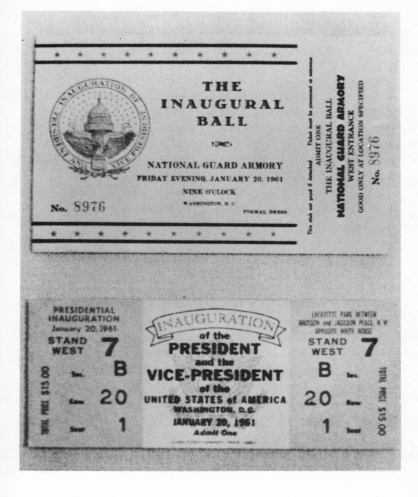

Tickets for the Inaugural Ball and Inauguration.

INAUGURAL ACTIVITIES

Calendar and Information

RECEPTION FOR DISTINGUISHED LADIES

Wednesday, January 18   National Gallery of Art, 3 to 6 p.m.

By Invitation

RECEPTION HONORING THE
VICE PRESIDENT-ELECT AND MRS. LYNDON B. JOHNSON

Wednesday, January 18.   Statler-Hilton Hotel, 6 to 8 p.m.

$5.00

Public Sale

YOUNG DEMOCRATS' RECEPTION AND DANCE

Wednesday, January 18   Mayflower Hotel, 7 p.m. to 1 a.m.

$8.00

Tickets Available Through The Young Democratic Inaugural Festivity Committee

GOVERNORS' RECEPTION

Thursday, January 19   Sheraton-Park Hotel, 3 to 6 p.m.

By Invitation

INAUGURAL CONCERT

Thursday, January 19   Constitution Hall, 8:15 p.m.

$5.00, $7.50, $10.00, $12.50, $15.00, Boxes (seating 5) $125.00, if available

Public Sale

DEMOCRATIC GALA

Thursday, January 19   National Guard Armory, 8:45 p.m.

$100.00 Contribution to the Democratic National Committee

Tickets Available Through The Democratic National Committee

OFFICIAL INAUGURAL CEREMONY

Friday, January 20   The Capitol, 12 noon

By Invitation

PARADE

Friday, January 20   2 p.m.

$3.00, $5.00, $6.00, $8.00, $10.00 $12.00 $15.00,

Boxes (opposite Pres. Reviewing Stand) $25.00 per seat

Public Sale

INAUGURAL BALL

Friday, January 20   9 p.m. to 2 a.m.

$25.00 per person, Boxes (seating 8) $320.00, Box seats $40.00 per person

By Invitation

3.   EDWARD H. FOLEY, *Chairman*, Inaugural Committee 1961

1.

2.

1. Ticket for the Democratic National Convention.

2. The card that came with a dozen red roses from Jack Kennedy
   when Judith was ill—Evelyn Lincoln was Jack's secretary.

3. Inaugural activities Judith was invited to attend.

NO ADDRESS   **NO. PHONE**

RETIRED

NO BUSINESS   **NO MONEY**

Under the Fifth Amendment to the Constitution of The United States, I respectfully decline to answer, on the grounds that my answer may tend to incriminate me.

The two sides of Sam Giancana's business card.

JERRY LEWIS PRODUCTIONS
PARAMOUNT STUDIOS
HOLLYWOOD

INTER-OFFICE COMMUNICATION

TO: JUDY CAMPBELL   FROM: JERRY LEWIS   DATE: 1/11/61

RE: DEAR JUDY

PLEASE PLACE A LONG DISTANCE CALL TO SAM FOR ME IN

FLORIDA, FROM MY PORTABLE DRESSING ROOM ON THE SET, ANY

TIME BETWEEN 2 AND 4 pm TODAY.

WHEN YOU GET HIM ON THE LINE HAVE ME CALLED AND I'LL

TALK TO HIM.

JERRY

The Congressional Directory Jack autographed in a White
House bedroom during one of Judith's visits.

The memo from Jerry Lewis asking Judith to contact Sam
Giancana.

Judith, age six, was in her Little Bo Peep outfit, holding her cat, when this picture was taken on Pearl Harbor Day. The picture later appeared in *The Saturday Evening Post.*

Dan and Judith Exner.

1.

2.

3.

4.

1. As a young woman, Judith's mother modeled at Bonwit Teller in the days when that position was something special. She was five foot eight and had "the most magnificent red hair and soft blue eyes."

2. Judith's father, who was an architect, was a tall man with a barrel chest, whose "voice would rumble and richochet off the walls like thunder claps on a summer night."

3. During World War II, Judith lived in this twenty-four-room Mediterranean villa in Pacific Palisades.

4. Judith, age twelve, wearing her first fur jacket, with sister Jackie and brother Allen.

5. Judith at far right, with sister Joan at far left, sister Jackie, and friend in Balboa the summer Uncle Allen died.

A photograph of Judith taken in 1962 by
Mervyn LeRoy's photographer.

Dick Elwood and Judith at the Malibu luau
in the summer of 1961.

1.

2.

1. Sam Giancana's Oak Park home.

2. John Roselli and his nephew in a villa at La Costa.

3.

4.

3. The Sands, Las Vegas.

4. The Mayflower Hotel, Washington, D.C.

Next page: Judith, age twenty-four, dressed for an evening out.

the light bulbs flashing in her eyes and you could almost hear the bells going off in her head. "Boy, oh, boy," she's thinking, "Sam wants to get to me." She ran into the bathroom and a moment later emerged dressed to kill. She had on her tightest, lowest-cut dress, her longest eyelashes, her reddest lipstick, her shiniest hairspray, and her biggest mink coat. I was grateful that the invitation was for lunch. Otherwise she could have worn her red taffeta, which was skin tight, with special emphasis on her well-rounded derriere and forty-four-inch bosom. Seeing this voluptuous five foot nine creature undulating on spike heels was enough to give some men a coronary.

She wasn't quite sure about Sam, didn't have all the particulars, but I had told her enough to start her wheels spinning. She was a nightclub singer with two records to promote, and she had been around the business long enough to know that talent could carry you just so far. More often than not, and this was especially true with beginners, it was *who* and not *what* you knew that made that dream come true.

We were complete opposites, but I liked Toni. It was fine with me if she wanted to impress Sam. More power to her. Sam was just another friend. I had no claim on him, nor did I want one. As it turned out, lunch was pretty much a disaster. Toni talked about her records, talked about her career, talked nonstop from the time we sat down until we left. Sam didn't say more than five sentences. He listened, he was a good listener, and I could see him sizing her up. He would look over at me and wink. It should have been obvious even to Toni that he was not impressed.

That evening at the Latin Quarter Sam asked me, "What are you doing with her? How did you two ever get to be friends?"

"I think she's a lovely gal," I said.

"Oh, sure, she's a beaut. Did you see what she was trying to pull off right in front of you?"

I knew what he was getting at but I wasn't about to give him the satisfaction. "Whatever it was, I noticed you didn't miss any of it."

"I'm not talking about that. She thought I could do her some good."

I gave him my most innocent look. "How could you do her any good?"

That little smile was back on his face. He was happy to be still putting one over on me. "Well, people get funny ideas at times. Couldn't be anything you said to her, could it?"

"I told her the truth. What else could I do?"

"Yeah, go on. I'm all ears."

"I told her you either were a jeweler or a cat burglar."

There were two other men at the table with us, a Jimmy and a Tom—introductions by Sam seldom got beyond first names—and all three roared with laughter.

On April 27, Jack called from Hinton, West Virginia, with good news. He was coming to Washington the next day to vote on a mine safety bill. It was another opportunity for us to get together and because of his hectic schedule I promised to wait for him at the Mayflower Hotel, as I had done at the Fontainebleau, without setting a definite time for the rendezvous. Jack sounded cheerful, and well that he should, for he had just scored a major victory in Pennsylvania, receiving seventy-five percent of the Democratic ballots in a write-in campaign.

But late that evening, after I had returned from a dinner date with Charles Evans (Charles and Bob Evans owned Evan-Picone—that was many years before Bob became head of Paramount Pictures), Jack called to say that there had been a change of plans. He had to make a quick trip to Indiana before returning to West Virginia.

He sounded so sad. "It's not the end of the world," I said, trying to cheer him out of his doldrums. "It's politics that makes the world go round, not love. What do song writers really know?"

"They know how I feel about you," he said. "They just don't know about my other commitments. Fortunately, it's not a permanent condition. It may even be shorter than you think."

"In that event, I've got the island picked out."

154

"That's my girl. Wherever it is, it will be paradise with you there."

A week later I·was in Chicago, again at the Ambassador East, but I was experiencing severe abdominal pain, a condition that had been recurring for several months. There were cysts on my ovaries and I was being treated by Dr. Krohn, but the medication was not doing the job. I knew the answer was surgery, but I was determined to postpone the inevitable as long as possible, even if it meant living with pain.

As always, Sam wanted to show me a good time. He devoted nearly all of his waking moments to me. It was a flattering and convincing statement of his interest. We talked and joked and laughed and ate and drank and had a marvelous time. Somehow he conducted his business, meeting with people at the Armory and at the Villa Venice, a restaurant and nightclub in Northbrook, some thirty miles northwest of Chicago. My impression was that Sam owned the place, and the fact that the biggest names in show business played there, including Sinatra, was impressive considering that the Villa Venice was nothing more than a mammoth neighborhood joint.

Only three things annoyed me about Sam in those days. First, of course, was his need to shower me with gifts and the battles that would ensue when I refused to accept them; I hated the terrible little cars we ran around in, and I couldn't understand his racial prejudice, which seemed irrational and pointlessly cruel.

One example was the night we went to the Chez Paree to see Sammy Davis, Jr. Again Sammy directed his performance to our table, and again Sam ignored him. This time, however, Sammy came to our table after the show. He greeted us, a big smile on his face, and Sam turned away from him. Sammy caught the movement and quickly turned his attention to me, asking me when I got in, where I was staying, how did I like Chicago? It was polite conversation, but with a nervous edge as he kept glancing at Sam, who was impatiently drumming his fingers on the table.

"Hey," Sammy said, turning his full attention to Sam,

"would you good people join me and a few friends for a little *soirée*?"

Sam abruptly stood up. "No, no, we can't," he said. "We don't have the time."

"Well, I thought—"

"Just forget it, okay? I told you, we don't have the time!"

Sammy gave me an anxious look and backed away. "Sure, okay, see you good people later."

On the way back to the hotel I was furious. "What's the matter with you?"

"Why are you mad? What did I do?"

"You know what you did."

"I thought I was charming as can be."

"Don't be ridiculous. You were downright rude to Sammy."

"Aw, don't worry about that nigger. He can take it."

"That's disgusting."

"Aw, come on, don't get excited. You're too sensitive. I'll bet you anything Sammy didn't even notice it."

"Don't worry, he noticed it."

Sam started to laugh. "Did I ever tell you about the time I threw cherry bombs under Sammy's chair? Now, that he noticed."

"You're crazy."

"I got both Sammy and that fruitcake Lawford in Frank's suite at the Fontainebleau. I rolled a couple of cherry bombs under their chairs and scared the shit—excuse me—the bejesus out of them. They jumped so high their heads nearly hit the ceiling."

"But why?"

"Why not? One's a nigger and the other's a fruitcake. Gave them a little thrill. Nothing to get excited about."

The phone was ringing when I walked into my room and it was Sammy wanting to know why Sam was mad at him. "Did I do something wrong?" he asked.

"No, Sammy, there's nothing to worry about. Sam was just giving you a bad time, just horsing around."

"God, I was really worried. I thought I did something to offend him and didn't realize it."

156

"Forget it, Sammy, he was just showing his muscle."

The pain finally got the best of my determination. I returned to Los Angeles on May 7, moved in with my parents in their new home off Laurel Canyon, and began a series of tests, along with new medication, but the pain only got worse.

The only bright moments in my life were the calls from Sam and Jack, whose campaign was going great guns. He was sweeping every primary. He won in Indiana and Nebraska hands down. But West Virginia had him really worried. When he called on May 10, the day West Virginians went to the polls, he sounded so gloomy I couldn't believe it. I thought he was acting. He said he was in Washington, hiding from the press, because he was convinced he was going to lose the primary, and with it, his chances for the nomination.

"In that event," I said, "I better start packing."

"That's what I wanted to hear," he said. "To the loser goes the spoils."

"I beg your pardon," I said, summoning my most indignant tone.

He laughed and all was well again. And so it was in West Virginia that day. Jack won a smashing victory, knocking Humphrey completely out of the race. In the next few days, Jack won primaries in Maryland and Oregon, giving him seven straight victories.

Medically, I was not doing as well with my own battle. My gynecologist, Dr. Krohn, whom I had met when I was with Frank in Hawaii, finally decided that the inevitable day had arrived. The cysts were increasing and surgery was the only solution. I was admitted to Cedars of Lebanon on May 23 and was operated on the next morning. Almost all of one ovary was removed and some nerves in my tubes were severed because of scar tissue—I don't remember all the details anymore, it's all wrapped up in medical jargon. As a gratuitous gesture, they removed my appendix.

When I came to later in the day, my mother, father, sister Jackie, brother Allen, and Travis were all lined up on one side of the bed looking down at me. My first impression was that they looked frightened and I said, "My God, is something wrong?"

They smiled and I felt better, but only for a moment. I became so violently sick to my stomach, a reaction from the anesthetic, that the nurses couldn't hold me down, even when they warned me that raising my head could cause a spinal headache. And did it ever. I had to lie flat on my back for two weeks. Every time I raised my head I felt like the back of it was going to explode.

I was in the hospital seven days and on every single one of those days I received phone calls from Jack and Sam, along with Jack's one dozen red roses and Sam's five dozen yellow roses. Jack's card read: "Get well soon—Friends of Evelyn Lincoln." Sam's were in a more jocular vein. "I wish I could take a vacation," or "Some people know how to live," words to that effect. Then I received flowers from my parents, from Travis, from the Elwoods, from so many friends that the place looked and smelled like a funeral parlor.

Because of my spinal headache I left the hospital in an ambulance. I had rented one of those fine old houses on Roxbury Drive, between Santa Monica and Sunset Boulevards in Beverly Hills, and hired a practical nurse. I was settling down to the task of getting well before Jack and his Democrats came to town in July for their convention.

On May 31, the day after I checked out of the hospital, Jack came to Los Angeles to speak at a testimonial dinner for Governor Pat Brown. He called from the Hilton and said, "Can I stop by? I only have a few minutes, but I'd like to see you, make sure everything is fine, that you're doing all right."

I was so thrilled I sat right up and just about lost my head in the excitement. The explosion in the back of my skull knocked me right down again. Pain or not, there was no holding me back now. With the help of my nurse, I slipped into my most beautiful negligee and really primped for hours before I was satisfied with my appearance.

I heard the car stop in the driveway, heard the door open and close, the doorbell, voices in the hallway, then the bedroom door opened and Jack walked in with a dozen red roses. There was a big smile on his face as he leaned over to kiss me. As his lips touched mine, I could hear the motor still running in the driveway.

"God, you look great," he said. "You look like you haven't been sick a single minute."

"I've always been able to fool you," I said.

"I think you've been lying to me. You just want a little sympathy."

"Some day I'll show you where that butcher sliced me open like a chicken."

He took my hand and squeezed it. "I can't wait," he said. "You hurry and get well."

We had talked only a few minutes when he stood up and apologized for having to leave. "It just kills me to have to run like this, but I wanted to see you, to make sure you're okay. Take good care of yourself and I'll call you later on."

One moment he was there and the next he was gone. That's how fast it went. I heard his footsteps going down the hall, the front door opening and closing, the car door slamming shut, and the motor noise gradually fading down the street. I was in seventh heaven. How thoughtful that had been. With his busy schedule, he still had found time on a hot day to drive across town in that miserable Los Angeles traffic just to bring me flowers and a smile. I think I loved him more at that moment than at any other time I can remember.

Sam was also doing his best but in a different way. He sent John Matassa to see me. Earlier, while I was in the hospital, he had sent Joe Pignatello with instructions to pay for my hospital bill, but I quickly rescinded that order. Now it was Matassa with a white envelope in his hand. "Sam told me to give you this and he doesn't want any guff," he said, trying to hand me the envelope.

I was in bed, propped up on a couple of pillows, making progress in my struggle to once again become perpendicular like the rest of the human race. "What are you doing?"

"Don't get upset, you'll be happy when you look inside."

I opened it and saw a stack of hundred dollar bills. "I

don't want it," I said, trying to thrust it back into his hand. "You better take it back to Sam."

John looked like I had slapped him across the face. This was an important assignment for him, having to come out to see Sam's girl, making sure that Sam's wishes were fulfilled. "He's sure going to be sore if you don't take this money."

"It's not your fault. You've done your job."

"No, you're gonna get me in trouble because Sam told me, 'Don't you come back here unless she's taken this money.' Sam said, 'I'm worried about her. I don't see how she keeps herself going.' "

"That sounds like a rehearsed speech. Go back and tell Sam that I said he gave you a rehearsed speech and that you did very well but I'm not buying it."

He looked like he was going to cry. It was a strange scene. There I was in bed, propped up on silk pillows, the imperious queen, and there he was beside the bed, the big gorilla on the verge of tears. He could have throttled a man with one hand, and probably had for all I knew, but he would have kissed Sam's feet for one quick glance of recognition. Now he was failing in his mission. "All right," I said, taking a couple of bills from the envelope, "this will get you back in his good graces. Go back and tell Sam I took what I needed."

He must have called Sam the moment he left the house because Sam was on the phone within an hour. "You are unbelievable," he yelled. "A guy tries to do something nice for a gal and look what she does. She throws it back in his face."

His need to give me money and presents was becoming very frustrating to both of us. It was now an obsession with him. But it was far worse for him than for me. I wish I could remember some of his expressions in those heated moments. They used to knock me over. He would get so exasperated that his character would actually change. I could see, or visualize on the phone, his poise dissolving as he reverted to type, back to the mannerisms and colloquialisms made so popular in gangster films. What was there to fear from Hollywood? Sometimes it was all I could do to keep a straight face. It would crack me up. Even his appearance

160

would change. He became a different person. The little cigar that he constantly chewed on would slip to a corner of his mouth and flop up and down as the flurry of words, many incoherent, fought for expression.

I used to get the biggest kick out of him. He became a very special part of my life. I loved his phone calls. Even when he was exasperated, he was a joy. He demanded nothing from me, or of me, and he wanted to give me the world. That was supremely flattering. No woman, I don't care who she is, can help but be impressed by this quality of attention from a man.

VIII

Monday, July 11, the opening day of the Democratic National Convention in Los Angeles, was a good day for Jack. Like most Americans, I was glued to my television set, and no doubt as hopelessly lost in the nuance of politics as everybody else. What was Governor Brown up to? What about Lawrence of Pennsylvania? Would Humphrey deliver Minnesota to Stevenson? It was a day of nail-biting suspense. Yet the consensus among commentators was that Jack's chances for a first ballot nomination looked good.

Jack was running the show from suite 8315 in the Biltmore Hotel in downtown Los Angeles, miles away from the convention which was being held in the Sports Arena. And miles away from my home on Roxbury Drive. Jack had promised we would get together but I had not heard from him in two days. When the call came early that evening I nearly broke one of my own commandments. He invited me to have dinner with him at Puccini's, one of Frank's favorite restaurants and one I think he owned an interest in. I don't remember if Jack said Frank was giving a dinner for him, or that we would be dining alone, all I know is that the invitation threw me into a tailspin. I wanted to go so badly. That might be my only chance to see him that week, which had to be the busiest week of his life. On the other hand, it was such a reckless thing to do that it stunned me. I couldn't believe that a man in his position would take such a foolish chance at the most crucial time in his life. My thought then was that he wanted to demonstrate his love at any cost. This was his way of saying that I was more important to him than his career. I know better now, but at that moment I was overwhelmed.

Finally I said, "I'd love to go, Jack, but I can't really. It's not worth the risk."

"Don't worry about that," he said. "It's perfectly safe. There won't be any problem."

"I'd rather not. I'm sorry—"

"It's all right, Judy. Dinner is going to be early. Could you come over to the Beverly Hilton after? I'll send someone over to pick you up."

"I'd love to, Jack, but I'll come over myself. Just call me when you get back from dinner."

It was before ten when Jack called again. "Are you sure you don't want someone to drive you?"

"No, just give me directions."

"It's room seven twenty-four and it's listed under Peter's name. If anyone should ask you where you're going, just give them Peter's name and say that you want to see Kenny O'Donnell."

I said I would be right over and I was there within twenty minutes. I knocked at the door and there was no answer. I waited a moment and knocked again. Still no answer. Now I was getting angry. All of a sudden I didn't like being in that hallway. I wasn't comfortable. I knocked one more time, still got no answer, and I left. When I arrived home the phone rang. Jack said, "Where are you?" I was furious. "Jack, I was there and I knocked and there was no answer." He seemed shocked. "But, Judy, I'm here. I'm right here!" "Well, I don't know what the problem is." I checked the number and I had gone to the right door. He said, "Please, come back. I'm sorry that happened. I've been right here all along."

After some coaxing and more conversation, I finally agreed to return. This time the door opened on my first knock. The room was full of people and Jack came right over to greet me. When he escorted me to the couch he looked really pumped up. "I'm sorry about all these people, but have a drink and I'll be with you in a few minutes."

There were six or seven men and one woman in the room. She was a tall, thin, secretarial type in her late twenties, with brownish hair and rather sharp features. She kept circling the room like a bird of prey, never lighting anywhere.

Then Peter and Pat walked in and seemed absolutely stunned to see me sitting there. I said hello and it took them a moment to regain their composure. I caught Jack's eye and he smiled and went on talking to a heavyset man, not even acknowledging their arrival. They looked at me and looked at Jack and somehow figured out they weren't welcome because they didn't even sit down. The next time I looked in their direction, they were gone.

Jack came over and said, "I'm sorry about the mixup, but everybody's going now. Just hold on because I want to spend some time alone with you."

He went back and people started drifting out. As much as he wanted them to leave, he still had something personal to say to each and every one before they left. Then he came back to the couch and sat down, sighing with relief. The only person left in the room was Kenny O'Donnell, who was wandering around, nervous as a cat.

Jack took my hand and said, "Let's go into the other room, I want to talk to you."

We went into the bedroom and sat on the end of the bed. As I looked up, I saw that the tall, thin woman was standing at the other end of the room. She gave me a little smile and went into the bathroom, closing the door. While I was trying to figure out what she was doing there, I heard Jack say something about the three of us going to bed together. I will never remember his exact words because I just couldn't believe my ears.

I think I said something like, "Oh God, Jack, how could you?" He said, "But it's all right, don't be afraid, I know you'll enjoy it." I thought, "Oh Lord, what's wrong with me?" He tried to kiss me and I pulled away. There was an anxious look on his face and I could see that he was puzzled

164

by my rejection. I was crushed. I just couldn't believe it. He never stopped talking. He assured me the girl was safe, that she would never talk about it to a single soul, that there was nothing wrong with a *ménage à trois,* that it was practiced widely, and, over and over again, that I would enjoy it—"I know you, I know you'll enjoy it."

It was a repeat of the night with Frank and finally I found myself giving Jack the same lecture—if you like it, fine, do it, but leave me out of it. I also lectured him on having the girl there without first asking me about it. I said things like "having your nerve," and the next thing I knew I was crying from sheer frustration and anger.

Realizing the gravity of his mistake, Jack quickly shifted gears. He got up and went into the bathroom, and when he came back, he put his arms around me. "I hope you're not angry with me," he said.

"I can't tell you how disappointed I am in you," I replied, trying to pull out of his embrace. "You didn't have to present this the way you did. You could have first asked me about it," I repeated.

"I'm really sorry," he said. "It was a stupid mistake."

I couldn't let go. "If you cared as much about me as you say you do, how could you have put me in this position?" I wanted him to know that I was angry and embarrassed, but I didn't want to let him know how terribly he had hurt me. This was far more devastating than the experience with Frank, who has a reputation as a swinger, and though I liked him, my affection for Jack went so much deeper.

"I do care for you," he said. "Please don't let this make you doubt the way I feel about you."

I kept on with my tirade. "How can I help but doubt how you feel when you—"

"I can't tell you how sorry I am. I think you're reacting too strongly to it, It's not that important. It's something you have the right to decide for yourself."

I pulled away. "What's the use. You're just completely losing the point. I'm tired and I want to go home."

"I just hate to see you leave like this."

For a moment it was as though Frank was sitting there saying those exact words. "Stay a while. I've sent her away. We're alone."

"Jack, not in a million years." I stood up and straightened my clothes.

He looked up, and the tension and pressure of the past few months were etched on his face. For the first time that evening I felt sorry for him, and truly wanted to put my arms around him, to comfort him, to tell him that it was all right, but I couldn't do it. "Will you call me here when you get home?"

"No, I want to go home and think this over."

He shook his head and stood up. "I really did it, didn't I?" he said.

"You puzzle me," I said. "I would think you had enough on your mind without cooking up something like this."

He forced a smile. "It wasn't easy," he said.

I started toward the door and stopped. "Don't you say one word about this when we walk out of this room."

"I won't. But I still want you to call me when you get home."

"I'll see how I feel when I get home."

Kenny was still in the other room, and obviously waiting for us. As we walked toward the door, Jack stopped and said, "Would it be an inconvenience for you to drop Kenny off at Jack Haley's place on Rossmore?"

I said no, but of course it was an inconvenience, although one Jack no doubt thought would help cool me off. He was smiling, his old confident self, when he kissed me on the cheek and said goodbye. "Don't forget," he said, "I'm going to wait right here for your call."

Kenny O'Donnell is another refugee from Camelot who has suffered a lapse of memory as far as I am concerned.

AUTHOR'S NOTE: *In an interview published in the Boston Herald-American on December 23, 1975, O'Donnell labeled all reports about the former President's ex-*

tramarital sex life as lies. "They are all lies," he said, "but there is no way to stop it. They will keep it going. I think there is a campaign on to give it to the Kennedys." Later in an Associated Press *interview, he said, "I think the guy they are after is Ted." Asked about the "seventy or more" phone conversations between Judy and Jack reported by the Church committee, Kenny said it was ". . . ridiculous. Some gal in California would call Evelyn Lincoln and ask to speak to the President. Evelyn Lincoln, a nice lady, would take a call from anybody. But that doesn't mean the caller actually spoke to the President. No one outside of Bobby Kennedy and Vice President Lyndon Johnson had access to the President's office without first getting clearance from me. Every morning I would get a list of phone calls he had received the night before. I never heard of this woman who now insinuates she had been his mistress."*

Being Jack Kennedy's mistress is the last thing that Judy would ever want to insinuate because it would be as false as any of O'Donnell's insinuations. "She now admits she is going to write a book," he continued. "That's what this is all about. It's just a sex story now, and not a very good one at that." As far as Jack was concerned, Kenny said he was "very discreet and very proud of being President of the United States. There is not much he did in his life, after 1957, that I didn't know about or Dave Powers didn't know about." The Secret Service, he said, recorded every visitor and there are no records of women who visited Kennedy secretly. "There were no secret passages or anything like that."

But that evening he was full of questions disguised as chit-chat, a low-key pumping that never fools anyone but the pumper. He wanted to know where I was born, where I lived, what I did for a living, how long I had known Jack, a very curious man. I gave him nothing specific, and though he was persistent, he was careful not to push. He would change his line of questioning, rephrase the questions, all innocuous on the surface, but probing nonetheless.

Gently, I turned the tables on him. As much as I hate to pry, I felt I had to do something. I said it was a fine evening and then wondered what he did for a living, what were Jack's chances at the convention, and what role did he play in the scheme of things. As a result, I learned that he was a professional politician, that Jack would win on the first ballot, and that he, Kenneth P. O'Donnell, was the architect of the Kennedy phenomenon. "I traveled with him every day of his life," he said. "The chain of command is from Jack to me to Bobby." This was all very interesting, and in the meantime, the miles were spinning by without further interrogation. When I pulled up in front of the Haley apartment house, I was still fuming. Then I felt his arm on my shoulder and his face was right in front of mine. All I could see were those lips coming at me. I jerked my head back and his chin hit my cheekbone. He pulled away and there was the strangest expression on his face. The corners of his mouth had curled into a leer, but his eyes seemed to be pleading for understanding.

"What in God's name do you think you're doing?"

"Well, uh—wait, don't get excited, take it easy, all I—"

I don't know what he was about to say. He never got it out. His mouth was stuffed with my words. "Get out of this car this minute!" He moved, but not fast enough. "Go on, get the hell out!" By now he was tripping over his own feet getting out. I yelled, "Close the door!" Then I reached over and locked it.

How I got home is a mystery. My eyes were blinded with tears. All I know is that I am lucky I didn't kill myself. When I got home I couldn't remember anything about the drive. I couldn't remember any of the stop signs, lights, streets, turns—everything was a complete blank. All I could think of was that I had tried to do this *nice* gentleman who worked for *nice* Jack a favor and look at what had happened. I had driven twice to the Beverly Hilton and look at what had happened.

I filled a tumbler full of ice and Jack Daniels and sat in a hot tub. It all seemed so unfair. It was so exasperating to be so vulnerable. This was something that had troubled me for a long time. A woman seems to have no place to go in some areas. How do you make your position clear? All right, so I went to see a married man. I realize that is not right. I am not condoning it but why should it make me common property? Why all of a sudden should those around him think that I am fair game for anybody? Why can't two attractive women go into a restaurant at night without creating the impression that they are available? Women's liberation has changed some of the practices, but it hasn't changed the thoughts in men's minds. The evening, the booze, the hot bath, it was a good time for self-pity. I felt I had earned the right. When the phone rang, I scowled at it and took another swallow. This was not the time for lengthy explanations. I was beginning to revel in my misery.

I slept most of the next day. The phone rang several times and the one time I did pick it up it was Jack, sounding full of vim and vigor and pushed for time. "I called last night and there was no answer," he said.

My head was throbbing. "I didn't feel like answering the phone."

"You're really upset with me, aren't you?"

"I'm more confused than upset."

"God, I wish I hadn't done that. Will you please try to forget it?"

"We'll see if I can. I really don't want to talk about it anymore." I felt weird saying those words. It seemed like *deja vu* but it sounded more like a broken record.

"I'd like to talk to you some more, but it's impossible now. Are you coming to the convention? Evelyn is holding four tickets for you."

"I don't think I will but my mother wants to go."

"I wish you'd come with her. Whatever you decide, the tickets are waiting here for you. Call Evelyn and she'll make all the arrangements."

At the end I softened. "Good luck tomorrow, Jack. I truly mean it."

"Thanks, Judy. I'll call you the first chance I get. Just take it easy and think kind thoughts."

We said goodbye and I felt better. I called my mother and she was delighted. My father was tied up at the office and so my mother asked a friend, Marie Marz, to go with her. My mother later told me what happened when she and Marie went to the Biltmore for the tickets.

The place was a madhouse. But when she introduced herself to Evelyn Lincoln, Evelyn stood up and said, "Oh, Mrs. Immoor, you've got to meet Senator Kennedy." My mother was thrilled beyond belief because she adored him. To her he was not only a good Irish Catholic politician, which is high enough in her eyes, but she suspected I was in love with him and she saw how happy it made me. Evelyn opened a door and said, "Senator! Senator! Judy's mother is here!" Like that. Jack came bounding out and said, "Oh, I am so happy to meet you!" And just made a big fuss over her and Marie. Then he said, "Isn't Judy with you?" She could see that he was disappointed, and she said, "No, she isn't feeling well." My mother gave the best excuses in the world—she used to do it for me all the time. "She went through quite a bit when she was operated on and had quite a difficult time. She's not feeling strong enough yet." Jack commiserated with her. "Oh, I'm so sorry to hear that. I'll have to call and see how she's doing. She is such a wonderful girl." Mom said, "Yes, she is, and I'm sure she'll be happy to hear from you."

My mother thought the whole Kennedy family was magnificent. She was absolutely ecstatic at the convention when she found herself seated right next to them. Ted even autographed her ticket. My mother was proud as a peacock. She had no doubts ever that Jack would be nominated and become President. Once she got something in her head, there was no way in the world to change it. In the next two years she would talk with Jack on the phone many times, and love every minute of it. And she loved talking with Sam on the phone. She liked them both because they thought her daughter was "special." She was that kind of mother.

I received a dozen red roses on the thirteenth and all it said on the card was, "I'm sorry." What happened at the convention on that day is history now. Jack won on the first ballot. I sent him a telegram, addressed to Evelyn, congratulating him on his victory. When he called on Thursday, I said, "Thanks for the flowers. You must feel guilty."

"I didn't send them just because I feel guilty," he said, and I detected a little defensiveness in his voice.

"Well, if you don't you should." I laughed and it broke the tension. I knew he didn't have a great deal of time to talk but we had a nice conversation.

"I'm going to try to see you before I leave," he said in closing.

"Well, don't worry about it."

"Oh, I don't like the way that sounds."

"All I mean is that you're too busy right now to worry about things like that. When this is over, we'll see what we can do about seeing each other." We said goodbye on that note and I felt that the episode at the Beverly Hilton was behind us.

As much as my mother liked Jack and Sam, she despised Frank Sinatra and anyone with that kind of swinging reputation. Actually, she disliked and distrusted most actors. Both Jackie and I had married actors and with predicted results. In her opinion actors were shiftless egomaniacs, devoid of any ethical standards, and that's all there was to it. With me it was a little more complex. Two weeks later I was in Atlantic City with Frank, getting set up for another disastrous experience.

I flew to New York on the twentieth and went to visit Marty Tamambaum in Great Neck. Marty had an apartment in the Navarro, 17E, which was at 112 Central Park South, a marvelous location, and since he was going to hibernate on Long Island while recuperating from his heart attack, I made plans to sublease his apartment. New York was the ideal place for me, close to Washington and Chicago, and a place where I had many friends. I enjoyed the Eastern lifestyle, the restaurants, nightclubs, theater, the late hours, for I had become a night person. I loved going to Reubens or Lindy's or the Stage Delicatessen at four in the morning for pastrami and coffee. Those were the days when I never had to worry about dieting. It was as though my figure had been cast in a mold and there was nothing I could do to change it.

On the twenty-fifth Frank sent a limousine to the Navarro to bring me to the Claridge Hotel in Atlantic City. Joe Fish and Skinny D'Amato, along with others of the entourage, the faceless ones, were in Frank's suite when I arrived. Frank was in his Dr. Jekyll mood, although he couldn't have been too happy about appearing in Skinny's 500 Club, a booking that was as dubious as any he had in Chicago, I don't have any specifics, but from conversations between Sam and others, I have the impression that many top performers were forced to appear in certain clubs by underworld edict. In fact, Sam and Johnny Roselli used to laugh about the things they made performers do. Their control over jukeboxes and night-clubs, from the lowest to the plushest, is more pervasive than most people realize. This gives them power over certain recording companies, radio, television, and movie productions. I once heard Sam say that Tony Bennett was kept from working for a number of years because he wouldn't follow orders. When he straightened out and got on the circuit laid out for him, then big things began happening in his career. I have no way of verifying any of this beyond the fact that it was a favorite topic of conversation among Sam and his friends, and it involved a long list of famous entertainers. I saw enough of them pay homage to Sam and Johnny to believe there was some truth in it.

I was in Atlantic City three days, in a room connecting with Frank's suite, and each day Frank's kidding was becoming more amorous. On the twenty-seventh, as I was helping him get ready for his show, he said something that really stopped me. I remember I was straightening his tie, and he took both my hands in his and looked right at me. "You know, baby, if I marry again, you're the kind of girl I should marry."

"Thanks for the compliment," I said, a little flustered, but determined not to pursue that line, "but our tastes are not compatible."

"Well, maybe you'd be worth giving up a little swing-ing." He smiled and kissed me, still holding my hands, and I

172

kissed him back until I realized he had something else in mind. I pulled away and he said, "Come on, will you sleep in here tonight?"

"Oh Frank," I said, "that's such a corny line."

He looked at me, the expression on his face hardening, changing from a smile to a knowing look. "You'd be surprised how often it works," he said, turning away from me and calling for Tony, who hurried in with his whisk broom.

That evening, after the show, Frank wanted to go bar-hopping. Joe Fish, Skinny, three or four faceless ones, and I started out with Dr. Jekyll and ended up with Mr. Hyde in his most extreme transformation. Nobody dared say a word as he cursed and flailed at the faceless ones in one of the most obscene performances I have ever witnessed. In one terrible place with a large horseshoe bar, Frank picked up a couple of aging hookers and proceeded to demonstrate his command of their vernacular until finally dismissing them with, "Oh, shit, get the fuck away from me, you pigs."

That was my final outing with Frank Sinatra.

On August 2 I went to the Four Seasons and El Morocco with Eddie Torres and Charlie Kahn, who were as insepar-able as Siamese twins. You never saw one without the other. Eddie was tall, Latin-looking, dignified, quiet, reserved; Charlie was short, robust, red-faced, a Jewish Phil Regan type, happy-go-lucky, talkative, and knew everybody. They were the classic opposites, but I have never known two better friends.

When I first knew Eddie, he was connected with the Fremont Hotel in downtown Las Vegas. Later on he moved over to the Riviera Hotel on the Strip. I will never forget the time I called Eddie to place a bet on the election. That is how naive I was in those days. I called from Los Angeles to Las Vegas and wanted to know what the odds were on the election. Eddie said, "Well, I don't really know, Judy, but how are you?" "What do you mean you don't know?" "When are you coming over to Vegas?" "Eddie, I want to bet on the election." "Oh, that's very nice, Judy. Call again sometime, always nice hearing from you.'' ''But Eddie, where do I place my bet? I want to bet on Jack Kennedy. Why can't you take it?'' ''Look, Judy, I'm sorry but I've got a call coming in from Paris. Talk to you later, okay.'' The next time I saw him he said, ''My God, woman, what is wrong with you? Don't you know there's a law against interstate betting?''

I had known Eddie and Charlie for years, had met them through Marty Tannenbaum, and every time Eddie came to visit his family in New Jersey and I happened to be in New York, they would always give me a call to see if I was free for dinner. They liked to eat at The Colony and to drink at Elmers, the quaint name for El Morocco, which was a cha-cha-cha kind of in-place for jet setters and nouveau riche types. It was where everybody went to see and be seen by everybody else. I went for the same reason. That's why it was always too crowded.

On August 3, Jack called from Hyannis to ask if he could drop by the Navarro the next day. We had made our peace. I am not one to hold something inside and brood over it. He had apologized, had done all he could to make things right again, and I had only two ways to go—forget or forgive him. Once I decided on the latter course, I got it out of my head. I knew I cared deeply about him and wanted to go on seeing him.

Except that it would be later in the day, he could not give me a specific time for his visit. I said it was fine, that I was painting again, and I would be home all day. The day I moved into the Navarro I had bought two complete sets of oils, sable brushes, canvases, and an aluminum easel that folded up into a tube for traveling. I started work on a very skinny nude girl who was standing in front of a mirror with a towel wrapped around her. I had gotten the idea from a Walter Keane poster, but I did it entirely in shades of blue. My father used to ride me about the way I painted women. I never made them voluptuous, and my father called them banana tits and that's exactly the way they looked. They were terribly unsexy.

My deepest fascination was with children's faces. Again I owe it to Keane, who painted children with sad faces and wide-eyed innocence. I wanted to capture that sadness and innocence. Children don't know what is happening to them, are not aware of the sadness in their life. Little children in tattered clothes, emaciated, victims in a world they don't understand and yet there is a deep sadness in their eyes. The lost children of the world. Having been a timid and frightened child, I could empathize with that concept. I am very sensitive to the unhappiness of a child. Adults can take care of themselves, hopefully, but a child has no place to turn.

As I look back on my paintings of children in those days, there was nothing but sheer tragedy in most of them. I had a feeling that I needed to shake people up. I was involved with people who lived a kind of superficial life, and perhaps my judgment of them was superficial, but I had this feeling that there was a great deal of sadness in the world. Perhaps I felt that my own life was superficial. There had to be something more to care about and I think I recognized it in the sadness of children. Childhood is supposed to be a happy time, in the ideal fantasy, but there are far more sad children than happy ones in this world, far more of them go hungry than not.

So there I was, the poor, sad, little rich girl at the easel. With Rachmaninoff on the hi-fi, filling the room with his melodic beauty, I would sip *Clos de Vough* and paint my sad children. The more the image took on life, the more emotional I became, until finally I would become blinded by my own tears. I think it was an important release for me, because deep down, regardless of what I was doing, I was still a sad unhappy child.

I often painted through the night, sometimes I would paint for days without leaving the house. I became obsessed with what I was doing and wouldn't even answer the phone. Jack understood that kind of drive. I think he liked the fact that I could get so lost in my work, and recognized that there were times when I didn't want to do anything else. The difference between our drives, his for politics and power and mine for art and beauty, was that I didn't have mine all the time.

175

The moment he walked in that day I said, "My, that island of yours must certainly have been nice today." He had this great tan and looked like a million. "All that nice sand and ocean, so idyllic for a romantic interlude."

He grabbed me and laughed. "God, you really know where to get a guy, don't you? That's really dirty pool."

"It beats stuffy, greasy, smoggy, steamy old New York in August. I once knew a handsome man who wanted to take me away to a deserted island and make love around the clock—I think that is the way he phrased it—but that was a long time ago. Memory gets hazy—"

He was hugging me and laughing. "Don't worry, we may be leaving sooner than you think. This election is not won by a long shot."

"But that can't be any problem now," I said. "I just read in the paper only yesterday that Truman has given you his Presidential seal of approval."

"That old bastard," he said, but it sounded more like *bahstard,* "has no other option. I'm the only game in town. I think he'd support the devil before he would Nixon."

Later, after we had made love, and he was holding me in his arms, he said, "Wouldn't it be nice if we could have that time together."

I raised my head to look at him and there was such a wistful look in his eyes. Jack was very loving and attentive after making love. He said all the things a woman wants to hear, but that look was something that stayed with me a long time.

I was so confused about love. There are moments during and after the act of love when words are not to be taken to heart. Many times Jack said, "Oh, I love you." At those moments his feelings for me were strong, but there is love and then there is *love.* I don't know how much he loved me, or if he loved me at all. If I thought I knew then, I don't know now. After my divorce from Billy and my experience with Travis, I was skeptical of intimacies expressed in bed. Several people have told me they loved me, but I don't think I ever quite believed them. I don't think I believed that anybody ever really meant it. And if they did, I knew it wasn't going to last. No matter how much you loved someone and they said they loved you it still wasn't going to work out. So I took the words "I love you" and let them sit inside me just where they wouldn't hurt. Or so I thought.

Real love for me is all consuming. For Jack, as I was to discover after he was in the White House, love was just another element in his life. It was completely excluded from all the other items on his daily schedule. There was a niche for each one: his career, his Presidency, his political party, his family, his children, his wife, or perhaps the image of the First Lady, me, his cronies, and so on down the line.

Before leaving that day, Jack said, "Will you be home tomorrow?"

"Will I see you if I'm home?"

"I think so. At least, I'm really going to try."

"Then I'll be here."

"Good. I want to see as much of you as I can, but I know as the campaign heats up, it's going to get progressively more difficult to find the time. The idea is to make plans whenever there's the remotest possibility of a meeting. You're good for me, Judy, you really are."

And he was good for me. I painted through most of that night and slept late the next morning. When Jack came that afternoon, he looked sensational and his mood was absolutely irrepressible.

"Vell, how var you today, Mrs. Feinberg [or was it Steinberg]," he said, shaking my hand like an anxious politician. "How's de hosiery bizness?"

He flopped on the couch and roared with laughter.

"How about letting me in on the joke?"

"I can't," he said, pulling me down next to him, "you don't know the secret code. You're just a girl. You don't even have a code ring."

"Let me smell your breath."

A moment later he started getting amorous and I never did find out what it was all about. While in bed I told him of my trip to Atlantic City and about Frank's black mood. That tickled him. He thought Frank's temperament was a riot. He was amused at the havoc Frank could cause and at the way people around him would cower in fear.

On August 8 and 9, I again went to the Colony and El Morocco with Eddie Torres and Charlie Kahn. I saw Jack at the Navarro on the eleventh and not long after he left he called to ask if I would contact Evelyn at her home and tell her not to meet him because he would be delayed. When I called Evelyn, she thanked me for relaying the message and then she asked, "How is he?" That kind of stopped me for a moment. "Why, he's fine. Racing around. He dropped over for just a moment." Afterwards I wondered why I had added that little disclaimer.

Jack was back again on the sixteenth and on that day we made plans for another visit at his Georgetown house. I missed my plane on the eighteenth and Evelyn changed my reservation at the Mayflower to the nineteenth. That evening I again took a cab to his home.

What is remarkable about this visit is that it was almost a total recreation of the previous one. There was a guest for dinner, a man whose face and name I've long since forgotten, and again during dinner Jack brought up the question of Evelyn's competence to serve him in the White House. It seemed to be troubling him terribly and for some reason he thought I could shed light on the problem.

My response was the same as before. "She's loyal as you could ever want anyone," I said. "If she has been good enough for you all these years, she ought to be good enough for you in the White House."

Later, in bed, I kidded him about his going to Independence the next day. There had been a story in the morning paper about it. Jack called him that old *bahstard* again, but he seemed tickled pink at the prospect that Truman might take to the stump on his behalf.

It was early morning before the taxi came to pick me up. This time Jack waited at the front door until I rode away. He didn't wave, that wasn't his style, but I did. Before leaving for New York the next day I went to the Old Senate Office Building to pick up my train ticket from Evelyn because Jack had insisted on buying it. I didn't see Jack, for he had long since left for Independence.

By nightfall I was back on the Manhattan merry-go-round. A few days later Marty Tannenbaum introduced me to Jerry Lewis, who immediately wanted to know all about my *shtick*. He obviously did not remember our meeting years before. When I said I was a Sunday artist, he asked if I would be interested in working for him. He explained that he had a picture coming up, *Ladies Man,* and he thought he might be able to find a way of utilizing my artistic "proclivities." Jerry, when he was being the debonair ladies man, had his own proclivity for big words. He would never use a small word when three big ones would do the job. When Jerry is coming on, he quickly goes overboard. You expect him to start speaking French. Although he is very serious about his flirting, from a woman's viewpoint it is funnier than his pratfalls.

He called six or seven times the next day with invitations for lunch, cocktails, dinner, theater, nightclub, and struck out each time.

Then on the twenty-third he came up with a novel idea. He called and said, "Would you come over for lunch?"

"I'm afraid not."

"Well, what about later? I have to go see someone very interesting. I could pick you up in my limousine and on the way over there we could talk about that job I offered you. I'm going over to Sophie Tucker's. Have you ever met her?"

"No, I haven't."

"Well, would you like to meet her? She really is a legendary figure. One of the greatest living stars of our time."

Now he had me. How could I refuse to meet this fascinating woman? So Jerry picked me up in his limousine and immediately got on the phone, playing the important executive to the hilt. As the limousine pulled up in front of her apartment house, Jerry said, "Damnit, I didn't get a chance to call England. That's all right, it'll keep. Did you know that tomorrow we're previewing *Cinderfella* here in New

179

York? I've got a million things on the agenda but this old gal is so marvelous that I can't come to this city without paying my tribute. For me it's like returning to—to—you know, oh, what the hell, you know the place I mean."

I thought, the womb?—but I didn't say anything. He ushered me into Sophie's presence and said, "This is Judy, my secretary."

My mouth must have dropped open. Sophie looked at me and at him as if to say, "I know what your act is, sonny."

Walking into her apartment was like stepping into an old Gloria Swanson movie. The motif was Roaring Twenties, and it even smelled like it. There seemed to be a lot of doillies, knick-knacks, end tables, floor lamps with fringe on the shades, throw rugs, pictures and doodads all over the walls, and heavy plush furniture. The only thing missing was wax fruit in a hobnailed milk glass bowl.

Sophie was everything I expected. This big broad with a face sculptured in concrete. When she laughed that whole room was filled with her sound, and when she talked the lamps quaked. They heard what she had to say. She didn't care what anyone thought of her. If she wanted to use a four-letter word, and you didn't like it, then you had better put cotton in your ears or leave. Because she was going to say whatever she pleased. She really made my day.

I went to Jerry's preview with Morris Levy and Marty Tannenbaum. From there we went to Danny's Hideaway and on to the Imperial where we met with Jerry and his entourage, which was bigger than Frank's, probably bigger than anybody's.

Jerry went back to Hollywood the next day and called me several times in relation to the job. He was beginning to sound sincere. His offer came at a time when I needed help. I was experiencing frequent depressions. My drinking had increased, I wasn't eating properly, and I would go for days without sound sleep. When I did finally sleep, my dreams were terribly disturbing. I would wake up completely exhausted. I began calling Dr. Sherman in Beverly Hills, who was the psychiatrist I had consulted after my breakup with Travis. I should have been happy, but my life was crumbling. I didn't know what was happening to me.

Basically, I am meant to be married. I am meant to be with one man and to give my whole life to that one man. My marriage had failed, and the pain it had caused me in those early years when I still thought I loved Billy had gone so deep that I couldn't bear to think about it. My relationship with Travis had also failed. I was falling in love with Jack, but I still thought I could stop it. I was almost glad that I couldn't see him more often. That's probably why I missed so many trains and planes going to see him. It wasn't a conscious effort, but perhaps I was trying to keep myself at arm's length.

I was a bundle of confusion. As I said, I hated his being married and I liked his being married. I wanted to see him and yet I didn't want to be in that situation. But I continued because I knew this was really my only protection. I didn't have to commit myself to him. If I didn't give all of me, I couldn't be hurt all that much.

In the event that he lost the election, I was afraid to contemplate what would happen between us. Would he get a divorce? What did he expect of me? Could I commit myself completely to him? It was all too new, too close to Travis, and in a way, even Frank, too close to the pain of failure.

I was living in an artificial world, one created in self-defense. "Look, see, I'm on my own. I'm my own boss. No one can hurt me. I can come and go as I please. If you don't like it, so what!" The problem was that I couldn't function very well that way. Being alone, without a man of my own to share my love, left a void that no amount of running could fill.

My painting was not filling the void. I was doing it to please myself, and Dr. Sherman suggested that I find another form of expression. I needed to do something more constructive with my life. So I decided to accept Jerry's offer. Up to this point, nothing in my life had worked out as anticipated, why I then found this prospect such a pleasing one shows the degree of my desperation.

Jerry came to New York on September 2 and I flew to

California with him on September 4. He sat with me for a while, trying to "visualize" for me the "concept" of my "project" with his production of *Ladies Man;* he dictated a flurry of memos to his secretary; he discussed musical arrangements with someone else; he never stopped talking or moving the entire flight. His attention span where others were concerned was severely limited. He concentrates best when he is listening to himself. He may have been listening to himself talking to someone, listening to a record of himself, reading something he had written, or listening to someone reading it to him, listening to someone compliment him or discuss him or his movies. He would listen to you on other subjects, but better make it quick if you don't want to get caught talking to yourself. Jerry had a million things to do and many miles to travel before he lay to rest—each day.

His Jekyll-and-Hyde syndrome made Frank's seem like a model of stability. Jerry could swing from the heights of euphoria to the depths of hell in the blink of an eye. This could happen many times in the course of a single day. He was one of those people who was happiest when he was unhappiest. He could make a problem out of just absolutely nothing, and carry on like he was demented, cry like a baby, then snap right out of it, laugh and joke, and the next moment he was right back in the doldrums.

Jerry was another one who flagellated those closest to him, but he made up for it by giving expensive presents to the victims. He kept one Beverly Hills jeweler busy engraving gold lighters, tie tacs, cuff links, pencils, bracelets, earrings, key chains, charms, etc. to reward those he had punished. Anyone around Jerry for any length of time had to collect tons of this stuff. The difference between Jerry's and Frank's flunkies was that Jerry was a workaholic. Jerry worked until midnight, and later, and when Jerry worked, everybody worked.

I don't mean to analyze Jerry, but having known Gary Morton and other comics, it seems to me that comics generally have one thing in common—insecurity. They clown to gain attention but it is also a clever camouflage. When they make people laugh it covers up for other inadequacies. Their clowning as they walk into a room throws people off balance. No one is looking at them for anything else. They are not looking at them for interesting conversation, for good manners or proper conduct. They are looking at them to laugh, to be entertained, and comics learn that trick in childhood. Nobody cares if they are unattractive. How many comics look like Johnny Carson? Most of them look like Milton Berle, Buddy Hackett, Gary Morton, Henny Youngman, Danny Thomas, Jerry Lewis, Bob Hope, Jimmy Durante, Alan King, Paul Lynd, Jonathan Winters—the list is as long as you care to make it.

Before leaving New York, Sam had asked me to deliver a message when I arrived in Los Angeles. He wanted me to contact Red Skelton's manager and instruct him to call Sam at the Armory, which I did the moment I checked into the Beverly Hills Hotel. That evening I went to my parents' home to help celebrate Allen's birthday. He was seventeen, a sweet little boy who towered over me.

I had several meetings with Jerry at Paramount to discuss the concept of my "special project." He hadn't yet "formulated" it in his mind, but he wanted some kind of booklet that would "commemorate" the work that went into designing the sets for *Ladies Man,* but the "germ" of this idea was still in a "formative state."

"Don't worry," he said, "I will get it settled in my mind before long. What I want to know now is whether you'd be interested in tackling it."

"Yes, I'm interested," I said, "as long as I don't have to punch a clock."

"Oh, don't worry about that. This is a special assignment. You can come and go as you wish. All I ask is that you get the job done on schedule."

"Of course," I said, not having the faintest notion of the job or schedule involved.

"I'm going to give you your own office," he said, "with your name over the door in bold type. Unfortunately, I can't pay you much at this juncture—that's the only problem. I've already got so many people on my staff, so much dead wood, that I've got to start chopping it down pretty soon.''

How much do you charge someone to give you therapy? ''I'm not interested in a big salary.''

''What's the minimum you would need?''

''Is a hundred a week all right?''

''Oh, that's fine,'' he said, jumping out of his chair. ''I'm going to have that office readied and the sign made for you right away.''

''When do I start?''

''Well, as you know, we're not clear yet on the concept. We need to clarify that somewhat before we put you on the payroll. But it won't be long. We're going to record some music tonight. Why don't you come over around ten-thirty?''

I had another session with Dr. Sherman that evening. He thought the job was tailor-made for me. ''I don't want to steer you,'' he said, ''but I think you need to do something constructive at this time in your life. You're not happy and this will give you an opportunity to concentrate on something else besides Jack Kennedy.''

Instead of going to the studio that evening, I called Sam and we had a long talk, the kind that was always so relaxing for me. Sam was good for me, as I said, because I was not emotionally involved with him. He was a friend, one that I was beginning to rely on more all the time. His advice was simple: ''Come to Chicago and relax for a few days.''

IX

The next morning, September 14, my mother had breakfast with me at the hotel and then took me to the airport. Sam and Joe were waiting at O'Hare when I arrived and we went directly to the Armory. Doris fixed a superb antipasto—everything imaginable—and we began on martinis. Thus started five exquisite days.

As always I had my suite at the Ambassador East, but we were together from early afternoon to early morning every single one of those days. There are moments from that trip I will never forget. There was the night we had dinner at the Singapore and the bowing and scraping reached new heights. At least four people greeted him when we entered: "Would you prefer your usual table, sir?"

Sam barely nodded his head and the *maître d'* called out, "Clear that table over there." Waiters and busboys were falling all over themselves. Sam didn't say a word. The more they kowtowed the more aloof he became.

They seemed terrified of him. I felt like I was watching the Three Stooges in a haunted house. I knew something disastrous was going to happen, somebody was going to stumble and spill something, and Sam was going to be furious. Then all hell would break loose. It had never happened in my presence but there had to be a reason for this performance. It reminded me of the times my father wanted silence at the table and said, "No laughing." You knew the first thing you were going to do was laugh. When my cousin Patsy lived with us for a while, she spilled a glass of milk every single night at the dinner table because she was so afraid she was going to spill that glass of milk. This was the same thing. You knew something had to happen.

Although nothing happened that night, I was sure something did the moment we walked out. Sam's favorite table probably collapsed. The kinetic energy released by the management probably ignited and the whole building blew up as we rounded the corner.

Later in the car, I said, "You must be some kind of bully. That was a comic opera in there. They were falling all over themselves."

"What a thing to say," he said. "I was so good, so humble, so quiet. I never said a word to anybody. You had my undivided attention."

It was true. I started to laugh and then he was laughing. We had the greatest time reenacting that comic opera—the Singapore fugue, as we called it.

What was so refreshing about Sam was that he didn't have those highs and lows of so many people I knew—Travis, Frank, and now Jerry. Whatever was going on inside of Sam, if it was something other than what I saw, was carefully concealed from me. I liked what I saw in him. I was always sure of how things would go when I was with him. I felt—and this may sound strange knowing what I know now—safe and secure. My head would be free of doubt and of the pressure that brought on the depressions. I was happy when I was with Sam.

We were at the Armory one afternoon and Sam said, "Come on, I've got a stop to make." So we jumped into his little black car—I was now calling it his "limousine"—and drove to 1147 South Wenonah Avenue in Oak Park. We pulled into the driveway of a red brick house, walked down steps, and entered a basement that had been converted into a kitchen and family room area. Sam introduced me to his sister Rose and her husband Richard Flood, which gave me food for thought. My first impression was that I had misunderstood him—that Rose was his sister-in-law and Richard his brother.

I asked him about it and he said, "No, Rose is my sister."

"That's strange," I said, "her marrying someone with the same surname. Is Richard a cousin?"

"No, no," he said, and there was that twinkle in his eye.

I thought, "Oh, no, I'm not biting this time." "That's very interesting," I said, as he led me up the stairs to what was the main floor.

"If you want to see something interesting, look at this," he said, pointing to a glass case and his magnificent collection of china figurines, the same kind I had seen in his Florida home. They were his wife's and he seemed especially fond of them. He was so careful in handling them.

Although he never said anything about it, I soon realized that this was his home. It surprised me because it was such an ordinary place, with typical heavy Italian furniture. Years later I used to get hysterical whenever I read about Sam's "Oak Park mansion." This was in the same category as his "pink Cadillacs" and "flashy convertibles." Sam was either playing games with me or somebody out there, probably the same somebody that wrote so many lies about me, has a fertile imagination. From the books and articles I've read, it only takes one fertile imagination and hundreds of copycats to turn fiction into fact.

What was not ordinary, however, was Sam's collection of jewelry. He showed me through the whole house, including his bedroom suite on the second floor, which didn't run the full length of the house but was more like a large attic. He had a bedroom, sitting room, bathroom and large walk-in closet to accommodate his extensive wardrobe.

I waited in the sitting room while he changed and when he came out there was a mischievous twinkle in his eye. There was an even brighter twinkle in his hand. It was a ring with a twenty-seven-carat canary diamond with blue white diamonds circling it. It was magnificent.

"Put it on," he said, handing it to me. I did and he said, "It looks beautiful on you."

"God, it would look beautiful on Tugboat Annie." I started to take it off and he said, "Don't, I want you to keep it." That ring looked so beautiful on my hand I didn't know what to say. Finally, I said, "Sam, you're crazy."

"I'm serious about this," he said. "This belonged to my wife and I would like for you to have it."

"I adore you for offering it to me. I understand the sentimental attachment you must have for it, and I can't tell you how flattered I am by your offer, but, please, don't ask me to accept it."

"Why not, honey. It's only a ring, a piece of jewelry. It's no big deal. You're just too sensitive about these things. Nobody is trying to buy you. I wish you'd get that out of your head. This doesn't entitle me to anything special. I'm not trying to trap you into anything. Okay?"

"Sam, I wouldn't be comfortable accepting a valuable ring like this on that basis. And I don't want you to be offended. We're good friends and I just love being with you. I love our relationship."

"I do too and it's great. Who's complaining."

"It would be different if our relationship was more intimate—"

"Well, you know we can change that anytime you're ready."

"I understand and I appreciate your feelings, but this has to be the way it is for now." Possibly I was leading him on. I used the words "for now" quite often during similar discussions. Somewhere in the back of my head, I was using Sam as my ace in the hole, the relief pitcher warming up in the bullpen. This was not a conscious effort at the time, but something arrived at now in retrospect.

My feeling about Sam was that he had had a good marriage. I think this not only because of the way he talked about his wife, but from observing his youngest daughter, Francine, who just adored him. Ordinarily, when parents don't have a good marriage it is reflected in the children.

We had a busy five days. We shopped on Michigan Avenue. We lunched and dined in places like Mike Fish, the Imperial House, the Trade Wind—not exactly Pavillon or The Colony, but interesting all the same. We spent the late

188

hours in smoky piano bars. Sam's favorite song was *You're Nobody 'Till Somebody Loves You,* and wherever we went he would always request that song. One big blond with a gutsy voice in a Little Italy bar sang it from the time we walked in until we left.

Sam was feeling pretty happy by now, and the first thing I knew he was singing right along with her. Usually something like this would embarrass me, but he was having such a good time, and he thought he was being so subtle that I could only laugh. Of course, no one would dare even say a single word to him.

Then he began to play with the words, wanting to make sure that I got the message: "I'm nobody 'till somebody like you loves me—all the way," and "You're nobody 'till somebody like me loves you—all the way." He twisted it every which way. As if that wasn't enough, he would lean over and whisper: "When are you going to make me somebody?" I would shrug and smile at him over the rim of my champagne glass—the strangest little places would come up with Dom Perignon when Sam ordered it.

It was that evening that he showed me his money clip with the initials SMG and said, "I'll bet you don't know what that means?" When I shook my head, he laughed and put it back in his pocket. He wasn't about to tell me his real name. That privilege would be left to the FBI at a future time.

Sam was a pretty fair drinker, but I never saw him sloppy drunk or mean drunk. There were times when he was happy-high that he liked to ride me about the Kennedy family. It was obvious that he didn't like them. He used to say that Joe Kennedy was one of the biggest crooks that ever lived.

My response was, "I don't want to hear that, Sam."

He'd say, "What's the matter? Can't you stand the truth."

"That's not what you're doing, you're trying to get my goat."

"No, I'm not. I'm giving it to you straight. He was a big thief."

"Be that as it may, I'm not seeing Joe Kennedy."

"The problem is that you can't separate one Kennedy from another. Maybe Jack would be okay if you could get rid of that damn family."

Whatever Sam had to say about Jack and his family, it was done in a teasing way. He never seriously discussed Jack with me. He never directly attacked him. It was always through his family. He often intimated that he knew a great deal of derogatory information about Joe Kennedy's background. I didn't want to hear it and I doubt that he would have told me even if I had asked him. There were areas that were automatically *verboten* without his having to articulate the guidelines.

Before returning to Los Angeles I went to New York because Jack thought there might be an opportunity for us to see each other. I drank and painted and talked to Jack, Sam and my psychiatrist on the phone. After ten days I realized that Jack, like God, was everywhere except at the Navarro. In that brief period, he was in Charlestown, West Virginia; Washington D.C.; Johnson City, Bristol, Kingsport, Knoxville, and Memphis, Tennessee; Sioux City and Ford Dodge, Iowa; Sioux Falls, South Dakota; Billings, Montana; Cheyenne and Casper, Wyoming; Denver, Colorado; Salt Lake City, Utah; Chicago, Illinois; Cleveland, Ohio; Chicago and Cleveland again; Painsville, Lorain, Elyria, Mansfield, Akron, and Canton, Ohio; Albany, Buffalo, Rochester, Lockport, Troy, Schenectady, Amsterdam, Ilion, Utica, Rome, Oneida, and Syracuse, New York.

Jack's second visit to Chicago, as noted above, was for his first television debate with Nixon on September 26. Jack stayed at the Ambassador East—we met there once after he was President. Perhaps I am prejudiced, but the contrast between Jack and Nixon on television was startling to me.

Jack's performance was flawless. He came across as a man who was calm, deliberate and mature far beyond his years. Besides appearing unshaven, Nixon was haggard, perspiring, and nervous as a cat. While Jack ignored Nixon's comments and addressed himself to the audience, Nixon's attention was riveted on Jack, as he took issue with every position expressed. This defensive attitude made him sound like a high school debater, one more interested in scoring points on little details than in proposing political solutions for the future. Jack was concerned about peace and freedom and getting "America started moving again." Nixon lauded the "progress" of the Eisenhower administration. It was no contest. Jack went into the first of the four debates as the underdog and when it was all over the positions were reversed.

I gave up my vigil on the twenty-ninth and returned home, except that I had no home of my own. I moved in with my parents and started apartment hunting. In the meantime, Jerry's concept was slowly evolving. In it's final evolution, after at least a score of "in-depth brainstorming" sessions, the concept became a booklet that would contain photos, sketches, articles and descriptive copy to "dramatize" everything that happened on the set from beginning to end. It was to be used for publicity, but I had a feeling that years later Jerry would sit back and relive those great moments when he produced, directed, wrote and starred in *Ladies Man*.

While I waited to become a paid member of Jerry's staff, I continued seeing Dr. Sherman. I painted, shopped, went to Palm Springs, dated almost every night, and even went to cocktail parties given by Kennedy supporters like Barry Sullivan. I saw Ted Kennedy at one of Barry's parties. He did a double take and just as he said, "Hey, hi there, how are you?" somebody whisked him away before I could answer. With all of these diversions, I was still confused and depressed. Fall was a long, painful season.

I finally found an apartment at 1200 North Flores Avenue, below the Sunset Strip and east of Doheny, and moved in on November 3. My apartment was on the second floor, number 201, and I took great delight in decorating and furnishing it. It was a fairly new apartment, not as large as I would have liked, but I was able to take it with the understanding that I would move when I found a larger place. This meant that I was shopping more for the future than the present. It was a one-bedroom apartment, with an L shaped living-dining room and a nice size kitchen.

It was here that I received my first visit from the FBI. There was a knock at the door and when I asked who it was, a man said, "Judy Campbell?" I said, "Yes," and he said, "We'd like to talk to you. This is the FBI."

When I opened the door there were two men standing there and both simultaneously flashed their identifications. One was named Dodge and the other was Vern Lynch. I didn't learn until some time later that Lynch was with the Internal Revenue Service.

It was obvious from the beginning that Dodge was in command. Lynch hardly spoke. He just sat there looking very menacing and Dodge conducted the interrogation. I had quite a few of my paintings around and Dodge wanted to know if I had sold any and before I could answer, he said, "Do you know Sam Giancana?" When I replied no, he looked at me like I had lost my mind. "Do you know Sam Flood?" I nodded and he said, "Well, they're one and the same. That's Sam Giancana. Do you know what he does for a living?" I shook my head and he said, "What do you do for a living?" Again before I could answer, he said, "Has Giancana ever given you any money?"

I began to say, "I beg your—" and he said, "Does he pay your rent? Does he flash big money around? Do you know Tony Accardo?" and he reeled off a long list of names.

I felt threatened. They were not two nice men who had come in to have a conversation. Whatever was on their minds, it was not something I wanted any part of. "Just a moment," I said. "What is your interest in Sam Flood?"

"Giancana," he said. "Salvatore Momo Giancana, better known as Mooney, and he's not the kind of man a nice girl should be running around with."

"What do you mean?"

"Tell me something, how do you support yourself? Are you an heiress?"

"I don't know what you mean by an heiress, but I have inherited money from my grandmother."

"Then you are an heiress."

"Whether I am or am not, I don't see how it concerns you.

What is it that you want to know? I don't understand any of this."

Dodge said it was in regard to an organized crime investigation, and he made it sound like I might be involved in it. I didn't have anything to hide but I realized they were trying to implicate me with their questions. At this point I didn't like those two men—the one with the long grim face seated on the sofa and the other with the sarcastic questions and abrupt manner who never stopped moving. From then on I kept my answers to a simple no. When they realized they weren't going to get anywhere they finally left. Dodge's parting words were, "Think about what we told you, we'll talk to you again."

I locked the door and leaned against it. My knees were so weak I thought I would collapse before I could reach the sofa. I was shaking like a leaf. I sat as rigidly as I could, fighting to maintain control of myself. I was terribly frightened. At that moment, those two men appeared as a far greater threat to me than whatever it was Sam represented. I had gradually come to accept Sam's way of life. I was not worldly, but neither was I stupid. I had seen my share of gangster movies, and the people who bowed and scraped before Sam were not doing it for ordinary reasons.

Perhaps my reaction would have been different if the FBI had approached me when I first met Sam. The idea of associating with an underworld boss might have frightened me. But now that I *knew* Sam, they were whistling in the dark. I wouldn't have told them anything about Sam if my life depended on it. Sam was my friend, and regardless of what anybody said about him, he had my loyalty. He may have been with the underworld, but you can put me on a cross, and I'll fight you, and you still won't make me betray a friend or family. It's not anything for which I claim credit. Or something I have to work at. It's part of me, my nature, something I have no more control over than breathing.

Later after I had calmed down I called Sam, and by now I was very indignant over their gangbuster methods. How dare they do this to *me,* a free law-abiding American citizen. It shocked me that the FBI, whose public image then was that of gentlemen, would act this way. I kept thinking, "So this is how they treat innocent people." I thought of myself as innocent, which I suppose was open to debate. Still their hostile, antagonistic approach was designed to intimidate and not to induce cooperation.

When I got Sam on the line, I just blurted it out: "The FBI was here asking all kinds of questions about you." His immediate concern was whether I was all right. Other than being boiling mad, I told him I was fine and then proceeded to reconstruct the encounter. Sam was very calm. He said it was typical harassment and nothing for me to worry about. They were on a fishing expedition and the safest way to handle that was to clam up, to completely ignore them, to act like they weren't even there. That was precisely what I did from that day forward.

November 8 was judgment day. By five o'clock Pacific time, CBS had predicted Jack's victory. The polls had closed in the east when President Eisenhower came on television and pleaded with party workers in western states to "keep fighting right to the last minute." By the time the polls closed in California, the projection was that Jack would win by a margin of five million. That was not the picture the next morning. Jack squeaked by on a prayer and a few thousand stolen votes in Cook County, without which Nixon would have awakened that morning as the next President of the United States. Mayor Daley has quietly taken credit for Jack's victory, but Sam often told me, "Listen, honey, if it wasn't for me your boyfriend wouldn't even be in the White House."

AUTHOR'S NOTE: *I explored that possibility in my research for* Captive City *and concluded that the election could not have been stolen in Cook County without Giancana's approval. First of all, Daley's victory edge in 1955, the year he first became mayor, came largely from the West Side river wards, the citadel of the old Capone bloc, which later became known as the West Side Bloc. What* this meant in terms of underworld control in the political hierarchy was not lost to Chicagoans who were (and still are) daily briefed on the latest intramural antics of their favorite gangsters and politicians. I went on to write the following:

"The Syndicate's trail of influence in both political parties is a well-lighted path. Its domination of politicians in at least half of the wards is a virtual dictatorship over the voters in their domain. 'The bloc's hold is so powerful,' the Daily News concluded in 1963, 'that people in its territory are afraid to vote against it—on the rare occasions when they are given a choice . . . The ease with which the West Side blocsters get elected and re-elected to the Legislature is another indication of their strength. Six legislators linked to the bloc have served a total of 109 years in Springfield. Thanks to an unspoken deal between the two parties, they don't even worry about token opposition on election day.' To Cook County Sheriff Richard B. Ogilvie, a Republican, the Bloc was 'a festering sore within the body politics of this community.'

"But to Mayor Daley the Bloc is nonexistent—all politicians, that is Democrats and pseudo-Republicans, are fine, upstanding public servants, elected by the people who have the 'right to select their leaders.' At a time in history when other cities have been subjected to abrasive reforms, the results in Chicago remain dismally negative. The reasons for this opprobrious stalemate have their roots in the anachronistic power structure of ward politics vis-a-vis organized crime."

After his nationwide investigation of organized crime, Estes Kefauver had this observation to make about Chicago in his book Crime in America:

"Everywhere we went the committee found a certain amount of political immorality, but in Chicago the rawness of this sort of thing was particularly shocking. . . . There was no doubt in the minds of any of us, after the sort of testimony we heard in Chicago, that organized crime and political corruption go hand in hand, and that in fact there could be no big-time organized crime *without a firm and profitable alliance between those who run the rackets and those in political control."*

In his book, Conversations with Kennedy, *Benjamin C. Bradlee recounts a story told by Jack Kennedy on election night: "Over dinner, he told how he had called Chicago's Mayor Richard Daley while Illinois was hanging in the balance to ask how he was doing. 'Mr. President,' Kennedy quoted Daley as saying, 'with a little bit of luck and the help of a few close friends, you're going to carry Illinois.' Later, when Nixon was being urged to contest the 1960 election, I often wondered about that statement."*

Nixon carried 93 of the state's 102 counties and lost Illinois by 8,858 votes. A switch of 4,500 votes in Cook County's 5,199 precincts would have given Nixon the state's twenty-seven electoral votes. An unofficial GOP check of only 699 paperballot precincts showed a net gain for Nixon of 4,539 votes. An official recount was not permitted by the Daley machine and the original election figures remained on the books.

However, Kennedy's narrow victory was not due alone to Illinois. Kennedy won Texas by only 28,000 votes. If the combined fifty-one electoral votes of Illinois and Texas had gone to Nixon, he would have become President with an electoral majority of two. As it was, Kennedy's margin of the entire popular vote was one-tenth of one percent.

I would smile and say, "Oh, sure," but I wouldn't pursue it any further. I didn't really want to know the details of anything. I liked being kept completely away from the seedier side of whatever his life may have been.

As the returns came in over television, the one thought that kept going through my mind was "where do we go from here? How the devil do you carry on a love affair with the President of the United States." I couldn't picture myself going to the White House for a rendezvous. I couldn't even fathom it. This troubled me but not enough to spoil the pleasure of his victory. I was so very proud of him. He had worked his heart and soul out for it. He was a very special person. There is nothing in this world that I would want that badly.

Before going to bed early that morning, I sent Jack a telegram of congratulations addressing it to Evelyn in Hyannisport. Later in the day I called her and we both reveled in his victory.

Whatever fears I had concerning the future of our relationship were dispelled the next day when Jack called to ask if I was coming to the Inauguration.

I had already given this serious thought. "I would rather not, Jack. I just wouldn't feel comfortable with your wife and family being there. I'll watch you on television."

"I wish you wouldn't feel that way. Why don't you come with Frank. The whole gang is coming. Or bring some other friends, or your family. I want you to be there."

We had a number of discussions about it. After one of his persuasive calls I weakened for a moment and called Evelyn to say that I would attend. "Jack will be very happy," she said. "I'll make all the arrangements to get your invitations out to you. Unfortunately, since you waited this long to decide, I can't send you a personally engraved invitation. I want you to know that I had you down for one but Jack told me you weren't coming. I assure you that you will have the best possible available seat and, of course, you will have tickets for all inaugural activities."

The next day I received a telegram from Robert Burkhardt, the Executive Director of the Inaugural Committee, stating that "invitations and tickets" had been set aside for me at his office. Then I received a program and various tickets in the mail. Jack was delighted that I had changed my mind, but with all that fuss I still ended up not going. The night of the inaugural ball, I went to La Scala with Travis and someone there said, "Hey, I thought you'd be in Washington tonight." For me, this justified my decision. Too many people already knew about our relationship without my flaunting it before his wife on this most important day of their life. All I said was, "It's too cold for me."

About a month after the election I finally got on Jerry's payroll. But after four weeks without a paycheck, I asked Jerry about it: "What was it you said I was getting a week?"

"Oh," he said, "I forgot all about it. I'll get a memo out on it right away."

Jerry loved memos. In the course of a day he dictated more interoffice memos than any corporation president. He had a dictating machine and his secretary was constantly transcribing his little plastic discs. Jerry turned on the machine whenever someone came into his office and surreptitiously recorded everything.

For a while, at least, working for Jerry was good therapy. It made me feel that I was pretty healthy. Jerry was fascinating to watch—if you could do it from a distance and not become personally involved. His behavior was more erratic than any of the slapstick comedy he ever dreamed up. He could be furious one minute, and the next minute be yelling for everybody to come play basketball. God forbid if he lost or anyone criticized his style of play. Jerry was convinced that he could do everything well. There were stories about his yacht and how the operators of various marinas would shudder when they saw Jerry at the wheel because Jerry thought he was an expert skipper and the result was an endless string of disasters.

Work on the picture would stop when Jerry grabbed a basketball. Afterwards he'd disappear into his dressing room and though no one knew when he'd be out, the moment he did emerge everyone had better be ready. "Come on," he would yell, "let's get to work. Don't you realize how late we are on this picture?"

Most of the people working closely with Jerry were caught in a love-hate situation. They were kept in a state of chronic anxiety. I think many ended up either with a psychiatrist or an ulcer, or perhaps with both, because very few people can function properly when they never know what to expect.

On my birthday, January 11, columnist Harrison Carroll called me at the studio with a disturbing message for Jerry. "I know you're a good friend of Jerry's," he said, "and I'm also aware that you know influential people." He paused before going on to explain that Jerry was about to be named as corespondent in a divorce action filed by a wealthy young man who was divorcing his starlet wife. Fred Otash, a keyhole type of investigator, was the one who had collected the information. "I don't know what you can do for Jerry, but I thought you should know about it, and I would appreciate your passing this on to him."

For the first time since I had met him, Jerry had a legitimate reason for being unhappy. He didn't disappoint me. His emotions ran the full gamut of his repertoire. It was a dazzling performance. He ranted and raved. He would be ruined, his wife Patty would divorce him, his audience would desert him, his friends would hold him in contempt—the dire circumstances he envisioned were infinite.

"How can I stop it?" he moaned, wringing his hands. "Do you have any idea at all? Do you know anyone who could help?"

Jerry knew of my friendship with Sam, having learned of it either from Marty Tannenbaum or Morris Levy. And because of the calls that came to the studio from Jack, he also knew about that relationship. "Well," I said, ever mindful of what he knew, "I could call Sam in Florida." I certainly wasn't going to ask the President of the United States to get a comedian out of a sticky divorce suit.

"That's great, Judy, but first let me make a few calls to check this thing out. I'll get right back to you."

It wasn't long before I was handed a memo which read:

DEAR JUDY

PLEASE PLACE A LONG DISTANCE CALL TO SAM FOR ME IN FLORIDA, FROM MY PORTABLE DRESSING ROOM ON THE SET, ANY TIME BETWEEN 2 AND 4 PM TODAY.

WHEN YOU GET HIM ON THE LINE HAVE ME CALLED AND I'LL TALK TO HIM.

JERRY

After explaining the situation to Sam, I asked if he would talk to Jerry and he said, "Sure, I'll talk to him." I went out of the room when Jerry talked to Sam and we never discussed it. Much later I did hear that John Roselli had a conversation with Otash and the evidence against Jerry was destroyed.

As I was leaving the studio that afternoon, I was summoned to Jerry's dressing room. The place was crowded with his personal staff and when I walked in Jerry stood up and said, "Happy Birthday." There was a big cake and Jerry handed me a gold bracelet. Two weeks later I had to remind him that my pay was three weeks in arrears. I don't think I was ever paid on schedule.

Jerry's close call with the starlet did not cool his ardor. Jerry was a toucher. When he walked with a man his arm automatically went around the man's shoulders. With women he never stopped experimenting, always trying to see how far he could go. I didn't mind the arm around the shoulder routine, but I constantly discouraged the other games he had in mind. He was always telling me how much he respected me as a person and how deeply he cared about me as a woman. He never stopped trying to get something going, and I would cut it off short whenever he became too suggestive in his conversation. He would use corny lines like, "All work and no play is not healthy," and would then invite me for a cruise on his yacht. I was able to fend him off for a few months, and finally he got the message and gave up on me.

Jerry's first attempt to fire me was to send his bookkeeper to tell me that they were cutting down on the staff. I immediately called Jerry, who was in Phoenix, and he apologized, saying that they were cutting down, but it certainly didn't include me.

I lasted another month. The ax fell while Jerry was appearing at the Sands in Las Vegas. I was having a drink in the Sands lounge with Jerry's secretary, Doris, when Jerry came in with his wife Patty and walked by without saying a word. A moment later Doris was paged and when she came back to the table, she said, "Let's get out of here, I have to talk to you."

"What's going on?"

"I was just given instructions not to talk to you," she said. "You tell me what's going on."

Not knowing what else to do, I called Sam. His advice

was, "Get out of there. You don't need that crap. Come on up to Chicago."

Sam was really hot under the collar when he met me at the airport. He wanted to know if I was all right and I told him that other than being upset I was fine.

"Do you want your job back?"

I looked at him and realized that I had better be careful. He was angrier than I had ever seen him. "I don't think so. I wouldn't be happy going back after the way I was treated. I'd rather forget the whole thing."

"You listen to me. All you have to do if you want your job back is say the word. If you want more money, you'll get more money."

The moment we reached the Ambassador East, Sam called someone in Las Vegas and minutes later Jerry was on the line. Sam was calm and deliberate. "Tell me, Jerry," he said, "what happened with Judy?" According to what Sam told me later, Jerry blamed his wife, saying she was jealous and wouldn't allow me on the set. "Well, listen here, you son of a bitch," Sam said, "I don't give a damn about your stupid wife. All Judy has to do is give me the okay and she's got her job back. Do you understand me?" Sam listened patiently while Jerry went into a lengthy apology. He held up the receiver so that I could hear Jerry's whining voice—he sounded like he had gone into his spastic routine. I could just picture him, jumping around and perspiring, scared out of his wits. "You better thank God she doesn't want your stinking job back, because she'd have it back and with a big raise in pay. Stop sniveling and thank your lucky stars that this lady wants nothing more from you."

I must admit that Sam's phone call made me feel pretty good. I felt Jerry had it coming. He abused people every day—and got away with it. His treatment of me was inexcusable. Now he was getting it back from someone he feared, someone he had no control over. I thought, "You're getting yours, even if I'm not the one on the phone. The person talking to you is talking for me." I wish I could have done it, but unfortunately a woman is seldom listened to. It used to bother me a great deal. The prettier you are, the less people listen. You're supposed to be decoration. This is something I've always resented.

The final blow for Jerry came from Jack Kennedy. Jerry had to be in Washington for some appearance and Doris was with him when he saw Jack. She told me that Jack said, "Hi, Jerry, how's Judy? Have you seen her lately?" Jerry was beside himself. It infuriated him that the President had asked about me instead of making Jerry the focus of his undivided attention. Jack, who knew of my falling out with Jerry, did it to needle him. Jack loved to get people off balance.

Two days later, on April 27, as we returned to the Ambassador East from the Armory, Sam said, "We're going to put on the dog tonight and really do the town."

Dressing to go out with Sam was quite a challenge. I never knew what to expect. I wore a full-skirted black lace dress with a simple high neck, the pearls I had bought in Palm Beach, and a white mink jacket. When I came out of the bedroom, Sam nodded approvingly. "You look fantastic," he said. "You're going to knock them all dead."

We then drove to Sam's house and it was my turn to wait while he went into his bedroom to change. When he came out he was holding a large emerald-cut diamond between twelve and fifteen carats, and he said, "I want you to have this." After our usual squabble, I agreed to wear it for the evening."

"If someone hits me over the head, it's your fault because I'm wearing this big rock on my finger."

He looked at me as if I had lost my mind. "Do you really think you can get in trouble with me around?"

Sam drove his little black car that evening. He never said a word about our destination. I realized it was the Villa Venice when Sam turned up a long street and I saw the large stone archway over the entrance to the parking lot. Sam slowed down and then suddenly zoomed past. When I asked him what was wrong, he said, "See all those ants out there." I looked more closely and saw that there were men sitting across the entire length of the archway, and all down the sides. They even had a couple of ladders.

"What's going on," I asked.

"We're going to a wedding reception," he said, "and those characters are Feds and newshounds, and they all have cameras. But we've got to go in there. I'm going to turn around, and you just kind of look down so they can't get a good shot of you."

He was truly enjoying it. He swung the car around and he was ho-ho-hoing all the time, and I said, "You're crazy, Sam." "Don't worry," he said, "everything is all right."

We swung through the archway and it felt like a thousand flashbulbs had gone off in one giant blinding blast. Sam was still laughing when he stopped under the canopied entrance and the parking attendants opened the doors. I must admit it was an exhilarating experience. Although I never saw it, I was told that our picture later appeared in one of the Chicago dailies.

The wedding reception was for Tony Accardo's daughter, Linda Lee, and her husband, Michael Palermo. The Accardos and the newlyweds were greeting arriving guests and collecting white envelopes like crazy. It was simply "how-do-you-do" to me, but Sam got the full treatment.

We sat at a table with Sam's two married daughters, Antoinette and Bonnie, and their husbands. The first thing Sam did was to take my left hand, as though he were being affectionate, and casually display the ring to his daughters. Antoinette nearly dropped her fork. She looked at Bonnie and they looked at him, and I quickly dropped my hand on my lap.

Sam started to laugh. "What's the matter, honey," he said to Antoinette.

"Nothing, nothing at all," she said.

Bonnie said, "May I see your ring?"

Now that I knew his game, I gave him a swift kick under the table as I raised my hand to show her the ring. "That's beautiful," she said, and it was obvious that they both recognized it. Antoinette, Sam later told me, had been pestering him for her mother's jewelry, and he wasn't about to give it to her. She had gone about it in a greedy manner and now he was having the time of his life watching her squirm.

Throughout the evening an endless stream of people came to the table to pay their respects to Sam. From time to time he would introduce them, but always on a first name basis, or with just nicknames, "Judy, this is Potatoes, Crackers, Monk, Smokes, Teets, Nags, Fifi, Horse, Needles, Cowboy, Turk, Dutch—I always got the biggest kick out of those monikers. They represented more pushed-in noses and scarred faces, more dese, dem and dose sprinkled with Sicilian than all of Central Casting. They looked so tough and yet were so gentle in Sam's presence that I had the feeling that I was watching a scene from *Guys and Dolls*. There was a lot of noise and rambunctious dancing, but everybody was having a happy time.

The next day there was a pleasant surprise in the newspaper. Jack was in Chicago to attend a Democratic dinner at McCormick Place. I called Evelyn and told her that I was at the Ambassador East. She said, "Oh, Jack will be so thrilled!" She connected us and Jack said, "Can I see you?" I told him I was in suite 839-40 and I said I would wait for him if there was any chance he could make it. But I couldn't resist adding that his coming to the hotel might be too risky.

"I'll be over for sure," he said. "Don't worry about that. Everybody knows I'm in town and there's nothing unusual about my dropping over to see someone."

He made it sound so normal, but as I sat there waiting for his knock on the door I tried to envision what his visit entailed—the limousines, the motorcycle cops, the secret service, the mapping of the route, the control of traffic lights, the blocking off of streets, and Jack in his limousine discussing affairs of state, or politics, with men who would be left waiting while we kissed and talked of love.

Although we had been talking on the phone on a regular basis, I hadn't seen Jack in quite a while. I was beginning to think that our relationship might just quietly expire from

204

neglect. I knew that Jack was impossibly busy, and though I believed him when he said he missed me and was looking forward to a time when we could be together again, I couldn't help but think it was beginning to sound like empty promises.

There was a gentle knock and I was up in a flash. A moment later we were in each other's arms and it was like we had never been apart. The way he behaved there was no doubt that he had missed me. God knows I had missed him. If the love I felt at that moment could have been preserved within my heart, I would have been blissfully happy for the rest of my life.

There was no time to luxuriate in the warmth of our love. As he was leaving he said, "I want you to come to the White House." And before we reached the door it was agreed that I would come to Washington on May 4. We kissed and he was gone. The visit could not have lasted more than twenty minutes.

After Jack left I suddenly remembered I was going to Miami the next day. I was going at Sam's invitation, and I left on a late afternoon flight, traveling under the alias of Judy Norris. Sam took a later flight, arriving at one in the morning. As always, I stayed at the Fontainebleau.

The next evening, April 13, we had dinner with Skinny D'Amato at Nate and Art's, and later that evening Johnny Roselli and his girlfriend Genene Claire joined us for a drink in the lounge.

AUTHOR'S NOTE: *Born in Esteria, Italy, Filippo Sacco was six years old in 1911 when his mother brought him to the United States to be reunited with his father, who had emigrated earlier and was living in East Boston. Ten years later, Filippo was arrested as a narcotics peddler and promptly skipped bail. It was then that he changed his name to John Roselli, and would later tell the Kefauver Committee that his birthplace was Chicago.*

He served his apprenticeship in bootlegging with

Longy Zwillman's mob in New Jersey and later switched his allegiance to Al Capone, where he gained expertise in labor racketeering, extortion and gambling. By the early 1930's, he had earned a reputation as a smooth operator and he was transferred to the west coast to protect some of Frank Nitti's interests. He was given a percentage in Nationwide News, the only bookmaking wire service then in operation, and became an associate of Willie Bioff and George Browne in the International Alliance of Theatrical Stage Employees and Moving Picture Machine Operators. On the testimony of Willie Bioff, Roselli and six top Chicago hoodlums were sentenced to ten-year prison terms for extorting millions from the film industry. Nitti committed suicide to avoid prosecution and Bioff was later murdered. After serving less than four years of his sentence, Roselli came back to Hollywood as an "assistant producer" to Brian Foy, who headed Eagle Lion Studio. That was his cover while he represented Chicago interests in Jack Dragna's west coast organization.

When Dragna died of natural causes in 1957, Roselli was picked by Giancana and the Mafia's Grand Council as their top coordinator in Las Vegas and Southern California. Don Giovanni, as he was known in the brotherhood, became a man of respect. He prided himself on his ability to settle disputes without raising his voice. Slim, medium height, with sharp features, iron-gray hair and icy blue eyes that turned black whenever he had to raise his voice, Roselli had reached the peak of his profession by the time he became involved with the CIA.

As Senator Frank Church's Intelligence Committee unhappily discovered in 1975, Giancana and Roselli had been recruited by the Central Intelligence Agency to arrange for the assassination of Fidel Castro. The middle-man in the operation was Robert Maheu, a former FBI agent who later gained notoriety when he was fired as Howard Hughes's alter ego in Las Vegas. From the testimony of CIA officials, Maheu and Roselli *before the Senate committee, the code name for the operation should have been Keystone. It was the greatest slapstick conspiracy ever conceived in real life.*

It has been described as a plot, but Webster's says that a "plot suggests careful foresight in planning and a continuity or complexity of positive action by one or a number of persons . . ." So a plot it wasn't. Fiasco is the word. No one knows how many fiascos there were between March of 1960 and the end of 1965—they began before and ended after the Kennedy administration. The original objective was to "dispose" of Castro before the Bay of Pigs invasion.

Even the committee's report was hard pressed to describe the fiascos: "The proposed assassination devices ran the gamut from high-powered rifles to poison pills, poison pens, deadly bacterial powders, and other devices which strain the imagination."

One wild scheme was "to spray Castro's broadcasting studio with a chemical which produced effects similar to LSD, but the scheme was rejected because the chemical was unreliable. During this period, TSD [Technical Services Division] impregnated a box of cigars with a chemical which produced temporary disorientation, hoping to induce Castro to smoke one of the cigars before delivering a speech. The Inspector General also reported a plan to destroy Castro's image as 'The Beard' by dusting his shoes with thallium salts, a strong depilatory that would cause his beard to fall out. The depilatory was to be administered during a trip outside Cuba, when it was anticipated Castro would leave his shoes outside the door of his hotel room to be shined. TSD procured the chemical and tested it on animals, but apparently abandoned the scheme because Castro cancelled his trip."

Unable to destroy Castro's image, the CIA decided to go all out on destroying the person. The cigars were now impregnated with a botulinum toxin so "potent that a person would die after putting one in his mouth." The cigars were delivered to an "unidentified person" and that was the last anyone heard of them. Various other fiascos resulted before August 1960, at which time "the CIA took steps to enlist members of the criminal underworld with gambling syndicate contacts to aid in assassinating Castro. The origin of the plot is uncertain." The committee was not noted for its use of hyperbole.

Colonel Sheffield Edwards, Director of the Agency's Office of Security, picked Maheu for the job because he was "tough enough" to handle the assignment. Maheu picked Roselli, who in turn picked Giancana, his old boss, as the "back-up man." Maheu, who had known Roselli prior to this time, denied that he was aware of the extent of Roselli's underworld connections and activities, but recalled that "it was certainly evident to me that he was able to accomplish things in Las Vegas when nobody else seemed to get the same kind of attention."

Maheu's cover story, as outlined by the CIA, was that he would "approach Roselli as the representative of businessmen with interests in Cuba who saw the elimination of Castro as the first essential step to the recovery of their investments." Maheu was told to offer $150,000 for Castro's assassination, which made it pretty high as hit contracts go in the Mafia.

In his testimony, Roselli said that Maheu's approach was that "high government officials" needed his expertise in recruiting Cubans to knock off Castro. Following that first meeting, which was at the Beverly Hills Brown Derby restaurant on September 14, Roselli went forthwith to Miami to work out the details for the first officially approved hit of his career.

At this point, I should explain that there is nothing clear-cut in the committee's report. It is one long collection of conflicting testimony presented in glorious confusion. Any writer could take this report and arrive at any conclusion he wished without any concern for the truth and still be in the committee's ballpark. It is simply a question of multiple choice.

Roselli and Maheu were registered at Miami's Kennilworth Hotel from October 11–13. On the eighteenth,

Roselli introduced Maheu to a Sam Gold (Giancana), who would be his "back-up" or "key" man, and to Joe (Santos Trafficante), who "Gold said would serve as a courier to Cuba and make arrangements there." Trafficante, whose specialty in recent years has been the drug traffic, had been the Mob's top gun in the good old days of Batista.

Although it was Giancana's job to locate someone in Castro's entourage to make the hit, Roselli testified that none of the Cubans eventually used in the fiascos were acquired through Giancana's contacts. There is persuasive evidence that Giancana thought the whole thing was a lark. Consider what happened when Giancana talked Maheu into putting a bug into the room of comedian Dan Rowan whom he suspected was having an affair with Phyllis McGuire, who was then having an affair with Giancana.

Bear in mind that the committee presents several versions of this fiasco. In one version, we are told that Maheu took the problem to Colonel Edwards, who concluded that the CIA did not have "the capability of accomplishing this," but gave Maheu a thousand dollars to hire Arthur J. Balletti, a private detective, for the job. Instead of the requested bug, Balletti decided to install a tap on the phone. The ensuing events were described by a CIA official as a "Keystone Comedy Act."

The report states that "On October 31, 1960, Balletti, believing that the apartment would be vacant for the afternoon, left the wiretap equipment unattended. A maid discovered the equipment and notified the local sheriff, who arrested Balletti and brought him to the jail. Balletti called Maheu in Miami, tying 'Maheu into this thing up to his ear.' Balletti's bail was paid by Roselli."

Giancana thought it was hilarious when Roselli told him about Balletti's arrest. "Giancana laughed," Roselli said. "I remember his expression, smoking a cigar, he almost swallowed it laughing about it." This upset Roselli no end. "It was blowing everything," he said, "blowing every kind of cover that I had tried to arrange to keep quiet." Only then, we are asked to believe, did Roselli tell Giancana that the CIA was involved in the operation "in order to have him keep his mouth shut."

What is intriguing here is that on the very day Giancana was supposedly introduced to Maheu, October 18, J. Edgar Hoover sent a memorandum to Richard Bissell, the CIA's Deputy Director for Plans, and reported the following:

"During recent conversations with several friends, Giancana stated that Fidel Castro was to be done away with very shortly. When doubt was expressed regarding this statement, Giancana reportedly assured those present that Castro's assassination would occur in November. Moreover, he allegedly indicated that he had already met with the assassin-to-be on three occasions. . . . Giancana claimed that everything has been perfected for the killing of Castro, and that the 'assassin' had arranged with a girl, not further described, to drop a 'pill' in some drink or food of Castro's."

In another part of the committee's report, from information provided in the Inspector General's Report, we learn that the CIA's "Support Chief contacted Roselli in early September 1960, and during the week of September 25, the Chief, Maheu, and Roselli met with Giancana and Trafficante in Miami."

With the FBI on the scent, the boys started manufacturing alibis. Again the Senate committee was presented with a multiple choice situation:

—Roselli said that Maheu gave him two explanations for the tap: First, that Giancana was concerned that Phyllis was having an affair; and second that he had arranged the tap to determine whether Giancana had told Phyllis about the assassination "plot," and whether she was spreading the story. Maheu later gave the FBI the second explanation.

—In a memo to Bobby Kennedy, dated May 14, 1962, Colonel Edwards stated that "At the time of the incident neither the Agency nor the undersigned knew of the proposed technical installation."

—The CIA's Support Chief testified that Maheu had informed him of Giancana's concern over Phyllis and his request for the bug. Otherwise, Giancana had threatened to fly to Las Vegas himself. Because Giancana's departure "would disrupt the negotiations," Maheu "secured the Support Chief's permission to arrange for a bug to insure Giancana's presence and cooperation." Balletti's boss told FBI agents that Maheu paid him a retainer of a thousand dollars for the job, and the Support Chief confirmed that the CIA "indirectly" paid for the tap because "we paid Maheu a certain amount of money, and he just paid it out of what we were giving him."

—Joseph Shimon, an acquaintance of Giancana, testified that Giancana told him he had gone through Roselli in his request for the bug. Shimon said Giancana told him he had paid Maheu five thousand dollars for the tap, that the CIA had not known about the tap in advance, and that Maheu subsequently decided to use his connection with the CIA operation to avoid prosecution for his involvement in the tap. Maheu testified he didn't remember receiving the money.

—Edwards told Maheu that if he was "approached by the FBI, he could refer them to me to be briefed that he was engaged in an intelligence operation directed at Cuba."

—On April 18, 1961, Maheu informed the FBI that the tap involved the CIA, and suggested that Edwards be contacted.

—On April 20, 1961, the final day of the Bay of Pigs fiasco, Edwards told the FBI that the prosecution of Maheu might reveal sensitive information concerning the Bay of Pigs invasion.

—In a memorandum to the Attorney General, dated May 22, 1961, Hoover summarized Edwards' statements which spelled out Giancana's CIA link. The CIA had relied on Giancana because of his contacts with gambling figures who might have sources for use "in connection with CIA's clandestine efforts against the Castro government." Although none of Giancana's efforts had "materialized to date," there was hope that his work "may eventually pay off." Edwards had never been "furnished details of the methods used by Giancana and Maheu because this was 'dirty business' and he could not afford to know the specific actions of Maheu and Giancana in pursuit of any mission for the CIA." Hoover went on to state that Edwards had acknowledged the "attempted" use of Maheu and "hoodlum elements" by the CIA in "anti-Castro activities" but that the "purpose for placing the wiretap . . . has not been determined." There was no mention of assassination attempts in Edwards' statements, nor was there any indication that Hoover had connected Giancana's CIA link with his boast to kill Castro that Hoover had reported on October 18, 1960. See pages 5–7 for the committee's analysis of whether the President or the Attorney General ever learned from Hoover of the underworld's involvement with the CIA in assassination attempts.

—Whatever the Attorney General did or did not know, the Justice Department decided that it would not be in the "national interest" to prosecute Giancana or anyone else involved in the wiretap incident.

—After considering the above contradictions, plus many more, the committee observed that "There is some evidence, however, suggesting that the CIA itself may have instituted the tap to determine whether Giancana was leaking information about his involvement" in the fiascos.

In a way it is fitting that the report is as confused as the operation it investigated.

The Bay of Pigs invasion, April 17–20, was considered by President Kennedy to be the worst defeat of his administration. While he publicly assumed "sole responsibility" for the fiasco, he privately confided to Ted Sorenson: "How could I have been so far off base? All my life I've known better than to depend on the experts. How could I have been so stupid, to let them go ahead."

According to the Senate committee, "There is some

evidence that Giancana or Roselli originated the idea of depositing a poison pill in Castro's drink to give the [assassin] a chance to escape." Roselli wanted something "nice and clean, without getting into any kind of out and out ambushing," preferably a poison that would disappear without a trace. Giancana had ruled out any notion of ambushing Castro. At first the CIA was under the impression that Castro would be gunned down in gangland style, but Sam pointed out that although popular in Chicago, this method presented a recruitment problem in Cuba.

The first batch of pills was rejected because they would not dissolve in water. A second batch, containing botulinum toxin, "did the job expected of them" when tested on monkeys. After a "contact inside a restaurant frequented by Castro" was found, money and pills were delivered to Roselli, Trafficante, and the Cuban with the contact at the Fontainebleau. Roselli testified that "Maheu opened his briefcase and dumped a whole lot of money on his lap . . . and also came up with the capsules and he explained how they were going to be used. As far as I remember, they couldn't be used in boiling soups and things like that, but they could be used in water or otherwise, but they couldn't last forever. . . . It had to be done as quickly as possible." Maheu denied any knowledge of this incident.

Testifying to the same incident, Robert Shimon said that he was present with Giancana at the time of the delivery. He had accompanied Maheu to Miami to see the third Patterson-Johansson fight (March 12, 1961), and he shared a suite with Giancana, Roselli and Maheu at the Fontainebleau. Maheu, Shimon said, told him that he had a "contract" to kill Castro, and that the CIA had given him a "liquid" to put in Castro's food that would kill him in two or three days without leaving a trace. The Cuban was contacted outside the Fontainebleau's Boom Boom Room, and when Roselli left with the Cuban, Maheu said to Shimon that "Johnny's going to handle everything, this is Johnny's contract." Giancana later

213

told Shimon that "I am not in it, and they are asking me for the names of some guys who used to work in casinos. . . . Maheu's conning the hell out of the CIA." A few days later, Shimon received a phone call from Maheu, who said ". . . did you see the paper? Castro's ill. He's going to be sick two or three days. Wow, we got him."

The attempt to poison Castro's drink either failed because the Prime Minister stopped patronizing that particular restaurant, or because somebody forgot to give the "go signal" to the contact, who subsequently returned the cash and the poison. Maheu did not know who was responsible for giving the signal. Another prospective assassin, an official close to Castro, was fired before he received the poison.

In the fall of 1961, the CIA placed William Harvey in charge of the continuing fiascos. In April 1962, Harvey instructed Roselli to maintain his Cuban contacts but not to deal with Maheu or Giancana, who were described as "untrustworthy" and "surplus." There were more fiascos, with three-man teams being dispatched to poison Che Guevara as well as Fidel and Raoul Castro. Harvey was getting discouraged. "There's not much likelihood that this is going any place," he told Roselli, "or that it should be continued." In January 1963 Harvey terminated the underworld phase of the operation and directed Roselli to "taper off his communications with the Cubans." Roselli broke off contact but neglected to tell the Cubans that the hundred fifty thousand dollar bounty had been withdrawn.

Maheu testified that "Giancana was paid nothing at all, not even expenses, and that Mr. Roselli was given a pittance that did not even begin to cover his expenses."

Roselli, who at the time of his appearance before the committee was fighting a deportation order, told the committee that he paid his own way, paid for his own hotel and travel expenses, and never "took a nickel." "No, as long as it is for the Government of the United States," he said, "this is the least I can do, because I *owe it a lot." His motivation, he added was "honor and dedication."*

When the FBI threatened to have him deported in 1966 unless he talked about some of his Mafia associates, Roselli did not forget those years of dedication. He contacted Edwards, who told the FBI that Roselli wanted to "keep square with the Bureau," but was afraid that his associates might kill him if he talked. Then the next year when Roselli was arrested for a million dollar card-cheating scam at the Beverly Hills Friars Club, he asked Harvey, who had left the Agency, to represent him. Harvey tried his best to have the CIA stop the prosecution, but to no avail. Roselli was convicted and sentenced to five years, with a concurrent six months on the alien-registration charge. He was released from prison in September 1973, but things were never the same again for Don Giovanni. On August 8, 1976 his body was found stuffed in a chain-wrapped oil drum floating in Biscayne Bay off Miami. The cause of death was asphyxiation and the modus operandi, said the police, clearly earmarked it as a "true gangland-style killing." But the police always say that when they don't know what else to say. Chances are we will never know the who or why of it.

But that was all in the future. Back in April 1961, Johnny Roselli was enjoying the best of both worlds.

I had met Johnny once briefly years before when Billy was at Warner's, but I had forgotten until Johnny reminded me of it that evening.

"Don't you remember," he said, acting surprised at my faulty memory, "I was standing with Briny Foy and I said you were prettier than Elizabeth Taylor."

I laughed. "How could I forget such a generous compliment. I happen to think she's a great beauty."

"Well, she's no match for you."

"What are you trying to do," Sam said, "turn her head?"

"A fact's a fact. Listen, I think I know something about beauty. I know Liz and I'm telling you this gal has it all over her."

"What else is new," Sam said, giving me a big wink.

At nine-thirty on the morning of May 3, I left by train for Washington. I had a drawing room and I was so tired after three days of vacationing in Miami that I slept nearly the whole way, arriving at seven the next morning. Evelyn had made my reservation at the Mayflower, room 484, and when I called her later that morning she said that "The President" would not be able to see me until the next day. Was that all right with me? I said it was and not to worry because I had friends staying at the hotel.

As it happened, Dick Elwood was at the Mayflower and that evening we went to dinner with a Colonel Jackson from the Pentagon. Dick was in electronics and did considerable business with the Pentagon. Whenever Jackson and a General Meyer came to California, both Dick and Bob Whittaker entertained them in the most lavish manner.

The next morning Evelyn called to say that "The President" would see me at four-thirty that afternoon. I don't know what happened to me, but Evelyn's emphasis on "The President" began to make me nervous. Suddenly, I didn't want to go to the White House. It was not anymore the place where Jack lived. It was an historic landmark where the President of the United States resided. What it was, in fact, was a monumental stumbling block. As I think back on it, I realize that I was intimidated by "The President" and the White House. As it got closer to the appointed time, my anticipation to see Jack became completely overtaken by my anxiety over what would happen once I got there. The anxiety gradually turned to anger. The next thing I knew I was having a tantrum.

Dick Elwood, who had come to visit with a friend, couldn't believe what was happening. "You ought to be ashamed of yourself," he said. "How many people get a chance to even go to the White House, much less be *invited by the President*."

"Don't lecture me," I said, pacing the room, "I'm not impressed."

I was growling and grumbling up to the time the cab drove up to the West Gate, which leads to the Oval Office, and I had to identify myself to the security officer. As the cab drove up to the door of the West Wing, the anger was replaced by shame. How could I have been so childish? I thought, "You really have a lot of gall pretending to be so blasé about going to the White House." I was impressed!

It was a humbling experience to walk through that door and to show my identification to the policeman seated at the desk near the entrance. I sat on a leather couch in the reception room beyond the policeman's desk and wondered what would happen next. I wondered if my hair was all right, if my lipstick was on straight, or if the skirt to my magenta Dior suit was wrinkled in the back.

A black man came out and escorted me into the Cabinet Room. I sat in one of the chairs that were lined up against one entire wall. "The President will be with you shortly," he said. I thanked him and a moment later I was alone in that big room and thinking, "What's happening?" My head was swimming. How in God's name were we ever going to be alone together?"

Then Jack walked in and I forgot all about "The President." I said, "Hello, Jack, how are you?"

"Great now that you're here," he said. "It's so good to see you!" He leaned over to kiss my cheek. He took my hand and sat down next to me. "What a way to end a day! You look ravishing."

I thanked him and we exchanged pleasantries for a few minutes. He said there was something he had to do that evening and would I please stay over until tomorrow? "I didn't want to tell you on the phone," he said, "because I was afraid you'd leave. That's why I had Evelyn arrange this meeting. Something came up that requires my immediate attention. I'm really sorry. Will you stay over?"

"Yes, I will," I said, and then I told him about my tantrum. How angry it made me having to come to the White

House and how ashamed of myself I had been when I came through the gate.

He laughed and I asked him how he was handling his job. He said, "Well, I don't know. I'm so busy I haven't had time to stop and find out."

"How do you like it, sitting up here on top of the mountain?"

"It depends. There are times when I'd prefer to be somewhere else."

It was not a serious conversation. It was just two people very pleased to see each other. I knew he was terribly busy and so after thirty or forty minutes, I stood up and he put his arms around me. "It's been a long time," he said. "Far too long. But we'll fix all that tomorrow. Can you come at one-fifteen?"

"I'll be here."

He looked at me a moment. "I had forgotten how beautiful you really are," he said.

"I hadn't forgotten how handsome you are!"

We kissed, only lightly, because Jack did not show a great deal of affection unless he was assured of privacy.

A White House car drove me back to the hotel. I called Dick Elwood the moment I walked into my room. I was so keyed up I had to talk to somebody or burst. It took hours and a little help from Jack Daniels to calm me down. I was so grateful that Dick was there. He was the perfect confidant. After all those months of depressions, I could feel myself getting really manic. I don't know how many times I went over every minute detail of that visit, and through it all Dick just sat there smiling as though he were hearing it for the first time.

At one o'clock on Saturday afternoon, a White House car picked me up at the Mayflower and brought me to the West Gate entrance. I waited in the reception room only a moment before a short stocky man came in and introduced himself. His name was Dave Powers and he would later tell me that it was his job to put The President to bed each night and to get him up each morning. He made it sound like it was a sacred trust. Whenever he intoned "The President," you had the feeling that church bells would start ringing and that people in great numbers would kneel as Dave, in his Boston Irish brogue, began with, "Our President, who art in heaven—" and not certain of the words, the people would murmur their response as they had learned to do in Church.

"The President will see you now," he said, "come with me."

As we walked down a hallway, Jack came out of the Oval Office and waited for us. There was a big smile on his face and I quickened my step.

"Finally," Jack said, putting his arm around my shoulder, "I've got you where I want you."

We went down another hallway and as Dave opened a door, Jack said, "How about a swim before lunch?"

I looked at the swimming pool and couldn't believe my eyes or my ears. "Not a chance," I said. "I didn't get all fixed up to go swimming."

"It will relax you," Jack said. "There's plenty of time. There's nothing like a swim to sharpen the appetite and loosen the old muscles."

"My old muscles are plenty loose and don't worry about my appetite. If you have to worry about something, worry about my hair."

"Dave, bring her a bathing cap."

"Don't bother, Dave."

"We have all styles of bathing caps and every size of bathing suits."

"I don't doubt it for a minute—thanks but no thanks."

Dave said, "I don't think you're going to convince her. She's not going to fall for your line."

After a little more kidding, Jack asked if I minded if he took a swim, and I said, "Please, be my guest."

"Dave, take Judy upstairs and fix her a nice drink."

"That's the first sensible suggestion I've heard today," I said.

"Let's hope it's not the last," Jack said, as Dave escorted me out of the room. We took the little elevator to the family quarters on the second floor. As we came into the living room I had a familiar feeling, for much of the furniture was from their Georgetown home. Dave handed me a drink and what happened next was also familiar. Like Kenny O'Donnell before him, Dave wanted to know everything about me and my family.

Luckily, Jack did not take a long swim. All of a sudden, he seemed to burst into the room. He looked at Dave and said, "Well, Dave, what do you think of my Judy?" Like that. Those were his exact words. Dave said, "She's a very fine lady, very fine lady, and she sure loves her family."

Jack had a daiquiri and we talked for a while before going into the dining room for lunch. Jack sat at the head of the table, with Dave on his left and I on his right. Lunch itself was most uninteresting—a cold soup and hamburgers. It struck me funny that Jack had to ask for the ketchup, which he proceeded to load on his hamburger. It doesn't matter where you live, you still have your same old basic taste.

Almost immediately Jack started pumping me for gossip, most of it directed at Frank. What was Frank doing? Was it true that he was seeing Janet Leigh? We went through the same old routine. I denied I knew any gossip and he insisted that I knew plenty. It went back and forth in a lighthearted way until Dave said, "You're not going to get anything out of her, I can see it!" Jack said, "Come on, now, Judy, just a smidgen, nothing shocking or disgraceful, just something amusing."

"As I've said before, Jack, pick up a movie magazine."

"Thanks a lot," he said, turning to Dave with a helpless gesture. "Doesn't she remind you of a career diplomat?"

When lunch was over, we went back into the living room and Dave excused himself, alluding to something or other that needed his attention. Then Jack said, "I want to show you the other rooms." He took me into their bedroom and again I noticed that the furniture was from the Georgetown house. The twin beds were on the right and we turned left, into a small alcove leading to another bedroom with a large double bed. There was a stereo in the alcove and Jack put on the music from Camelot.

We stood beside the bed and he put his arms around me. "What a way to spend Saturday afternoon," he said, hugging me. We were standing close to a window and I could see the Washington Monument in the distance. But directly below me was the south lawn, which is known as the President's Park, and it gave me the strangest feeling to be standing there in the arms of the man I knew as Jack, but that the whole world recognized as the thirty-fifth President of the United States.

Then he kissed me and I forgot about monuments and parks. It was not long before I went into the bathroom to undress. When I came out Jack was already in bed, lying on his back, and this was the first time that he remained completely on his back. He was having trouble with his back, but there is something about that position, if not arrived at naturally, that makes the woman feel that she is there just to satisfy the man.

At first that was not the feeling I had with Jack. Because of his back problem there were times when there was nothing else he could do. On this day, he held me, he kissed and caressed me, and gently maneuvered me into that position. By this time I was familiar enough with Jack to feel completely free and uninhibited in making love. At this point in a relationship, all positions are beautiful expressions of one's love. Whatever brings two people pleasure is beautiful. It is the only way it should be with lovers.

After making love, as I mentioned before, Jack said and did all the right things. He was so relaxed, so tranquil, so serene that he became an entirely different person. For that brief moment, I don't think Jack Kennedy had enough ambition to carry him an inch beyond that bed. The fire in the dynamo that so impressed the world had been momentarily banked and he was like any other man luxuriating in the warmth of a woman that had brought him pleasure.

We talked, we dozed, we casually caressed, but as time passed I began to feel uneasy. I felt I was not where I belonged; that when I left it would seem like it had never happened. The feeling of unreality that began then was something I was never able to shake whenever I was in the White House. It was fine when he came to see me. Then he was Jack, who had to find his own way home.

Finally, I said, "God, I have to go or I'm going to miss my plane."

"I wish you didn't have to leave," he said. "I wish you could be here in Washington all the time."

"I've thought of it," I said, "but it just wouldn't work out."

"Wouldn't you like to come to White House functions? I want to put your name on the list. You wouldn't have to come to all of them but at least you could select the ones you want. That way we would see each other a lot more often."

"Jack, I know it's an honor to be on that list, but you know I couldn't attend functions with your wife there. I've told you before, Jack, it's something that I just will not do."

"I know how you feel, but give it some thought, will you?"

"My God, Jack, I would be so uncomfortable. I couldn't survive one of those evenings."

We exhausted that subject, as we did so many others, without arriving at any real decision. By now I knew I would never make my plane to Chicago unless I got out of there in a hurry. Jack was not in the least perturbed. "Get dressed," he said, "I'll take care of everything." And, my God, did he ever.

A White House car zipped me to the Mayflower, and while I settled my account with the cashier, my bags were loaded in the car, and we made record time to National. I raced through the airport only to discover that not only were they holding the plane for me, but it had been called back to the terminal after it had started to taxi out to the runway. I have never received so many dirty looks in my life. Those were the days of bomb scares and people were terribly nervous about flying. When the plane returned to the terminal, everyone was thinking that something was wrong. Then I stepped into the plane and if looks could kill, that would have been it for me. The only amusing moment was when I noticed that Eunice Shriver was on the plane. It was the kind of irony that I could appreciate at that moment.

222

X

The plane landed in Chicago at six-forty. Actually I was on my way to Las Vegas, with an hour layover in Chicago—just enough time to have a drink with Sam and discuss the plan he had in mind. This trip was his idea. While in Miami I had told him about my experience with Jack Entratter at the Fontainebleau, and the fact that ever since then I had been *persona non grata* at the Sands. They were always sold out when I called for a reservation. But the main reason for going to the Sands was that Jerry Lewis was appearing in the Copa Room. "You're going to sit right up ringside with Joe, and if that doesn't make that little son of a bitch a nervous wreck, I'll eat my hat. This is your chance to get back at him. With you sitting there with Joe, he won't know what to expect."

As far as I was concerned, Jerry Lewis was a dead issue, but I could see that it was important for Sam to make this last gesture at squaring things for me. Also there was the matter of Jack Entratter. "I've had a little talk with Jack," Sam said, "and I don't think you'll have any more trouble at the Sands. In fact, Jack insisted on personally picking up your tab, and, listen, I don't want you disappointing him. Give him a chance to make it up to you."

Before going to the show the next morning, I had dinner at the Angus with Johnny Roselli and Joe Pignatello, who was now operating an Italian restaurant in Las Vegas.

Joe and I saw the late show and I doubt that Jerry ever had a more miserable time. Joe and I never took our eyes off him. We just stared and didn't laugh once. It was a terrible show.

Jerry doesn't function well when he's nervous. He spotted us almost immediately and from then on it was downhill all the way. He is a worrier and I am sure Sam was right. He didn't know what to expect.

After the show Joe had a good laugh. "You really got back at him, didn't you?" he said. "Boy, just leave it to Sam. If you ever got a problem, just leave it to Sam. He knows how to fix things real good. You couldn't have done nothing better than that. The guy really panicked. He was sweating bullets. That was the longest show of his whole life."

I left for Los Angeles the next day and was met at the airport by Dick Elwood. Since Travis's marriage and Dick's divorce coincided almost perfectly, Dick was now my closest male companion. Every single woman needs a Dick Elwood in her life. He is the man who is always available when you need an arm to lean on or a sympathetic ear. He is the escort who makes no demands, who loves you in his own quiet, patient way, hopefully awaiting the day when the man *you* love leaves you and he can move into the breach. It never occurs to him that you may never love him, no matter what happens to the man you love.

Knowing how Dick felt about me, I spent entirely too much time with him. I cared a great deal about him as a person, but I knew I could never love him. By remaining aloof, I think I fed that love he had for me—there was no way he was going to get over it. I was close and yet so far out of reach that I became an irresistible challenge to his male ego.

Dick was a sharp businessman, strong-willed, hard-headed, and tremendously well liked by all who knew him. I certainly enjoyed being with him. He moved in fast company. He worked hard and he played hard. Taking the lead from his wealthy friends in Palm Springs and Beverly Hills, he entertained lavishly on a regular basis.

Now that I knew Johnny Roselli, he began calling me quite regularly to inquire about my health and state of mind. I noticed that his calls were more frequent when I was not in contact with Sam, who would occasionally disappear for periods of time. Other times he would call and ask me to relay a message to Sam: "When you talk to Sam would you have him call me at such and such a place, at such and such a time." Then Sam would do the same thing. The first thing I knew I found myself relaying messages back and forth. But that was the extent of anything that I consciously did for them. Occasionally I would have dinner with Johnny and Genene, usually at Perino's. They treated Johnny like a king at Perino's. They were not as obsequious as the Singapore with Sam, but not too far removed from it.

I flew to New York with Dick on June 6. He was going to New York and from there to Washington on business. He had a reservation at the Plaza, but I couldn't get one. The hotel was booked solid for the entire summer. So I talked to Sam. "Don't worry about it," he said. "I'll make a reservation for you at the Lexington. When you get there, call Joe DiMaggio. It might take a couple of days but he'll get you into the Plaza."

I called DiMaggio and he said I could move into the Plaza on the eighth. My brother Allen was to join me on the thirteenth and I had already arranged to take him to the Bahamas as a high school graduation gift. But on the tenth, while he was entertaining friends in New York, Dick Elwood suffered a heart attack. I rushed to the hospital the moment his doctor called me. I visited him daily and after he was well enough to eat solid foods, I had the Plaza prepare a special lunch for him every day which I carried to him on those heavy silver platters.

When Allen arrived on the thirteenth, we both went to see Dick at the hospital. Allen liked Dick and he knew how I felt about helping a friend in trouble. I didn't know what to do. I didn't want to disappoint Allen because I knew how much he had looked forward to this trip. On the other hand, Dick needed to see a friendly face every day. Who else would bring him lunch from the Plaza? Allen solved my dilemma by saying that he would be just as happy staying in New York.

That evening we had dinner at the Round Table with Morris Levy and did the town until the early hours. On the fifteenth Morris gave a party at Birdland. It was Count Basie's opening, and there was a big celebration. We sat at a long table with about forty interesting characters. There were bottles of booze and mixers the whole length of the table. I was sitting between Morris and Allen, and across from Allen was a blonde in a low cut dress with a bosom that looked like it was the biggest silicone job on record. She looked like she was going to explode with every breath she took. She focused on Allen and his eyes were about ready to pop out of his head. Every time she moved I thought her plastic balloons were going to knock over the bottles sitting in the center of the table. The more nervous Allen became, the faster he drank. I didn't pay too much attention at first. I was enjoying Count Basie and Joe Williams. By the time I did realize what was going on, she was trying to get Allen up to her place, and he was falling completely apart—a six foot three bruiser turned to Jello. Suddenly I was coming on like mother hen, but every time I tried to talk to him all he'd say was, "Leave me alone." Finally I said, "Okay," and by now I was furious. "You're going to get rolled. That is, if you're lucky. Otherwise, you're going to get something a lot more painful."

"Leave me alone."

Morris kept glancing at me and shaking his head. "Will you leave the kid alone?" he said. "Let him enjoy himself, let him have a good time."

"What are you talking about," I whispered fiercely. "Have you looked at that thing?"

"That thing," he said, "happens to be a very sweet gal."

"Jesus!"

"Calm down. Everything's taken care of. It's my little graduation gift for the kid. She'll either make a man out of him or kill him trying."

After that I kept Allen's glass full. Before long he was gulping down straight Jack Daniels like it was Dr. Pepper. Around four o'clock a whole bunch of us loaded Allen into Morris's limousine, feet first. He was still saying, "leave me alone," but you had to pay close attention to make out the words. He sounded like his tongue was too big for his mouth.

While in New York I saw *Camelot* twice. It starred Richard Burton, Robert Goulet, and Julie Andrews, and I was just in love with it. Of course, the music had a special meaning for me. It was thrilling to sit in the darkness of that theater and dream my own version of *Camelot*.

Before going to New York that spring I leased a two-bedroom house in Malibu Colony for the summer. It was Dick Elwood's idea that a small group of friends spend the summer together. Dick leased a big old mansion that was right on the beach, and my house was across the street from his, so his friends used my tennis court and my friends used his beach. All the parties were held at Dick's place. Bob Whittaker was Dick's guest almost every weekend, and on many of those weekends they entertained colonels and generals from the Pentagon, with Colonel Don Jackson and General Lou Meyers frequent guests. There were a lot of pretty girls and wining and dining and extravagant presents. It was hard to say which came first, business or pleasure.

I had talked it over with Sam before taking the Malibu house.

"What do you think about it?" I asked.

"I'm not too sure," he said. "Are you going to be down there alone?"

"No. My brother Allen is spending the summer with me. He's going to take care of the place for me, sort of earn his room and board."

"I'd like for Johnny to look the place over from time to time."

"Why don't you come down and look it over yourself? It's really very nice."

"Not me," Sam said. "I'm staying out of California."

Sam had often told me that the Los Angeles police had the most relentless intelligence system in the country. It was impossible for him to come into any part of Southern California without being harassed.

Others who took houses in the Colony that summer included Albert and Joyce Linnick—everybody called him Albie, and he was a lawyer in Los Angeles; Paul and Renon Ross—he was a Hollywood publicity agent; Lionel and Louise Steinberg—I can't remember his specialty; Diane

Gussman and her husband who was seldom there—the house belonged to her family and she later sold it to Lana Turner.

It was a crazy drunken summer. From just the small group named above, there were two divorces and one suicide attempt. The worst tragedy was Dick Elwood. The change that came over him after his heart attack was shocking. He became a weakling overnight. He seemed to thrive on sympathy. He became a little cocker spaniel around me, sitting at my feet and whining all the time. He wanted me to love him and I couldn't stand even to look at him when he acted that way. It was pitiful the way he walked around moaning and groaning over me all the time. By the end of the summer everyone thought I was a real heel. They felt sorry for him. They didn't know about my relationship with Jack, and they would say, "She's always running off, just leaving him alone all the time." They thought we were lovers.

I became very impatient. His weakness disgusted me. I have a tendency to need strong people around me. If a man is wishy-washy with me, I will walk all over him. It's a bad trait but I can't help it. I respect strength. I don't like a bully, but if a man doesn't like what I'm doing, then let him speak up and we'll talk about it. I am not the strongest woman that ever lived but I can't stand a man who is weaker than I am.

His mooning over me was so grotesque that even my parents began referring to him as my "little puppy dog." I regret today that I treated him so badly. I wish I could have been more compassionate. But I was having my own problems that summer.

I was never at the beach for more than a week or two at a stretch, but whenever I was there the partying and drinking were constant. I think we were all drinking with a vengeance. I drank Jack Daniels until dinner and then I switched to Green Chartreuse, which is a hundred and ten proof, and drank it straight up. I gained more weight that summer than I ever had before. I wasn't fat—I could still wear a bathing suit without looking too terrible—but I wasn't Miss America either.

I remember waking up with some of the most horrendous hangovers. I could hear people on the tennis court and it sounded like a bomb going off every single time someone hit the ball. Besides the drinking, I was taking Percodan to kill the pain caused by adhesions from my operation. The day was divided into two parts—mornings and early afternoons were for sobering up, and the rest of the time was devoted to drinking.

One of Allen's eighteen-year-old school friends, who came down to spend a week with my brother while I was in Washington, ran away to San Francisco with Joyce Linnick. Joyce was thirty and had two small children—a girl and a boy who had cystic fibrosis. I was blamed for that marriage breaking up.

Johnny Roselli took Diane Gussman and me to dinner at Romanoff's one evening. After dinner we stopped at the bar for a drink and someone called out, "Hey, Campbell, what the hell are you doing here?" I nearly fell off the bar stool. I turned and it was Frank Sinatra. He was just beaming as he walked over to us.

"You look like you're in a good mood," I said.

"What do you mean by that crack, Campbell?" he said, narrowing his eyes to simulate anger. "Are you implying something nasty?"

"You better watch it, fella," Johnny said. "I don't think you realize who you're hustling here."

Frank raised his arms, executed a graceful salaam, and everybody laughed. The two men shook hands and we all went over to Frank's house for a nightcap. When we got back to the beach, Johnny asked to bunk on the sofa for the night, but not long after I was in bed, I heard him sneak out the front door and walk across the street to Diana's house. That was the second divorce.

Renon Ross was pregnant that summer and she and Paul were going through a terrible time. She was having emotional problems and Paul had no patience with her. She got drunk one night and ran into the ocean. The water was rough and it was pitch black. She was rescued two or three times before she became too exhausted to try again. There is no question in my mind that she would have drowned if someone hadn't gone in after her.

I saw Jack in the White House five times that summer but the most memorable visit was on August 8. I arrived in Washington the day before and as usual Evelyn had made my reservation at the Mayflower—room 353—and there was a "WH" notation on my bill indicating that the White House had requested the reservation. When I called her, she said Jack would see me for lunch the next day and that she would send a White House car.

The eighth was a Monday and it was hot in Washington. I wore an apple green Chanel style silk suit, with a straight skirt and a very simple square-cut jacket. Evelyn met me in the reception room and escorted me down the hallway past the Oval Office and around toward the main part of the White House. Jack and Dave Powers were standing together, near the pool area. Jack had his arms folded across his chest and watched me very intently as I walked toward him.

"Well, that's a nice quiet color to wear to the White House," he said.

He was smiling, but not enough to get away with that kind of a crack. "If you don't like it, I can always leave."

He laughed. "You look gorgeous!"

"Fine," I said, "but that's still no way to open a conversation."

"Really, Judy, I was giving you a compliment."

We kidded back and forth. He wanted to take a swim and again I refused. This time he passed it up. We went upstairs and sat around and talked for a while. He wanted to know if I was enjoying my summer at Malibu and I asked him how he was enjoying his at Hyannisport. He asked about Frank again, and although I felt that his interest in Frank was genuine, I found it a little annoying that I always seemed to remind him of Frank. Then as we walked into the dining room, he said, "Have you heard from Teddy?"

That stopped me. "You mean your brother?"

"Yes. Has Teddy called you?"

"Of course not," I said. "You should know that."

"Well, I just wondered."

Jack never forgot what Teddy had tried in Las Vegas.

Several times when we were in bed he said, "Boy, if Teddy only knew, he'd be eating his heart out." I think he got a big kick out of the fact that he had succeeded where Teddy had failed.

Just as we were finishing lunch, Jack said, "I want to ask you something that's quite serious." He paused, glanced at Dave, then looked directly at me. "Did you repeat a story to the effect that I had tried to get you into bed with another woman?"

I looked at him and almost died. The combination of being Irish and German is a disaster at such times. My temper flared instantly. It was inconceivable to me that he would approach this subject in front of Dave Powers. The way he phrased the question, his tone of voice, implied that I was lending credence to a malicious story someone had invented.

"Jack, you know damn well I would never repeat that story to anyone." Of course, I had told Dr. Sherman and Travis, and possibly Dick Elwood. It was the kind of thing I couldn't hold inside of me. I was so upset I had to talk to someone. I just couldn't stew in it alone. I have often wondered how Jack could have gotten that information. I must have discussed it on the telephone and now that I know as a fact that the FBI surveillance included wiretaps, that's another possibility.

At that moment, however, the very fact that Jack was right made me all the more furious. I said, "How dare you discuss this with me in front of *him*."

AUTHOR'S NOTE: *"The only Campbell I know," Dave Powers told the press when the story broke in late 1975, "is chunky vegetable soup."* Newsweek *reported that Judy Campbell's name did not appear in Powers' White House logs. Yet when I interviewed Powers for my biography of J. Edgar Hoover, he had this to say about his record keeping: "Ken O'Donnell and I had the job of keeping the President on time. Every minute of the President's day in the While House is accounted for in these books. Now, when the President would leave the*

231

I stood up, nearly knocking my chair over. "I'd really like to leave, Jack. I'm very upset about this."

"Well," he said, and seemed embarrassed, "I just wanted to talk to you about it. A story got back to me."

"Well, that's what you get when you want to hear gossip all the time. But I'm not going to discuss it with you. If you think I'm running around telling tales, then it's time we call it quits. Perhaps you should behave; you should conduct yourself in another way."

"Oh, Judy, please calm down a little."

"Listen, Jack, this stems from one place and that's you."

Jack stood up and came around the table. "Come in the other room," he said, taking my hand. "I want to talk to you."

Dave casually left the room. By now I knew what it meant when Jack said he wanted to talk to me. I let him lead me to the bedroom because I didn't know what else to do. I was fighting mad and yet I felt guilt and shame. And fear. How had the story gotten back to Jack? I had told three or four close friends in California, people I thought I could trust, and the story had gotten all the way back to the White House. It frightened me to contemplate what that involved.

We sat on the bed and he kissed me, but it was hopeless. I can't control my emotions that easily. I was in no mood for love. When he became more amorous, I said, "Jack, please, I can't—not after what just happened. I really would rather leave."

"Wait a couple of minutes, you'll feel better. I was so looking forward to this afternoon."

"You should have thought about that before embarrassing me like that in front of Dave. I just don't understand you, Jack. Why couldn't you have waited until we were alone? That would have been fine. But this way doesn't even make sense."

"I'm sorry, Judy, if I upset you. I feel very badly about it."

"You're damn lucky I didn't blurt out in front of Dave how I felt about your behavior that night. You made it sound like I was spreading lies about you."

"I'm really very sorry," he said.

"But I have more respect for you than to do something like that," I said, forging ahead, determined to say my piece at any cost. "And I have more respect for myself, too."

We talked it out, or I should say, I talked it out until I felt a little better about it. But I still wanted to leave. Finally, he said, "I think I'm going to take a nap. What would you like to do?"

"I'd like to leave."

"Would you let Dave show you through the White House?"

I agreed and we walked out to the living room and Dave was sitting there. Jack said he was going to take a nap and would Dave give me the grand tour. Dave said he would be delighted and he started out, all chipper like nothing had happened, rattling off historical data as we moved from room to room, but none of it was registering. We looked at portraits and at the dishes used by each president. I was not seeing or hearing anything, and finally I asked if he would get me a car because I was really tired and would he tell Jack that I would talk to him later.

"Oh, I wish you weren't so upset," he said. "Come on, walk around a little, you'll calm down. Let me show you the White House the way no tourist ever sees it."

"Thank you, but I really need to get back to my hotel and just think a little by myself."

All the way back to the hotel I kept telling myself that I was making too much out of it, but that didn't help either. I think I might have been more reasonable if I hadn't felt so guilty. If only he had gone about it more discreetly, I might have apologized because I knew I had talked out of turn. I knew I should have kept my big mouth shut. But coming out with it in front of Dave just got my back up. There was no reasoning with me after that. I was young and immature in so many ways, but even now I think it is human nature to look for ways of excusing one's own mistakes. I made a mistake and Jack made a mistake, but I forgot about mine and wouldn't let him forget about his. I wonder what Jack really thought about my tantrum. Did he realize I protested too much? If he did he never let on. But Jack, I suppose, was a pretty fair actor.

When Jack called later in the day, he seemed surprised that I hadn't come back with Dave to wait for him. I said I thought it was pretty obvious why I hadn't and he said, "The day sure didn't pan out the way I had planned it."

"Well, I'm not too impressed with your planning."

He asked if I was leaving and I said I hadn't made up my mind. "May I call you tomorrow?" I said yes and he paused a moment. "Any chance of your having dinner with me tomorrow evening?" "I don't know," I said. "Ask me again tomorrow. Maybe I will have calmed down a little."

Around eight o'clock that evening Sam knocked on my door and I nearly fainted when I saw him standing there with his son-in-law, Anthony Tisci, who was married to Bonnie—Tisci was then administrative aide to Congressman Roland Libonati. Sam was the last person in the world I ever expected to see in Washington. He had never mentioned ever going to Washington. I was pleased to see him but for the life of me I couldn't figure out what he was doing there or how he knew that I was there. Knowing what I know today, I should have been terrified.

I said hello and Sam sent Anthony on an errand before coming into the room. As soon as we were alone, I asked him what he was doing in Washington and he said he was attending to some business. When I inquired as to how he had found me, he just gave me that same little smile that said, "I've got ways of finding out." I should have been more suspicious of his actions. Instead I took it as a compliment. I was pleased at the lengths he would go to find me.

He wanted to go out to dinner but I suggested room service. He said that was fine because he couldn't stay long. I

234

was relieved to see him after what had happened that afternoon. At that moment he was a joy to behold. He was so easy to handle: a little peck on the cheek, a little squeeze, and he was happy. The way Jack was behaving, and with Dick Elwood groveling at my feet, Sam was the only stable part of my life. I have said it before and I can't say it too often: he was there when I needed him; he solved my problems, he gave me wise counsel, he would have given me millions if I had asked for them—from what I now understand, he had the millions to give—and he never caused me any problems. Although he wanted a more intimate relationship, he didn't pressure me. When I think of it now, I realize it was all too ideal, all too studied and planned, but for me at that time Sam was winning his way into my heart.

I was in a better frame of mind when Jack called the next morning. We had a friendly chat and Jack made the right move. He said he wouldn't be able to see me that day, but could I make it on the twenty-fourth? I didn't want to be angry with him so I said I would be back on that date. By the time we hung up the relationship was back on an even keel.

I arrived back in Malibu on August 10 and two days later we had a sensational luau at Dick's place for about two hundred guests. The caterers, who also provided the entertainment, arrived early in the morning and cooked a pig in the sand. They fenced in a large area with bamboo, erected a dance floor, covered the ground with grass mats and with colored pillows to sit on, and everywhere were flowers and fresh fruit. There were sword and torch dances, and hula lessons for anyone brave enough to face the onslaught of inebriated critics. My parents came and had a great time. It was the best night of that whole summer.

On the fourteenth I was back in Chicago. I was at the Ambassador East nine days, and saw Sam every one of those days. A few days after I arrived, my mother called early one morning to say that my sister Jackie was in the hospital. She was pregnant and the doctor thought she was going to lose the baby. The whole family was frantic because she had had about five miscarriages and one in approximately the seventh month. She wanted a baby so desperately that if she lost another one I don't think that emotionally she would have been able to handle it. I wanted to come home but my mother advised against it.

Usually Sam picked me up around noon but I was beside myself after my mother hung up. So I called Sam. "I'm coming right over to get you," he said. "I don't want you to be alone." He was at the hotel within a half hour. Johnny Roselli was with him and we drove directly to the Armory. Once ensconced in Sam's booth with them on either side of me, Sam said, "I'm not going to let you think today."

The martinis started coming and Sam said, "Drink up, it's going to be a long day." We had left word with the hotel to switch my calls to the Armory. I think I talked myself out about Jackie in the first two hours. We were drinking head-to-head and after a while they were coming pretty fast. I was a pretty fair drinker but I have a good biological alarm system that slows me down when it gets a little too frantic. After a while I had three and four drinks lined up before me.

"Come on," Johnny said. "A little less talking and a lot more drinking."

By midafternoon, when we were all pretty well into our cups, Sam said, "Come on, let's get some fresh air." We piled into his little black car and the next thing I knew we were in Queen of Heaven Cemetery. Johnny and Sam started running around looking for the name Roselli on tombstones. Every time they found one, Johnny would say, "Ah, I remember him well," and would go into a long story about this uncle or that aunt, or niece or nephew, and it was a riot to see them having so much fun. "Ah, poor Uncle Giuseppe," Johnny said, waving us toward a large tombstone. "Died of lead poisoning. What a prince among men he was, my Uncle Giuseppe. Very rich, big man in olive oil and machine guns, wanted to put me through college, embalming college, but I preferred the other end of the business." That had them both going hysterical. I was laughing right along with them, but they knew something that made it much funnier. I had no idea that Johnny's real name was Filippo Sacco. It is quite possible that Johnny was trying to connect himself with fake relatives. I wonder if he tried to use some of those names when the FBI later got him on the alien registration charge.

It was a crazy day and by evening the news about Jackie was more encouraging. Although she was in the hospital several days, the baby was born later that month.

A couple of days later while I was riding with Sam, there was a show tune on the radio and he started after me to sing. He had been trying to get me to sing ever since I had mentioned that I had an operatic voice as a child.

"How do you expect me to do anything for you if you won't sing? How do I know you can carry a tune without a bucket?"

"I don't want you to do anything for me. And besides, what can you do for me?" I said, teasing him back.

"You'd be surprised what I can do for you."

"All right," I said, "I'll sing but only if you promise not to do anything—and to not mention it again. I'm sick of hearing about it."

"You've got my word."

It was a defiant type of singing. I was tired of being teased about it and I thought I'd show him once and for all. It was a light operatic show tune, and I started to sing along with the music. I hadn't sung in a long time, and I dreaded the high notes coming up. I have three separate ranges, and when I broke for a high note, Sam said, "Oh, that's falsetto." I stopped and looked at him. "What do you know?" We kidded about it, and he said, "You have a beautiful voice. Let's do something about it."

"Sam, you promised."

"Wouldn't you like to cut a record?"

"No!"

"Don't you want a career?"

"No. And must you always act the impresario?" I said this for a reason. The first time Sam saw some of my paintings at the Navarro he wanted to fill every restaurant in Chicago with them, and with outrageous price tags. They would have been sold if he had to buy them all himself. Sam wanted to create a career for me—acting, singing, painting, I could have had my choice. I think he truly felt that a career in the arts was the ultimate accomplishment.

My lack of interest puzzled him. Whatever Sam did for a living, he was a product of the work ethic. He couldn't understand a life of idle luxury. To paint was self-indulgent unless you put a price tag on it. Some people will tell you that work is good for you, but that is in the same category as exercise—it's good for *you* if *you* like it. As one comedian wisely observed, if everybody had the same taste, we'd all be killed in the rush.

When we got to Sam's house that day he took me to the basement kitchen-family room area and opened a door that was always kept locked. It led to a large room which he used as a den, and where he kept his safe. He opened it and took out a solid gold charm bracelet that had been his wife's. "You won't take diamonds," he said, "so how about a little trinket, something to remember me by."

"Thank you," I said, "it's beautiful."

"Well," he said, rubbing his hands in sheer delight, "I've finally got you to accept something without an argument."

August was my month for accepting gifts without an argument. Jack had something for me when I saw him on the twenty-fourth. The ritual was the same as before: Evelyn made the reservation at the Mayflower, arranged for the White House car, and Jack was waiting for me in the hallway near the Oval Office. This time, however, he was alone. Dave Powers was nowhere in sight. We went straight upstairs and had daiquiris which were brought out by the same black man who always waited on us. As soon as the drinks were served, Jack said, "I have something for you."

"Oh, oh," I said, "big chief has a little conscience medicine."

Jack leaned back in his chair and laughed, "God, you don't let loose very easily."

"I don't know what you're talking about."

"Just for that, I'm going to make you wait for it."

"That's not fair."

"It's something very special. I hope I can give it to you today."

"Oh, that's really cruel."

"There's not another one like it in the whole world."

"Well," I said, "why don't we have lunch and go talk this over in your private office."

"Great idea," he said, taking my arm to escort me into the dining room. I haven't the faintest notion what we had for lunch that day. Whatever it was, rest assured that it was bland and totally uninspired.

When we entered the bedroom I took a small Congressional directory from my purse and handed it to him. "Would you do me a favor," I said, "and sign this for my mother."

"Well, since you put it that way, how can I refuse? I think your mother is lovely. I have great sympathy for her. I can't understand how she ever raised such a brat."

"My God, you think my mother's lovely and feel for her. Can you imagine how I feel for your mother, who is a saint in my mother's eyes, having a son who misbehaves like you do."

We bantered back and forth while he walked over to the window and signed the book on the page opposite his picture. The signature is just a mish-mash. He could just as well have signed J. Edgar Hoover for all I know. Since then I have read that Jack's signature was never the same twice.

After he handed me the book he said, "Now, I have something for you!"

We both were in a light, happy mood, and I just looked at him, and we were standing beside the bed, and I said, "I know, Jack, you've given that to me before."

He roared with laughter. "That comes later. I really do have something for you."

He handed me a nicely wrapped box and inside was a velvet case. I took a deep breath and raised the lid. I almost fainted when I saw a large diamond and ruby brooch. The design was similar to a daisy with four rows of petals. Each petal was eighteen carat gold, and each had a cluster of nine or ten rubies in the center and about thirty full-cut diamonds set in platinum along the edge. I was speechless and confused. It was the same old problem: Where do you draw the line? I looked up and there was such a look of pride on his face that I knew there was no way in this world I could refuse it. This was his peace offering, his way of saying he was sorry, and I was touched deeply by it.

"Oh, Jack," I cried, putting my arms around his neck. "It's magnificent."

And it truly was magnificent. I have seen enough jewelry to know that it takes more than gold and precious stones to make something beautiful. Some of the most expensive jewelry can be the ugliest.

"I thought it would look beautiful on you."

"But why, Jack? You didn't have—"

"Just a minute," he said. "Things haven't gone the way I had hoped for us. It's my way of saying how much I care for you."

"But it's not necessary, Jack."

"As a rule I don't give a lot of presents," he said. "It's something I don't think about. But I wanted to do something special for you and I know how you feel about accepting gifts. Wear it and enjoy it. Let this remind you that if my intentions go astray from time to time, my heart is in the right place."

I was thrilled with it, delighted he thought this much about me. It was just a marvelous day. We lay in bed for the longest time after making love. He got the biggest kick when I jumped out of bed to get the brooch. I was just ecstatic about it and I kept opening the case and looking at it.

"Oh, I love you," he said, and it was like a wave of warmth washing over me.

Sometimes Jack would become wistful and talk about the constricting nature of his office. He seemed to yearn for the ordinary pleasures of the average mortal. He liked to walk in bare feet, to loaf around in old slacks and a sweatshirt, to go sailing, to feel the wind and sea on his face. There was a tremendous conflict going on within him. I think he had a natural desire to be just an elegant bum, to be on the sea under the sun, to play games and to make love. But there was this other drive for power and the two drives were in constant conflict. He was either running to or away from his job. The real problem came when he tried to run in both directions at the same time.

The job was keeping him away from me, and I was keeping him away from the job. I would tease him about loving his country more than me: "Well, you made your choice. I know where you stand—you love your country more than me."

"Just like a woman," he would say, "to put it in that light."

Whenever we fantasized about what he would like to show me, it was never Paris or Vienna; he was always going to take me someplace where we could be alone. I could understand that when I thought of what he had to cope with in that office. He was constantly surrounded by people, being clocked and watched all day long, until he had hardly a minute to himself. The time we spent together was not all that much in the framework of an eighteen-hour day in a seven-day week. It was a brief diversion, a momentary escape from organized bedlam. In a way, I was a refuge. He could hide from the rest of the world and have a good time doing it.

As I was leaving that day, I told Jack I would be at the Plaza until the thirty-first and he promised to see me if at all possible. He was commuting to Hyannis every weekend and he said he would drop over at the Plaza either on his way down or back from the Cape.

Dick Elwood was in Washington and that evening we went to dinner with General Lou Meyers. Throughout the summer, Dick had been forming a new company called Magnatronics—it had something to do with new transistorized military equipment. Dick had been discussing it with Jackson and Meyers, and he had been after me to become a member of the firm. He even had my name printed on business cards. As it turned out, he wanted me to present some papers about the company to Jack, and I didn't like the idea at all. I wanted to help him because I knew he was having financial problems, but there was no chance that I would ever directly approach Jack. Dick indicated that it could mean quite a sum of money for me, and I told him, as I had from the very beginning, that I wanted nothing to do with his company. I did agree, however, to give the papers to Evelyn Lincoln.

Before leaving for New York the next morning, I called Evelyn. "I've got an envelope that a friend wanted me to present to Jack," I said, "but I would rather have you read it and decide whether it is something you want to give him." She said, "Fine, I'll arrange for them to expect you to come through the gate." I dropped it off on my way to the airport. I was in her office two minutes and that was the last I ever heard of it.

Suite 1529-31 at the Plaza was elegant. But instead of waiting in lonely splendor, I did what comes naturally for night people in New York. I dined late and drank until early morning. Whether it was The Colony or the Round Table, El Morocco or Birdland, the result was the same. It kept me from having to spend too much time with myself.

Even Jack was impressed with the size of the suite. "I could hide in here for a week," he said. "I must say this is an improvement on the first night I was here. There's room to breathe." He toured the whole place, inspected the kitchen, bounced on the bed, stretched out on the living room sofa and nibbled on hors d'oeuvres.

"Yes, I wish I could hide you for a month, but what about the guys in the hallway. Wouldn't you worry about them?"

"Depends on how preoccupied I am," he said, pulling me down on the sofa next to him. A moment later he picked up a magazine and began reading. I sat with my head on his shoulder. It was a comfortable intimacy. We kidded and kissed and as we grew more passionate love took its natural course—at the right moment we just naturally flowed into the bedroom.

There was nothing forced or awkward or vulgar about any of it. Time was the only enemy. He acted like he had all the time in the world. I was the one who watched the clock, always wondering how much time this busy man could spend

242

with me. Sooner or later, depending on where we were, one of us would have to leave. We would never spend a full night together. We often talked about that at the White House. "If only I could keep you right here, and have you waiting here for me when I came back. Then in the morning we could make love before breakfast, and after lunch, of course," And I'd say, "Oh, sure, and before and after dinner." It was a longing that could never be satisfied because of his other longing.

The happier the visit with Jack the greater was the emptiness afterward. My emotions were so mixed up. I felt fulfilled by his love and by my love for him and yet at the same time I was empty because that wonderful moment together was gone again until the next time—and when would that next time be? Toward the end of our relationship, even the phone calls began to irritate me. What good does it do to keep telephone contact with someone you care deeply about if you can't touch him, you can't see him? It is more emptiness.

I used to detach myself from the reality of his wife. Jackie Kennedy did not exist for me. I deceived myself into thinking that he rejected that part of his life; that he wanted to be with me but there was nothing he could do about her. That was my way of rationalizing, of being able to live with the situation. If one can live with emptiness? I wanted to love and be loved on a daily basis, but I was closing the door to that possibility. You can't find it by going with a married president, not in a million years.

XI

Throughout the fall of 1961, winter and spring of 1962, I continued to see Jack at the White House. The routine never varied except that in the evening the White House car deposited me at the East Gate, which is the one used by tourists in the daytime. Either Jack would meet me in the entrance hall near the door or an aide would escort me to the little elevator and Jack would be waiting in the family quarters. I would arrive at seven or eight, and we would have a couple of drinks before dinner, most often frozen daiquiris.

Evening was a more relaxed time for him. It seemed like his time was more his own. I don't ever remember anyone barging in with messages. The only interruption was the telephone. Nothing drastic ever happened; he never had to be called away. We would have a relaxed dinner, the usual meat-potato dish. Later we would make love and spend the rest of the time in bed. I was always the one who decided it was time to leave. I'd say, "It's getting late and I really think I should go," and he'd say, "Stay a little longer."

Some nights when he wasn't feeling too well, when his back was bothering him, you could tell it by his face. He looked haggard and worn. Gradually, over this long period of time, I began to notice a change in his attitude. I understood about the position he had to assume in lovemaking when his back was troubling him, but slowly he began excluding all other positions, until finally our lovemaking was reduced to this one position. It is impossible for me to pinpoint when I first realized it, because it was such a gradual process, but slowly I began to feel that he expected me to come into bed and just perform. There would be a moment of stillness when I came into bed and it was almost like he expected me to roll over and put my arms around him and make love to him. I knew I was through the minute I did that, which is a bad way to have to feel. Perhaps other women were that way with him, but that is against my nature.

I think that Jack's natural preference, which he had tried so hard to repress early in our relationship, was for the woman to be the aggressor in lovemaking. He wanted the woman to make love to him. I had sensed it for a long time. Sometimes I could almost feel him shake himself out of it when he felt me withdraw from him. He would look at me and reverse his action. He would roll over and kind of smile, as if to say, "I've got to meet you halfway or you're not going to make a move."

But the move that he did make was not spontaneous, and the feeling that I was there to service him began to really trouble me. I tried to excuse it. I realized that the pressures of the office were probably getting progressively more demanding. He had been sitting in that chair now for quite a while. The weight of his office was getting heavier on his shoulders, and he was changing. He wasn't as happy-go-lucky, not as relaxed and cheerful. He was somber, sometimes downright solemn. He would drift off into his own private world, and I could feel him a million miles away. He had more important things on his mind. The excuses that I invented didn't make me feel more sympathetic. I've always been overly sensitive about being rejected. I would instinctively draw back from him and he would ask me, "What's wrong?" And I would say, "If you're really not here with me, I'll leave."

Then he would come back from wherever he had been and apologize. Other times, when he was particularly tired, he would get short with me. "You're hard to please," he'd say. "You're absolutely right," I'd say. "I'm very demanding. When I'm on that plane tomorrow, I'm going to feel very guilty about having taken up so much of your time."

"Oh, Judy," he'd say, "I'm sorry. Please forgive me."

This conversation, with variations, happened several times.

By early 1962, I dreaded going to the White House. I wanted to see Jack, but not in that place.

What is strange to me is that Jack was a different person when away from the White House. For example, there was the evening in mid-November 1961 when he came to my apartment on North Flores. He had come to speak at a dinner at the Hollywood Palladium. I remember he had been in Texas the day before for the funeral of Sam Rayburn, and I think he had made a speech in Seattle just before going to Texas. He had called me in Palm Springs every day for a week to make sure that I would be in Los Angeles for his visit. He wanted me to attend the dinner and I said, "Shall I call Evelyn?" and he said, "No, I'll take care of everything."

Jerry Nathanson, who was in real estate and politics in Palm Springs, was seated next to me and Evelyn at a table that was directly in front of the speaker's dais. Whenever I caught Jack's eye, he would raise an eyebrow in recognition. After a while it became hysterically funny. I am sure Evelyn and Jerry wondered what was wrong with me. I am afraid that I don't remember a word that was spoken by anyone at that dinner. There is just something about a political dinner that trigger's some little mechanism in my ears that make the words bounce out before they can register on the brain.

For the first time since I had known Jack I did something that took him completely by surprise. Before I showed him through my apartment, I sat him down and handed him a pencil sketch of himself which I had done on canvas with the intention of later doing it in oils. He was floored by it. It seemed to shock him that I had taken the time to draw his picture. He was flattered by the compliment. That is how ingenuous he could be at times. Having painted a number of portraits, I think very few people are flattered by the image reflected by painters—or cameras, for that matter. I don't like photographs that look like me. I only like the ones that look glamorous and not like me at all. It's a natural reaction. Jack was vain in that he liked things to compliment him. So it was a compliment to me, too, that he liked the sketch. It's possible, of course, that he liked the idea that I was home thinking about him when he wasn't around. After Jack's reaction to the sketch, I just left it that way instead of going to oils.

I gave him a tour of my apartment and tried to mimic Dave Powers, describing various pieces of furniture and fixtures as though they were historical monuments. I took him into the bathroom and explained that many movie queens had sat on that throne. Jack immediately got into the act. He inspected closets and admired a hanger, a garment bag, making a great fuss over little things because it was not all that large an apartment.

Once in the bedroom, he completely ignored the bed—which was not easy. It was a massive bed with a tremendous headboard. The bedspread was a heavy beige brocade, and if not obvious in color, the bed was obvious in size. Jack walked around it like it wasn't even in his path. Then suddenly, "Hark! What have we here?" "Sire, this is a President-size bed, circa 1961, a mysterious contraption designed for the dubious pleasures of our ancient leader. As you will note, sire, it is grander than the less important king-size antique used by the limited rulers of the pre-atomic age. I beg thee not to sit on it, sire, for it is possessed of an evil spirit that makes the strongest men go ape."

Before the words were out of my mouth, Jack had me down on the bed, rolling and laughing. There was nothing wrong with his back that night. It was a joyous reunion, as though two lost lovers were meeting after a long separation. Before leaving that evening, he made me promise to come to Florida in late December.

This was my second visit to see Jack in Palm Beach. I had seen him in early spring that year, but that was before my first White House visit and at a time when he was still a neophyte at his job. Both times I was picked up in Miami and driven to the same house in Palm Beach which I have described as similar in appearance to Sam's place. It was the typical Floridian one-story-pastel-colored-upper-middle-class-subdivision-retirement-haven. The house Jack used was on a fairly flat area and near the water. There was a large green lawn, large swimming pool, and it was all enclosed by a shoulder-high wall.

I arrived around one that afternoon. Jacked opened the door and there was not another soul in sight. There may have been an army of Secret Service men hiding in the bushes and closets, but to the naked eye, we were completely alone. Jack was wearing light tan casual slacks, a yellow short sleeve sportshirt, and beige canvas shoes with no socks.

He was in great spirits as we strolled leisurely toward the water. He loved the sea. I don't think any man ever loved it more. When we came back some invisible cook had prepared a seafood salad. We sat at a glass-topped table which was almost identical to Sam's. It gave me a weird feeling.

I remember lying in bed with the windows wide open and the sun warm on our flesh. He couldn't have been more attentive and loving. It was an idyllic afternoon, one that left me with renewed hope for the future of our relationship. I was able to kid myself a little while longer about an impossible situation. The problems in my head and the emptiness in my chest would not disappear by becoming more deeply involved with a married President who could cheat on his wife but who was becoming irrevocably wedded to his job.

Again gradually, I got the feeling that he was planning for his family to be in the White House for quite some time. I think that's why he worried so about Teddy being immature. It was a concern of his that he expressed on numerous occasions. It was concern and not criticism. I can't recall specifically what it was that Teddy had done to cause this concern, but whatever it was, Teddy had failed in some areas of responsibility, and it had made a strong impression on Jack.

It was also my feeling that Jack was leaning less on the family and making more of his own decisions without the family pow-wow. His father had suffered a disabling stroke and Jack was almost totally his own man. I say this not from any political knowledge, but from the impressions I got from hundreds of casual conversations over a period of nearly two and a half years. For whatever it's worth, Jack believed in a Kennedy dynasty, and he was going to be the patriarch.

By this time, Jack was beginning to reflect the importance of the office. That was the feeling he conveyed to me. He became more impressed with the fact that he was the President. Not anybody around him, not his aides, not his advisers, not his father, not his family—*he* was the President. Whereas before it had always seemed like a joint effort. It may well be that he finally had to have that attitude because the responsibility did lie on his shoulders. When the problems came, they came to him. When something went wrong, it was his mistake. He became very sensitive about what was said about him. And sensitive about his appearance because he was unsure of himself in the way he looked and the way he dressed. This was a likeable quality. He was a handsome man and he was a charming man but still he was not a vain man.

Although he was feeling more important, he could conceal it. He could fool the best of them. He could be so humble when he didn't feel it, and he could charm the socks right out of your shoes. He had an incredible talent in that direction. He knew just what he could do with people.

I was not as aware of this talent in the beginning. That was something that started coming through after we became more comfortable with each other. It was like any other relationship. You see your mate differently after you've been intimate for a long time. You see him in good and bad moods, and when the pressures get heavy on him, you sometimes get the brunt of it at the least expected moment. I was seeing different sides of Jack. I was seeing a more real Jack. In the beginning, he was all charm and romance, just sweeping me right off my feet. When a romance is in first bloom, your total concentration is on the other person. You try to impress him; you want him to like everything about you. As you become more comfortable with each other, the concentration falters.

As he started to be more sure of me, I sensed that he was taking me for granted. He had won me over and I was going to stay won as long as he so desired. This feeling could have come from my own insecurities. There is no reason why he should have had to woo me constantly. Yet I didn't want to be a possession, someone he could command to appear in various places whenever the urge struck him.

I used to agonize over his phone calls. The tone was getting more imperious. He would call and say, "Can you be in Washington on Sunday?" Sometimes it was within a day's notice. Either I wasn't up to making a trip or I'd just gotten back from someplace, or I was in Palm Springs and I didn't want to leave. I didn't appreciate being beckoned. I realized he was probably in the middle of some world-shaking decision, and he didn't have time for polite amenities, but it didn't help my disposition. There were times when I really wanted to go, but I'd say no because his tone hit a wrong chord. He didn't have any patience with it at all. He wanted a reason and sometimes I was good at inventing excuses and other times I was very bad. I didn't think fast enough for him. He knew exactly what I was doing.

"Well," he would say, "if you don't want to come, then don't!" And hang up!

I would sit there and stew. I was angry and I was hurt. But I was becoming ambivalent about our relationship. If he called and I wasn't at my place he would call my mother, and she would call me, and sometimes I would avoid calling him back until the next day. When I did return his call, he would want to know what was wrong, and I would invent more excuses.

If I said it was too short notice, he would say, "You know what my time is. I have so little time to spare," and the attitude was that because he was the President, because he had so little time, I was supposed to jump every time he wanted to see me, and I found myself getting irritated with the situation. I would hang up after one of his calls and say to myself, "What the hell's the matter with you? What are you so tense about?" I realized that flying all the way across the country just to see him for two hours was not worth it. Being in love with him was becoming too much trouble.

After a while I began pushing the situation until I was

250

daring him to get mad at me and yet I didn't want it to end completely. I was so confused about everything that at certain times I felt guilty about the way I was treating Jack. I would think, "This is dumb, and what are you doing?" I'd call Jack and say I could be back at a certain time and leave the decision up to him. It never worked out on that basis, but at least I felt better about it.

Whenever Jack got short with me, my first instinct was to make him feel foolish, and a good way with a man in that position is to tell him he's acting like a child. I would say, "Don't be so childish." I'm afraid he didn't appreciate that at all.

For a long time he could still laugh at me and kid himself out of the doghouse, but by late spring 1962 he was less inclined to agree that he was being childish. I began avoiding his calls and avoided calling him back, and his calls became less frequent, but there was never any definite break-off point. I didn't know I no longer loved Jack until I realized I didn't care if I never saw him again. I didn't wake up one morning and say, "I no longer love Jack." It happened so gradually that I wasn't really aware that it was over until long after it had ended. It just dwindled away and at one point the telephone finally stopped ringing. The last conversation could have been, "Can you be here on Tuesday," and I said, "No, maybe in a couple of weeks." But that was at least three months after the March 22, 1962, White House luncheon between Jack and J. Edgar Hoover, who supposedly told the President of my relationship with Sam. The Senate committee's report states that "According to White House logs, the last telephone contact between the White House and the President's friend [me] occurred a few hours after the luncheon." The inference is that Jack immediately contacted me and said don't ever darken my door again. Nothing could be further from the truth. If what the committee says about the White House logs is in fact true, then it is pretty obvious that Hoover spoke to Jack about me. It is too much of a coincidence that it would happen on the same day. The only explanation I can offer is that our calls were either no longer

251

recorded in the logs, or they have been deleted. The point is that Jack never mentioned any of this to me. I saw Jack in March and April and the calls did not stop until sometime in June. And they stopped, not because of any outside force, but because of natural attrition. The spectre of the White House killed the romance. Not J. Edgar Hoover.

XII

I found that I was happier with Sam. It was a more natural relationship. We spent days and weeks at a stretch together. There was that quality about Sam that made me feel that he would move mountains for me. He was a widower with a family, and in a sense I felt he was faithful. I didn't believe that any man was ever completely faithful to any woman, but whatever Sam may have been doing on his own, he managed quite well to create an illusion of fidelity.

In mid-October 1961 I leased a house in Palm Springs for three months. I kept my North Flores apartment and commuted quite regularly—that is, when I was in California. I got back to painting. That was when I did the sketch of Jack. By now there seemed to be countless people who knew about Jack. Complete strangers would come up and say, "Are *you* the Judy that's going with Jack Kennedy?" The "ladies" at the Racquet Club, particularly Gloria Cahn, who had a terrible crush on Jack, would always ask me about him. Gloria would be sitting by the pool and as I walked by, she would say in her bitchiest tone: "Been to Washington lately?" I would look directly at her and sweetly reply, "Oh yes, just returned." That was my way of turning the knife a little. The talk was going like wildfire. Even Walter Winchell got his two cents in. In his May 8, 1962, column, he wrote: "Judy Campbell of Palm Springs and Bevhills is Topic No. 1 in Romantic Political Circles."

It took such a long time to work up to an intimacy with Sam that I don't remember just when it happened. I always enjoyed being with Sam but now I was anticipating seeing him. I completely stopped thinking about Jack when I was with Sam.

I must say that Sam was entirely different in my eyes than anything reported in the press. He was so gentle with me. I have since read that he and Phyllis used to have rip-roaring battles. I never once had any kind of a battle with Sam, and I've got a pretty fair temper. I would be angry with him about one thing or another, but it never amounted to anything. He never abused me physically or mentally. If he got mad at me for any reason, or if my being upset over something annoyed him, he was silent. But it was a strong kind of no nonsense silence.

Only once did he walk out in anger. We were kissing and it became a little too passionate, which was something I had always tried to avoid, and when I refused to go any further, he walked out without saying a word. I left for New York the next morning, and no sooner had I walked into my room at the Plaza than he was on the phone apologizing. A moment later he had a piece of jewelry delivered to my room.

It was not long after this incident that we made love for the first time. He had become more difficult to restrain, but also it had reached the point where I wanted him to make love to me, and I wanted to make love to him. When it happened, it was that simple. Yet it had taken over a year and a half to get to that moment. For the first time since I had left Travis, I had my man with me when I woke up in the morning. Love with Sam was not as exciting as it had been with Jack, but it was gentle and tender and emotionally fulfilling. It left me with a comfortable feeling instead of a gnawing emptiness. I felt like I really knew how to handle Sam. Once we became intimate, Sam did not change with me, he didn't revert to some unreasonably possessive creature. If possible, he was more attentive.

Was Sam using me because I was the President's girl, as many writers have suggested? All I can say is that Sam had been after me to leave Jack for a long time. He would point out that Jack was married and try to make me understand the futility of the situation. Sam couldn't have been more delighted when I finally stopped seeing Jack. As I said, I had a hard time letting go of Jack. I liked the feeling that he was there and still wanted to see me. That's the way it was. I don't understand it when I look back on it. I guess Jack represented a form of emotional security.

Sam was not too thrilled the few times I saw Jack in 1962. Before we were intimate he would kid me about Jack, but now it wasn't funny anymore. I could tell by his silence that he didn't like it. But he listened when I explained that I was confused, that I needed time to work it out. He promised to be patient, but I knew it was eating away at him.

Sam wanted to show me Europe, but I was sensitive about traveling with a man who wasn't my husband. I didn't like the way it looked. I've always been overly concerned about appearances. Having been exposed to people in show business, I've seen what reporters can do to the most innocent situation, and I've seen what is done to situations that are not so innocent. It is shocking to see the lies the press can get away with. I could imagine what would have been written about my traveling in Europe with Sam Giancana. I think I was on a plane with Sam only twice the whole time I knew him. And that was twice too often as far as I was concerned. We never shared the same hotel suite. In New York we didn't even share the same hotels—mine was the Plaza, his was the Hampshire House. When he stayed the night, it was in my bed, and not I in his. I may have been involved with public figures, but I have always been a private person.

For example, several times Jack suggested that I fly with him on Air Force One. I could have met him at a certain point and we would have flown the rest of the way together. He had no qualms about asking me. It wasn't maybe it could be done this way or that way—he had it all worked out. But I knew I wouldn't be walking out with him. I would be hiding back there in the plane until the excitement of his exit had died down. That was so far out of character for me that instead of being flattered by the offer, I was insulted and told him so in no uncertain terms. But Jack could laugh at me at times like that. I think he just loved intrigue.

Whatever Sam's intentions may have been in the beginning, he fell in love with me. In a nice way he did become possessive. He wanted me to live in Chicago but I refused because I still wanted my independence. Whenever I was with him whether it was in Chicago, New York or Miami, and I talked of returning to California, his mood would change to one of displeasure. But instead of arguing about it he would say he had to leave for a while. A few hours later he would be back with some extravagant gift. "This is for the birthday I missed in 1958," he would say, or it was for prior Christmases, Easters, Valentine's Days—he would always have an excuse for the presents.

I could understand the pleasure Sam derived from giving me lovely presents. As I said, it makes me happy to give someone a present. But what do you give someone like Jack or Sam? They can go out and buy the world. One day I got this brainstorm. They both smoked Schimmilpenninck cigars, which are imported from Holland, and are quite thin and short. I went to a jeweler in Beverly Hills and had two solid gold cigar cases made and gave them each one.

In March 1962, I moved into a new apartment at 8401 Fountain Avenue. It was in a new four-story building with four large apartments on each floor. Johnny Roselli considered moving into the building himself. "Christ, with the both of us living here," he said, "this has got to be the safest place in town." He was referring to the FBI surveillance which intensified until they were watching our every move. "With the FBI watching it all the time," he said, "you don't have to worry about anybody breaking into your apartment." As it turned out, every apartment except mine was broken into during the time I lived there. The only burglars who ever broke into mine were FBI agents, and I caught them in the act.

I had left for lunch with Johnny at the Beverly Hills Brown Derby, when I realized that I had forgotten a piece of jewelry I wanted to have repaired. I drove back to my building and when I walked into my apartment, there were two men standing in the middle of my living room. I took a step back, ready to scream, as they both fumbled around for their identification folders. When I saw they were FBI agents, I completely lost control over the situation. Instead of writing down their names and calling the Beverly Hills police, I screamed for them to leave. They were out of there so fast it took me a moment to realize that I was screaming in an empty room. When I told Johnny about it at lunch, his first question was whether I had recognized the agents. He advised me not to do anything about it until he had a chance to talk it over with someone. That evening, when I talked to Sam, his advice was to let Johnny handle it.

By the end of September that year I was again experiencing abdominal pain. I had been planning on going to Chicago for a long visit, and since I needed an extensive diagnostic examination, my doctor suggested Billings Hospital at the University of Chicago. I felt a little better when I arrived in Chicago and I postponed the examination.

Sam had to be in Florida on business and I went to join him at the Eden Roc. The day after I arrived Sam said, "Come on, I have to go somewhere." I had long since stopped asking where we were going. Whatever answer he gave me we would end up somewhere else. So I'd grab onto his arm and we would be off.

We came to a beautiful residential area and Sam stopped in front of a new house. It was a huge place, very modern, with lots of glass and stonework, and a swimming pool that was half indoors and half outdoors. It was very plush but not my cup of tea. I prefer older houses. I like warmth in a home. This was a Miami house, too cold, too stark.

"What do you think of it?" Sam asked.

"I think a lot could be done with it," I said, not know ng what he had in mind.

"Pretty swanky, don't you think?"

"Are you thinking of buying it?"

"I'll tell you something," he said. "I'll buy it if you decorate it for me."

I just jumped at that. I love interior decorating. I have done it for many friends. At one time I had checks printed up that said "Judith Campbell Interiors," so I could shop in wholesale houses. I even had my license. "That's something

I'd love to do," I said, and from the look on his face, I knew he thought he had me hooked.

He had a couple of aces up his sleeve. He played the first one when we got back to the hotel. We were having a drink and I said, "Are you really going to buy it?"

"Like I said, if you decorate it."

"You really know how to get to me."

"Yep, I figured that would please you," he said. "But there is one other condition—"

"I just knew it. What is it?"

"Well, if I buy it and you decorate it, you have to live in it."

"Sam, for God's sake, I don't want to live in Florida."

"No, wait, I want to give you the house. You only have to live in it when you want to, like in the winter when the weather's great here. Whatever you do, it'll be yours. I'll see that all the papers are in your name and I'll even pay the gift tax."

"Oh, no, the deal's off," I said.

"But why can't I give you something like this," he said, and I could see he was getting frustrated. "You can't buy it yourself."

He was getting frustrated and I was getting irritable. I would reach a point in a discussion where I didn't know how to handle it. It went around in circles until finally Sam gave up and said he had to go somewhere.

I took a hot bath and tried to calm down. I knew I hadn't heard the last of it. Sam was persistent. Sure enough, it came up again at dinner that evening. We covered the same ground, with the same result.

When we got back to my suite after dinner and a few drinks in a couple of bars, Sam said, "I want to talk to you seriously about this house."

I was exhausted. "Oh Sam, no more, please."

"No, I mean in another way," he said. "Would you live in it if we were married? Would you accept it as a wedding gift?"

That just about knocked me right off my feet. "That's not a fair question," I said, and I know my voice was shaking.

"Well, honey, I am asking you, and I know it's a stupid way of saying it, but will you marry me?"

To this day I don't know exactly what I said at that moment. I know I told him I needed time to think about it. I mentioned my disastrous marriage and my fears of getting married again. I know I brought up the fact that he had to be away so much of the time. I didn't think I could sit somewhere and wait for him. To me that was a lonely way of life.

Sam agreed that I should think about it. "You don't have to tell me now, you don't have to tell me tomorrow. I want you to think about it until you're sure of your decision."

After Sam left that night, that called for another hot tub. Deep down I knew I wasn't ready to get married. I didn't believe in marriage, not with the people I was seeing—there had to be something very wrong with it. I wished that Sam hadn't forced the situation. As things were we had a marvelous relationship. There was, for me I know, a total kind of fulfillment. I recalled how it had been before we were intimate. I was like a child going out to play; there was something shallow about it that I realized only after we became closer. There was a different feeling between us. The anxieties vanished. I knew I had been right in the choice I had made. Sam was the better man for me.

The way he treated me, the way he talked about his feelings for me, I knew that Sam loved me. He told me often enough. Sometimes I could feel him watching me for the longest time and then he would say, "You are really beautiful. Would you believe it, I really love you." Other times he would say, "What is this you think you've got? Who do you think you are? Why should I love you?" With Sam, "I love you," came out very often and in many different ways.

Feeling the way I did made my decision that much more difficult. Sam called around noontime and I invited him to my room for brunch.

"I'm not going to press you," he said, the moment I opened the door.

"Am I glad to hear that," I said, "because I've been thinking about it all night and it's troubling me."

259

"Okay," he said, and he was in a good mood, "not another word about it."

After we had eaten, he said, "Come on, I have to go somewhere." He headed straight for a jewelry store. "See anything you like?" he asked. I selected a pearl brooch and a pearl ring, and Sam picked a diamond watch for me, and all of a sudden I thought, "Oh, oh, what's going on?" He wasn't going to pressure me and here we are in a jewelry store. I felt like I was being set up for the slaughter. At any moment I expected him to buy an engagement ring. Sam excused himself and went in back with the owner. When he came out there was that little mischievous grin on his face.

He was up to something all right, as I discovered that evening when he picked me up for dinner.

"Ah, I see you're wearing your ring and brooch," he said, casually reaching into his pocket and handing me something wrapped in the jeweler's tissue paper. "Well, wear this too."

It was a diamond bracelet over forty carats, with the center diamond about two carats, and a circle of baguettes perfectly graduated in size all the way around it. It was the most delicate, the most exquisite bracelet I had ever seen.

I just about died. "Sam, you didn't—"

"No, I didn't. I just asked you to wear it, just wear it. Is that asking too much after what you've put me through?"

So I didn't say anything more about it. I didn't even thank him. I thought to myself, "Okay, but you're getting it back tonight." But I couldn't take my eyes off it all evening. When we returned to my room after dinner, I took it off and said, "You take it, Sam. I don't want to keep this in here all night."

"You're not supposed to give that back to me."

I started to say something and he stopped me. "Don't, it's too late, I'm too tired, and I can't argue with you. You be a good girl and accept it." And I did.

I wish I could have postponed my decision forever. But I knew that wasn't possible with a man like Sam. So when he called me the next day about going out to lunch, I invited him to my suite. "Oh, that doesn't sound good," he said.

Over lunch I told him that I had made a decision and in

260

light of it, I didn't know how I could keep the bracelet. "My God," he said, "you're not going to start in on that again."

"I love you, I know I love you," I said, "but I just can't see myself getting married right now."

"Okay, but why don't you think about it a little while longer."

"That wouldn't be fair, Sam, because I don't know when I can ever face the prospect of marriage. I don't like saying this because I don't know what's going to happen. I love seeing you and I love being with you, but marriage is out of the question. I just couldn't cope with it."

He was quiet for a while and he just looked at me—he would get a look on his face sometimes that I couldn't figure out. I couldn't tell whether he was angry or just thinking. It was a subtle, deceiving look that was a little unnerving. After a long silence, I said, "I'm sorry, Sam. I truly am."

"You don't have to be sorry," he said. "I'm sorry, but that's the way it goes."

No more was said about it, but I could tell that he felt rejected, and terribly disappointed. I didn't know what to do. His mood changed and he said he had to go out. When he called later in the day to make plans for dinner, I asked, "Are you all right?" "Yeah, I'm fine," he said, and he sounded like he had been drinking. Nothing more was ever said about it again. As I look back on it now, I can see that our relationship started on the road to dissolution on that day.

At the time I went into Billings, on October 10, Sam said he would be away but that John and Maryann Matassa would look after me. In the hospital it was discovered that I had a chronic kidney condition. After I was released, I moved into the Oak Park Arms to be closer to Sam, but I didn't see him for several days. Then one night I went out to dinner with the Matassas and two minutes after we sat down Sam walked in, a big smile on his face, and I thought that everything would be fine, but it was never again the same. He would take me to his home and to dinner, but the marvelous times of being together all day every day had stopped.

It was around that time that I first heard about his relationship with Phyllis McGuire. I read something in the paper and mentioned it to John Matassa. "Oh, I was hoping you wouldn't see that," he said. I pressed for more information and he said, "You mean to say you don't know anything about it." When I shook my head, he said, "Well, everybody else does."

That was as far as he would go and I didn't want to pursue it further. I didn't like the idea. It was a blow to my ego. To be honest, I felt I had Sam right in my pocket. He wanted to marry me and I had rejected him. This gave me a feeling of power, of being one up on him. But the minute I heard about Phyllis I felt that little twinge of jealousy. It bothered me but I was vain enough to think that Sam was purposely making me jealous, that it was just part of his plan to bring me around to marrying him. What I didn't realize was that Sam's vanity and ego were far superior to mine. For a long time I had the feeling that he was trying to teach me a lesson: "You're the one that's going to be sorry!" Rejection is hard for anyone to accept gracefully, but a man like Sam, with his money and power, had to find some way of maneuvering around it.

When we went out in the evening it was usually to the Villa Venice. That was when some of the top acts in the country were appearing there. It was there that Sam introduced me to Eddie Fisher. Sam and I were sitting in a small banquet room when Eddie came in to see Sam, who was in one of his aloof moods. The more Eddie talked the more apparent it became that Sam didn't like him. It got downright embarrassing. On the other hand it was equally apparent that Eddie had come to pay homage to Sam. Throughout dinner Eddie kept looking at me and finally he said, "You look like my wife Elizabeth." He said his wife, but at that time they were either separated or divorced.

"Careful," Sam said, "her head is big enough now."

"No, really, I mean it. She has the same kind of beauty as my wife Elizabeth."

Sam clanked his fork on his plate and gave Eddie a look that is impossible to describe. "Shut up, kid," he said, "too many people tell her things like that."

I couldn't believe my ears. It was not the words as much as the look and tone of voice that surprised me. Eddie just froze in his chair and I could feel my pulse throbbing in my temple. Then Sam laughed and Eddie was very quick on the upbeat. A moment later we were all laughing.

I saw Eddie's closing show with the Matassas. It was very schmaltzy with heart tugging songs. He brought the house down. Between shows that evening Eddie sat with us, and it came up in the conversation that I was going to New York for a few days. Eddie asked if he could contact me there and I said it was fine, but after he left I asked the Matassas about it. "That's okay," John said, "Sam won't mind."

I left for New York on November 28 and at Sam's suggestion I stayed at the Essex House. The first thing Eddie wanted to know when he called was whether Sam was in town and the next was if Sam would mind if we had dinner together. I said no to both questions and that evening I went with Eddie and Dr. Max Jacobson to the Plaza's Persian Room to see Robert Goulet.

Max Jacobson didn't lose any time telling me that he knew about my relationship with Jack. "The Secret Service really have their hands full tonight," he laughed. "They're not only following Jackie, who's in town to see me, but they're following Jack's girl who just happens to be with me."

That kind of talk hadn't surprised me in a long time. What did arouse my curiosity was his comment that Jackie was coming to see him. Then he proudly explained that he gave her shots, which he described as vitamins and enzymes. I have since read somewhere that Max also gave the shots to Jack and was with Jack in Russia during his historic meeting with Khrushchev.

My first experience with one of Max's shots came two nights later. Eddie and I went nearly two days straight without sleep. We talked our problems out, letting our hair down, and poor Eddie was torching for Elizabeth in the worst way—he had an ache for her that just wouldn't quit. In the process, we consumed an unhealthy quantity of alcohol and very little food. It hit me when Eddie was taking me back to the Essex House. Suddenly, I thought I was going to faint. "My God," I cried, "I don't know what's happening to me."

"Hold on," Eddie said, "I'm taking you right over to Max."

Max looked me over and said, "Don't worry about it, you're all right. It's just a combination of the medication for your kidneys, no sleep and the drinking. This will fix you right up."

He gave me the shot and I instantly felt fine. He never mentioned that it contained amphetamine. Eddie had left for the airport to catch a plane for Los Angeles, and I took a cab back to the hotel. There was a mixup about my messages—I had called earlier and had been told that I had about fifteen messages, but now there were none. For all I knew, Sam or the FBI had stolen them. I was upset about the messages and then suddenly I could feel myself beginning to panic. I was on the thirty-fifth floor and got this irresistible impulse to jump out. I suffer from acrophobia, but now all I could think of was running across the room and leaping through the window. I could visualize myself tumbling through the air screaming, and splashing on the street. I sat on the floor of the bathroom, which was the farthest point from the window, and I was shaking so hard my teeth were chattering.

The phone rang and I nearly jumped out of my skin. I crawled to the nightstand and picked up the receiver. It was Uncle Armand calling from the airport. "You'll probably think I'm crazy," I cried, "but I feel like I'm going to jump out the window." And I was holding onto the phone as though it were my last hope on earth. "Oh, you're going to be all right," Uncle Armand said. "Now don't worry about it, you're going to be just fine." He couldn't get off the phone fast enough.

Finally I called Max and he was there with a psychiatrist like a shot. When Max realized that it wasn't a psychological problem, he gave me a shot to counteract the other one. I calmed right down. He made me swallow one sleeping pill, left another one on the nightstand, and confiscated the rest. I must have slept fourteen hours.

I went back to Max's office the next day for an examination and he gave me another shot. I started feeling better, stronger, more active, really alive. I thought it was the vitamins and enzymes, but it really was amphetamine. Whenever I felt low, I got one of Max's shots. Sometimes it was once a day; at other times it was once a week, depending on my state of mind.

I was in good company. Besides Jackie and Jack Kennedy, some of his other patients included Jay Lerner, Johnny Mathis, Margaret Leighton, Andy Williams—a veritable Who's Who of the entertainment world.

Max tried to teach me how to administer my own shots— made me practice on an orange so I could get the feel of the pressure needed to stick the needle in my buttock—but I never could do it. So when I was in Chicago, Max would mail the medication to a Dr. Yacullo. In California, I would see Max's son, Tommy, who was a doctor in Canoga Park.

In the meantime I was in contact with Sam, and he was after me to return to Chicago. I went back on December 8 and moved into the Sahara. Instead of a suite I asked Sam to get me a single room, and he couldn't believe it. I didn't realize it then, but the shots were making me jumpy. I felt more secure in one room. I didn't have to worry about a second room. As a child I was always frightened by darkness, and now I could feel myself becoming more insecure at night. Whenever I went out with Sam I always had him search the room when we came back. After my experience at the Essex House, I wanted something small and close to the ground.

I have always been fascinated by the way the press labels restaurants and hotels owned by the underworld. It can be the finest place in town, but, as far as the press is concerned, it's always a syndicate joint. The Sahara was a new garish multimillion-dollar hotel on Mannheim Road, which was described in publicity brochures as a "little bit of Broadway, a little bit of Hollywood, and a whole lot of Miami Beach and Las Vegas."

Whatever it may have cost, or imitated, the Sahara was

strictly a joint because the man who operated it, Manny Skar, was the typical joint operator. Manny belonged in a sleazy carnival. He was a crude, coarse, vulgar, loud, fast-talking, boorish simpleton who made the criminals who stayed and dined at the hotel look classy by comparison.

During the two months I stayed at the Sahara I became very fond of his wife, Bea—we spent a good deal of time together, enough for me to know that she was a lovely woman. But I never could understand how she could love that ridiculous clown, this *mamzer,* who took sadistic pleasure in humiliating her in public. He had a mistress by the same name whom he called Bea One and he referred to his wife as Bea Two, and this was quite a funny joke to Manny. He took delight in showing their wedding picture to point out the size of Bea's nose before her plastic surgery. Bea took it all to heart and still she loved that little worm. Even after his enemies gunned him down in his car one night only moments after he had let Bea out in front of their apartment building, she mourned him for years.

It was a cold winter, with leaden skies and wind-driven snow. I spent days on end in my room.

Except for Sam and Bea, the only other person who was able to penetrate beyond the blankness of my mind was Tony Bennett. We had much in common. We are both shy, reserved people, not at all outgoing. His awkwardness, his discomfort, his not knowing what to do with his hands on stage has become part of his personality, his style as a performer. Once you know him, he is a very gentle, warm, sensitive, unpretentious human being.

While he was appearing at the Sahara, his room wasn't too far from mine and we got together a few times and talked about art. I remember one time I had a greeting card from Sam sitting up against the mirror. It was one of those silly little cards and Tony sketched it in a couple of seconds. He is a fine artist and he tried to encourage me to paint again. "The thing to do," he said, "is to sketch everything you see. Take your phone over there. Sit down and sketch it from every possible angle. You'll be amazed at how many different shapes it presents. There's a hundred things in this room you could sketch, and all of them would present different problems depending on the time of day, on light and shadow, angle, perspective, and it's all fascinating once you really get into it." It was inspiring to think about, but I just couldn't muster the energy.

In a way, I was trying to make up my mind about whether to continue seeing Sam. I wasn't ready to go home. I wasn't ready to put all this behind me. I had to stay there to see what was going to happen. I suppose I wanted the decision to be made for me.

Sam and I were still intimate, but he never stayed the night anymore. He was pleasant enough when he was with me but it wasn't the same as before. I thought he was still playing the game of teaching me a lesson and that eventually things would work out.

At times I was convinced that there were other games being played. Ugly, frightening games. My room had been part of a suite but the connecting door was locked and Sam had promised me that the other room would not be rented. But some nights when my light was out, I could see a light coming from underneath the door. I would watch that light for hours, and sometimes a shadow would flicker across it and I was convinced there was someone in that room. Other times there would be a little tap or a bump on the wall, almost like an accidental sound, and I would have to talk to myself: "Stay calm, everything's all right, don't let your imagination run away with you."

When I couldn't stand my imagination any longer, I would call the manager and complain that someone was in the other room. "That's not possible," he would say, "we're not renting that room." "That's funny," I would say, "because the light's on in that room and I just saw a shadow underneath the door." "Oh, well, maybe someone just went in to check it." "At two in the morning?" "The room is checked periodically." I never got any other explanation.

I left for California on February 4, 1963, and on that day at least, Sam was his old self. My plane was leaving at six-fifteen that evening, but John Matassa picked me up at the hotel early in the afternoon and brought me to a coffee shop where Sam was waiting for me. There was another man sitting with Sam in a booth, but the moment I sat down, two men walked in and sat at the counter.

"It's the Boy Scouts," Sam said, shaking his head in disgust. He pulled out a miniature camera that was hidden in a Zippo-type lighter. He winked at me, lifted the top of the lighter and sighted through a tiny viewer. Aiming it at the two men, Sam snapped their picture and lighted his cigar at the same time.

By this time, of course, the FBI were all over Sam. There were carloads of agents parked near his house, the Armory, the Villa Venice, the Fresh Meadows Golf Club, the Sahara, the Fontainebleau, even St. Bernadine's Church—wherever Sam went, the FBI was sure to go, en masse. And they did the same thing to me.

AUTHOR'S NOTE: *In June 1963, Giancana petitioned the federal court in Chicago for relief. He charged the FBI with harassing him by keeping his house under constant surveillance and by dogging his footsteps even on the golf course. "How would you like it," his attorney told the judge, "if you were on the eighteenth hole trying to line up a putt, and there were six FBI agents watching you?" Because of the surveillance, Sam's score often soared to 115, some twenty-odd strokes above his normal score.*

Federal Judge Richard D. Austin granted an injunction limiting surveillance to a single FBI automobile, parked at least a block away from Giancana's home, or a block behind when following his car. He further stipulated that a disinterested foursome must play between him and the agents whenever he went to a golf course. "I know there are some not interested in civil rights and not concerned with privacy who will in the future approve of this type of harassment," Austin stated in his opinion. "I cannot give my sanction."

"If those two characters are in here," Sam said, "there's a bunch more around outside. "Come on," he said, "let's have some fun." Sam exchanged car keys with Matassa, and the plan was that John and the other man would take off in Sam's car. We went out and the two agents remained seated at the counter. The cars were in a huge parking lot, jam-packed with cars and people, which made it easier to switch them.

John and the other man roared out of there, tires screeching, and an FBI car was hell bent after them.

"We pulled a fast one," Sam laughed. But no sooner were we out of the parking lot than there was another FBI car after us. The chase that ensued was something out of *The French Connection*. We went around corners on two wheels, even up on the sidewalk a couple of times, and all the time Sam was yelling and whooping it up like a wild man. I think he was reliving the days when he was the fastest wheelman on the West Side.

"You're not scared, are you?"

"No," I cried, "it's great. Go faster!"

Dr. Yacullo had given me a shot that morning so I was in great spirits. (Unfortunately, it was not until years later that I discovered the shots contained amphetamine—naive me, I thought it was done with vitamins and enzymes.)

Suddenly, we came to a tire skidding stop behind a motel and Sam said, "We've lost the dummies!" We sat there for only a moment before Sam pulled out again. "The hell with

269

it," he said. "They know we're going to the airport, so let's give them a ride for their money."

And we were off again, with Sam whooping and slapping the steering wheel, and I whooping right along with him. After being cooped up for two months, I felt as frisky as a cub coming out of hibernation. That was probably the best time the FBI ever made going to O'Hare. There must have been four or five carloads of them at the airport. They were angry enough at this point to show themselves. They don't enjoy it when the prey plays games with them.

We got out of the car and Sam had his arm around me, smiling like he was having the time of his life. Although my legs were a little wobbly, I was smiling, determined never to let the FBI think that I was upset or afraid of anything, because that was giving them an edge they would use against me. I don't know about the rest of the Bureau, but I can tell you that I have no respect for the ones that hounded me to the very edge of my grave. Their behavior and tactics were ruthless. If they had suspected the smallest chink in my armor, they would have destroyed me on the spot. My motto was to keep my chin up and my upper lip stiff, but in the end it didn't work out quite that way.

We arrived at least an hour before my flight and naturally gravitated to the cocktail lounge. "I don't want you to worry," Sam said, "but they'll be on the plane with you. Is someone meeting you?" I said that my father would meet me, but that wasn't good enough for Sam. "Call him now and ask him to come right out to the plane. Have him tell them you're not feeling well and they'll let him meet you right at the door."

While I made my phone call, Sam went to talk to someone. When I came back he had another plan. We waited until almost flight time. Sam let me start down the ramp and then suddenly he was right behind me as I boarded the plane. I had never seen grown men scurry around like that before. Credentials were being flashed all over the place. Sam sat next to me and calmly carried on a conversation in a tone loud enough for at least six pairs of flapping ears to hear him.

270

"I just can't wait to get there," he said. "Now it's your turn to show me around."

"My mother will just love meeting you. She certainly has enjoyed you on the telephone."

Split seconds before the stewardess closed the door, Sam gave me a kiss on the cheek and darted out of the plane. It is impossible to describe the pandemonium that ensued—men frantically unbuckling seat belts, leaping out into the aisle, grabbing coats and briefcases, tripping and bumping into each other as they raced out of the plane.

Sam probably laughed all the way home. But for me, now alone on that plane, the harassment that would eventually lead me to a desperate suicide attempt was moving into its final stage.

XIII

I was followed, hounded, harassed, accosted, spied upon, intimidated, burglarized, embarrassed, humiliated, denigrated and, as I said, finally driven to the brink of death by the Federal Bureau of Investigation. Those were the days when special agents were thought of as Simon-pure guardians of our liberties. They followed me in cars with license plates that couldn't be traced through the Department of Motor Vehicles. They wiretapped my phone, my parents' phone, and only God and J. Edgar Hoover know who else's. They probably bugged every room I was ever in for more than two minutes. It was a cruel and relentless invasion of my person and privacy that kept scores of men illegally employed as burglars and eavesdroppers in an effort that must have cost millions and produced nothing of any value to anyone. They must have accumulated tons of reports and transcripts, all signifying nothing, and no doubt most of it long ago shredded. The only ones incriminated by the "evidence" were them.

My first reaction was, "Who do they think they are? What do they think they are going to find out from me?" I made up my mind that I would never talk to them. My other reaction was, "Okay, Sam, I'm with you. If you have to fight them, I'll fight them, too." I remember once telling Sam about the FBI following my mother and me one day while we were shopping in Beverly Hills. They used three or four cars and you could see them talking over their little microphones.

"My mother really held up," I said, and I was so proud of

her. "She was just an old trouper. You have a strong supporter in my mother." That's the way I felt about the whole thing. If that made me a criminal, then so be it.

Sam laughed, getting a real kick out of it, because he just loved my mother. He reached into his wallet and handed me a business card. "Whenever anybody gets too nosey, show them this card," he said.

I looked at it and burst out laughing. In the center of the card was the word RETIRED, and at the four corners it read: NO ADDRESS . . . NO PHONE . . . NO MONEY . . . NO BUSINESS. On the back were these words: "Under the Fifth Amendment to the Constitution of the United States, I respectfully decline to answer, on the grounds that my answer may tend to incriminate me." I have kept that little card all these years because it was exactly the way I felt.

The FBI not only questioned all my friends, but I think they questioned anyone who had the misfortune of riding in an elevator with me. And they were such hypocrites. Special Agent Dodge questioned Betsy Duncan, who was one of Johnny's many girlfriends, and she said, "If you want to know anything about Judy Campbell, I know she just came back from the White House. Why don't you go ask the President." Dodge let it go right over his head, acting like he hadn't heard a word she said. That was early in 1962, when Hoover ordered that top priority investigation of me. When Betsy told Johnny, he thought it was the greatest thing he'd ever heard. He's the one who told me about it, and his comment was, "Good for her."

I became very clever on the phone with Sam and Johnny, having a conversation about nothing and yet telling them what was on my mind. In a way, I was like a citizen in Orwell's *1984*. I was living in a dictatorship where your every word and movement were monitored and filed away for future condemnation. Hoover was God and the special agents were his avenging angels, recording everything in that big ledger up in the sky so that some day St. Peter could consign me to the fires of hell for all eternity.

There came a time when I was convinced that Jack knew everything about me and that he knew about Sam and

Johnny, because I couldn't picture the FBI doing all this to me without his knowing about it. The more I thought about it, the more it bothered me that Jack had never once asked me for the names of any of the people I was seeing in Chicago, New York, Florida, or any of the other places I told him about. All he ever asked me about was Frank, and all he seemed to care about was Hollywood gossip. Didn't the Secret Service want to know if I was safe?

Believe me, it is easy to get paranoid when you are being watched day and night, and the watchers make sure you know you are being watched. It makes you suspicious of the most innocent gesture or remark, and it calls for a lot of breast beating and soul searching.

Returning to California after my stay at the Sahara, I went to the Racquet Club in Palm Springs to soak in the sun and think things over. I wasn't sure about Sam any more. I wasn't even sure I wanted to see him again. I knew I didn't want to go back to Chicago. That was an abnormal way to live. I was seeing only the people Sam knew. They treated me as Sam's girl, and if I just blinked an eye at someone, everybody had better stand up and shout. These thoughts were an indication of the way I was beginning to feel not only about Sam, but about my way of life. I was so tired of being hounded, but I didn't know what to do. How to stop it!

I left Palm Springs on March 6 to visit Tommy Jacobson. I was getting depressed and I needed a shot. I stayed overnight with my parents and the next morning I drove my mother's Thunderbird to Canoga Park, which is at the extreme western end of the San Fernando Valley, a good twenty miles from Beverly Hills. Guess who was waiting for me in the parking lot? I came out the front entrance and had to walk around to the parking lot behind the building. I was about halfway to my car when I heard someone yell, ''Judy!'' Since I knew so many of the people who visited Dr. Jacobson, I immediately turned to acknowledge the greeting. God, it was Dodge and his buddy coming at me from either side and they were about on top of me. ''We'd like to talk to you about Sam Giancana and John Roselli.'' And they were waving their little folders with their badges and credentials in front of my face. I turned, got in my car and drove out of there without saying a word. Before now I had been accosted in familiar places—restaurants and stores I frequented—but here in this unexpected Godforsaken spot, it scared me more than ever.

All the way back home I tried to figure out how they knew I was there. I knew I hadn't been followed from my mother's home. FBI surveillance is not all that difficult to spot once you've been through it a couple of times. The only answer was that my parents' phone was tapped. Either that or Jacobson's.

I called Sam from a pay phone and he wanted to know if I was returning to Palm Springs. When I replied yes, he said, "Okay, someone will be in touch with you."

Back in Palm Springs I was immediately swept into the swing of it. The next evening I had dinner with Charles and Judy Offer—Charles was a wealthy banker—the Sontags, and Bo Bolinsky, who was then one of the Angels' hottest pitchers. In those days the Angels had their spring training camp in Palm Springs. Bo was a character. He should have been an actor instead of a ball player. He was tall and had this dark tan, but he was not the typical handsome man. He looked more like a good-looking boy. His problem was that his education had been neglected and he spoke with "dese, dose and dem" pretty much like some of the characters I had met at the Armory. But Bo had a flair; he was fun and charming, and pining something awful for Mamie Van Doren—he and Ray Anthony.

My life has either been woven in a blanket of coincidences, or it has been one monumental conspiracy. Frank Sinatra called on March 11 to invite me for dinner at his home. He said that Ruby and Connie (they owned Ruby's Dunes, the most fashionable restaurant in Palm Springs) would be there and asked if he could send his houseboy George to pick me up. I accepted the invitation but said I would drive my own car. An hour later, Sam called to ask if I would have Frank call him. When I told Frank about it that evening, he said, "Okay," and not another word. Although

Frank never mentioned Sam to me, Sam talked about Frank. Sam respected Frank and he liked the atmosphere around Frank. He knew Frank liked tough guys, and I've heard Sam say on numerous occasions that Frank was a frustrated gangster. Anyway, on that evening in Palm Springs, Frank was in his Dr. Jekyll mood which meant we had a pleasant relaxed evening.

The next evening I dined with Travis and his wife Carolyn, and Harry Gould, who was an executive with PepsiCola. Carolyn and I had worked out a momentary truce. The next night it was the Chi-Chi club with Jerry Nathanson, and so it went from night to night.

On the seventeenth I had dinner at Ruby's Dunes with Johnny Roselli and Peanuts Danolfo.

AUTHOR'S NOTE: *A former dealer in some of Moe Dalitz's old midwest illegal gambling operations, Nick "Peanuts" Danolfo's career at the Desert Inn improved considerably following a conclave of fourteen Mafia bosses, including Giancana, at the Jackpot Motel in 1960. Danolfo went from "host," a meaningless title, to general manager in one giant leap.*

To avoid being noticed leaving Las Vegas they had driven to Palm Springs in an old dilapidated car. Sam had sent them to tell me that Jimmy Cantillon would be handling my problem with the FBI. Jimmy Cantillon was Johnny's attorney in Los Angeles.

Jimmy is a good Irish Catholic boy with a taste for whiskey, a roving eye, and the face of an altar boy. But appearances can be deceiving. Jimmy can win you over in two seconds flat, yet he can be ruthless, cold, calculating and cruel at the time you need him most. Depending on some kind of reading on the meter in his head, Jimmy would either hum with enthusiasm when I needed him, or he just tried to fluff it off. The same set of circumstances on different days would receive opposite reactions. Jimmy was only available when it suited his purpose, whatever that may have been, from hour to hour. The reason I inherited his services, as I later discovered, was not because of my own problem with the FBI, but because a federal grand jury in Los Angeles was looking into organized crime.

Exactly eleven days after I gave Sam's message to Frank, I got the surprise of my life. That evening I went to see Bo pitch against the Cubs and then went on to the Key Club. They had pool tables and Bo, who was quite a pool player, had to sharpen his game for a charity match. We had a drink in the lounge and headed for the tables in the back. But as we walked past a closed door I heard voices, very faintly, and instantly knew that Sam was in that room. I got this terrible sinking feeling, but as Bo practiced, I kept telling myself that I was imagining it. It was nerves.

When Bo finished practicing we went back to the lounge and a moment later the door to the room opened and out came Frank, and right behind him was Sam, and some other men. My heart stopped beating when Sam looked directly at me and just walked past without a sign of recognition. The one thing that kept going through my head was that Sam knew I was seeing a lot of Bo and was not happy about it. It took a lot of Jack Daniels before I dropped off to sleep that night.

Sam worked in mysterious ways. He was on the phone the next day, acting like nothing had happened. I figured if he wasn't going to bring it up, I certainly wasn't. After the usual amenities, Sam said, ''A friend will be in touch with you tomorrow about that business. He, and that other guy, should be able to take care of things for you. Any more problems just give me a call.''

The friend turned out to be Sid Korshak, whom I had previously met with Sam in Chicago.

AUTHOR'S NOTE: *The underworld ties of Sidney R. Korshak are in every way as mysterious as those of Meyer Lansky. Born in 1907 and admitted to the practice of law in Illinois in 1930, his early background is pretty much a blank, except that he grew up on Chicago's West Side in the days when Al Capone ran the show in that town. As a young attorney, Korshak got to know a number of the Mob's captains and lieutenants, earning a reputation as a shrewd legal adviser, but there is no record of his ever being arrested. His close link to the gang was first revealed in 1943 during the celebrated movie extortion trial that sent John Roselli and six of his cohorts to prison. Willie Bioff, the stool pigeon in the melodrama (later murdered by a bomb), testified that he had been introduced to Sidney Korshak by Charles "Cherry Nose" Gioe, one of the defendants, as "our man." "Pay attention to him [Korshak]," Gioe had warned Bioff. "Remember, any message he may deliver to you is a message from us."*

Chicago columnist Irv Kupcinet, another good friend of Korshak, asserted that Korshak was undoubtedly the highest-paid attorney in the United States. This is especially impressive considering that Korshak does not practice law. He calls himself a labor-relations man, but the two most descriptive words would be "finder" and "fixer." Korshak has been involved in more "deals" than there is space in this book to recount. Somehow, whenever Korshak gets involved in any negotiation, his group usually comes out on top. His influence over the Teamsters' pension fund, over racetracks, Las Vegas hotels and casinos, the liquor industry, and the entertainment world, to name a few interests, are as mysterious as his ties to underworld bosses. The question today is not whether he has ties to them, but whether they have ties to him. It is quite possible that the tail is now wagging the dog.

I had seen Sid around the Racquet Club for years. He and his wife Bernice were very friendly with the Hollywood crowd.

We met at six for a drink in the bar at the Racquet Club and went on to Ruby's Dunes for dinner. Sid is tall, with a long face, large soft nose, and small eyes that never seem to blink. Everything about him is slow, deliberate, relentless. I had the feeling that he was just sitting back and watching and listening, and if it didn't go the way he wanted it to, he would just take his time and he would do something about it. No hurry. It can always be done—that kind of attitude. No one was going to stop him. No one was going to say anything unpleasant. No one was going to change his mind.

I was never afraid with Sam, but Sid frightened me. I could feel the power he wielded as he sat there watching me. This was not my first impression. It evolved over a series of meetings in Palm Springs, Las Vegas, and Beverly Hills.

That first night, after I had told him of my grievances against the FBI, he calmly informed me not to worry about it. It would be taken care of.

I was reaching a point where I didn't want much more to do with the situation. I would be loyal to Sam and Johnny because I had more feelings for them than I did for the FBI. I would have stuck up for them to my dying day. After what the FBI had done to me, I had no use for them. I wouldn't have talked to them even if Sam had been out to kill me.

At one point in our conversation I told Sid I knew Sam was in Palm Springs. "I don't like the idea that he came here without telling me," I said, "when he was on the phone with me just the day before."

Sid didn't even move his head. I had the feeling that my words were going into his little eyes instead of his ears. I had about as much chance of staring him down as I would have had with a lizard. "I don't like it at all," I repeated. I didn't say I was uneasy about it because that would be the last thing I would ever want Sid to think about me.

One day, Sid called and asked me to fly to Las Vegas so that we could talk. He had made all arrangements at the Riviera Hotel, with my suite down the hall from his. Vince Edwards was making his singing debut that evening, and I went with Sid, Stella Stevens, Betty Mahoney (one of Johnny's girlfriends), Tony Martin, and Allard Roen, an executive at the Desert Inn. I stayed three days and probably talked business with Sid three minutes.

Eddie Fisher started calling; we dated a few times and became good friends. Eddie was a great one with the phone when he got lonesome. I have a precious image of Eddie. It happened at his home one day when he was playing gin with Yul Brynner. Yul was smoking a huge black cigar and Eddie decided he'd light one. God bless him, he was such a little man, that cigar just overpowered him. He looked like a little kid smoking his daddy's cigar. Whenever I think of Eddie, I can see that cigar stuck in his face and I just have to smile.

On April 15, Eddie gave a cocktail party at Au Petit John in Beverly Hills. He had taken the place over completely and it was jampacked with people—even when he was having financial troubles, Eddie did things in a big way. After the cocktail party, he and I got into his limousine with Angie Dickinson and Alain Delon—we were going to Paramount Studios to see a private showing of *Come Blow Your Horn* which Eddie had arranged for his guests.

As soon as I was introduced to Angie, she let out a shriek: "You're Judy Campbell?" I told her I was and she said, "John has told me so much about you!" All I could say was, "Oh, really." At first I thought she meant John Roselli, but then I realized that she meant John Kennedy. She kept saying, "Oh, I'm so glad to meet you. I've heard so much about you."

After the movie the four of us went to LaScala with Bette Davis and her daughter, and again Angie started out on how much John had told her about me. I couldn't figure it out. Why would Jack Kennedy discuss me with Angie Dickinson? I had a lot of questions I would have liked answered, but there wasn't a chance I would discuss them with her.

I met Sid at his Beverly Hills office on the nineteenth—he had a small office on the second floor of a building that served as the reservation office for the Riviera Hotel. I said something to Sid that day that I will never forget. I was sick of the intrigue, of not knowing what was going on, fed up with men cheating on their wives—every husband I knew was making his grab at me if he got a chance. I was sick of conversations with Sam where I wasn't able to say anything on the phone. I couldn't blurt out something that was bothering me, everything had to be said in a roundabout way.

I looked at Sid and said, "You know what I want?" And

before he could answer, as if he would, I said, "I want some man to keep me!" I think he blinked. For a moment, I think I saw the wheels turning as he studied me with those little eyes. I did it deliberately just to see his reaction. It was the last thing in the world I wanted, but I was tired of all the shenanigans, of being kept in the dark. I wanted to throw a curve at somebody. I didn't know anything about any of them and they knew all about me, and it was bothering me. I felt like I was in a giant maze and they were watching me running around in circles.

Sid's reaction was to continue the conference for later in the afternoon. We would have cocktails in the Polo Lounge of the Beverly Hills Hotel. I kicked myself all the way to the hotel. I knew it would be repeated, but it is hard to explain the feeling I had when I said it. What I had wanted to say was, "Okay, all of you think I'm this way, let me throw a little shocker at you and see what you do." It was so totally out of character that I will never forget saying it.

I began spending more time at home, painting and ruminating about my situation. I was concerned about getting involved with other people. Some people, I realized, were afraid to be around me because of Sam. Others were avoiding me because the FBI had questioned them about me. I didn't like what was happening to me. My depressions became more frequent.

I developed female trouble and had a D&C on the morning of June 6. The next morning two FBI agents walked into my hospital room and accused me of having had an abortion. "A what?" I yelled, speaking to them for the first time since the day they had broken into my apartment. "An abortion," they repeated in unison. "You people are insane! I didn't have an abortion. How dare you walk in here and accuse me of that?" "Well," one of them said, "we think you did." They came at me from both sides of the bed, and they looked so menacing that I screamed out, "You get out of this room, right now!" "Take it easy, you're only helping yourself if you name the doctor who performed the abortion."

I think any female kind of operation does something to a woman's nervous system—there's a certain depression, a helplessness, and I got hysterical. I started screaming for help.

They turned and walked slowly to the door. Before leaving one of them said, "I wonder if the little guy, Jacobson, did it?" He turned and there was the most hideous leer on his face. If I could have killed that man, I would have on the spot. There is nothing heinous about an abortion today, but in 1963, my God, it was the sin of the century. They knew precisely what they were doing when they falsely accused me of something like that. As far as I know, they never talked to Dr. Jacobson or to my gynecologist. It was just another ploy in their vicious cat-and-mouse game.

The surveillance intensified that summer. I went to visit my sister Jackie in Cardiff-by-the-Sea, which is near San Diego, and a friend of her husband, Dick Taylor, rented a car for me. In no time flat, the FBI were at the rental agency wanting to know who had rented the car they had seen me in. The men at the agency told Dick, "Jesus Christ, what's going on? Do you know the FBI have been here several times asking about you and about the car you rented for the girl, causing me as much a hassle as possible."

Dick drove me to Pasadena and I hid out at the Arroyo Inn. Jimmy Cantillon took a sudden interest in my case. I would either go to his office or he would come to Pasadena. I went back to Cardiff for a couple of days and then back to Pasadena. To put it bluntly, they had me trying to hide from the FBI wherever I went.

As I later discovered in a front page newspaper story, this was happening at a time when Sam and Phyllis were vacationing at Frank's Cal-Neva Lodge up in Lake Tahoe. The incident not only caused a big commotion in the press, but because of it Frank was forced to sell out his interests in Cal-Neva and the Sands. It seems that Sam's name was in a "black book" in Nevada and that meant he was *persona non grata* in any of the state's gambling places.

It gave me something to think about. I was still talking to Sam on the phone, but except for that brief glimpse of him at the Key Club, I had not seen him since February 4. As far as I was concerned, the romance had vanished as completely as that winter's snow. For weeks, literally, I agonized over that damn diamond bracelet. I didn't want to send it back in the mail, nor did I want a confrontation with Sam, but suddenly, returning it to him seemed the most important thing in the world to me.

As it happened, I had left some jewelry in Chicago to be repaired, and so on September 29, I flew to Chicago and stayed with the Matassas overnight. The next morning I picked up my jewelry and John drove me to O'Hare. Just before boarding the plane I handed him the bracelet, which was gift wrapped, and asked him to give it to Sam. I was taking the coward's way out, but I didn't want any more meaningless arguments.

It was two or three days before Sam called, and I figured it probably had taken him that long to cool down. "You didn't have to do that," he said. "I know what you're thinking about, but none of it has anything to do with the bracelet. It was a gift and I know how much you love it. Would you keep it if I sent it back?"

"No, I don't want it back, Sam," I said. "It's not the kind of gift that I can keep. Our relationship was different when I accepted it. The less said about it now, the better."

For me, at that moment Sam sounded too reasonable. I guess I was getting cynical. After all, I would either be questioned by the grand jury or the FBI. No matter how interested he was in Phyllis, he wanted to keep me on his string. Perhaps my returning the bracelet made him think I was severing that connection.

I hastened to reassure him that I considered him a wonderful friend, that there would always be a warm place in my heart for him, and that whenever I had any problems he was the one I would call, because I valued his advice.

I continued hiding. Jimmy Cantillon moved me into the Airport Marina Hotel. Not only were the FBI looking for me to serve me with a summons to appear before the grand jury, but Jimmy and Johnny were keeping very close tabs on me. I was sick to death of it all, all those lonely nights in hotel rooms, and it began to dawn on me that I could go to jail. If the grand jury gave me immunity, and I took the Fifth

Amendment, as I knew I would, I could be imprisoned for contempt for the term of that grand jury. Jimmy didn't tell me that, but I was reading everything I could find on it; on the other hand, I didn't mention it to Jimmy, either. That was precisely what happened to Sam in Chicago two years later. They gave him immunity and he ended up serving a year in the Cook County Jail.

Someone worked a miracle. I didn't have to appear before the grand jury. As I look back on it now, I should have realized that there was no way the Justice Department would bring me before a grand jury and risk the possibility that my relationship with Jack would be revealed. I was never before a grand jury. Not in Chicago when Sam was jailed for contempt, not during Johnny's two trials in Los Angeles. I didn't know it then, but I had diplomatic immunity.

The questioning by the IRS and the FBI amounted to nothing. They never asked me anything about myself. The line of questioning was, "Do you know so-and-so?" One long list of meaningless names. "Did you ever see John Roselli and this so-and-so together?" "Do you know where John Roselli was on such and such a date?" They never asked me where I was on any date. Of course, I wouldn't have told them. I gave my name and took the Fifth Amendment on everything else, without a single objection from them. The interrogation, like the surveillance, was just another exercise in harassment. The questions were innocuous. They knew where Sam and Johnny were on the dates in question. They had been on top of them day and night. So I sat there with Jimmy and declined to answer silly questions from clerks, really, who were taking their orders from Washington. They didn't ask me about my income, my associates, my travels, my family, or my way of life. They treated me as though I had no existence of my own. The way I feel about it now, I think if I had volunteered to go before the grand jury they would have disbanded it—post haste.

AUTHOR'S NOTE: *At this point I would like to quote from an FBI document that has been in my files many years. It is dated October 23, 1963, and it is a report by Special*

Agents Andrew V. Furfaro and Clarence A. Turner. The subject of the report is Sidney R. Korshak. The opening paragraph reads:

"On this date, the witness appeared in the office of Assistant U.S. Attorney Thomas R. Sheridan to testify before the above agents, in lieu of appearing before the Federal Grand Jury which had subpoenaed him to appear on October 29, 1963. The interview was quite cordial and informal, and in most instances Mr. Korshak volunteered information without being asked."

If the report, which is five pages long, is a fair summary of the interrogation, then the information "volunteered" by Korshak was as innocuous as the questions propounded to Judy. Korshak talked about Jake Arvey's son, Irwin, whom he described as "presently a paranoid." Jake was "very ill" and had lost "¾ of his stomach," but Jake was still alive and kicking political asses at this writing.

Korshak was the "first person to be subpoenaed by the Kefauver committee to testify from Chicago," but "he was not asked to testify."

He admitted "he is a member of the Friars Club, but that he is not proud of, nor does he go near the place. That the Friars Club is a 'cesspool.' That the members are not a social and charitable fraternity but a collection of gamblers who wager on anything if the odds are right. That he suggested that they seal up the Friars."

In reference to the McClellan committee, "Robert Kennedy and Pierre Salinger appeared in his [Korshak's] office, and questioned him about sweetheart contracts between unions and management. He appeared before the committee for one hour, and Kennedy questioned him again, and then thanked him for appearing."

Korshak said "he represents racetracks in the Chicago area. Mervyn LeRoy called him one day before the expected employee strike at Hollywood Park and asked him to help. He went to Hollywood Park, and met

On November 19 there was a confrontation with Dodge in Jimmy's office. Jimmy had told the FBI about the two special agents who had broken into my apartment and Dodge wanted me to identify them. They threatened to subpoena me if I didn't consent to the interview, and Jimmy said, "All right, but she will not answer a single question." Dodge looked directly at me and said, "Will you identify the two men you found in your apartment?" I looked at Jimmy and he said, "She will not." I didn't open my mouth once—Jimmy had given me strict instructions not to say a word. He never explained his reasoning, but I think he and Johnny wanted something to hold over their heads.

Johnny reserved a room for me at the Beverly Crest Hotel on November 20, two days before Jack was assassinated. I was sleeping when my mother called to tell me to turn on the television. I couldn't believe it. I buried myself in that room for days, and all I could think of was "My God, Jack is dead!"

My escape when I couldn't handle an emotional problem

was to stop eating and drink myself to sleep. It took very little liquor to keep me in a stupor when I didn't eat. I would wake up, take half a drink and go right back to sleep again. It was the only way I could blot it out of my consciousness. Otherwise the horror would start happening all over again. By staying in a stupor, I wasn't bothered by dreams. In a natural sleep I would have been dreaming, aware subconsciously that something was terribly wrong. Every time I woke up from my stupor, the shock was there, the horror repeated again, and I couldn't get past the fact that he was dead, and all that death implies—the awesome finality of it.

I couldn't think of myself in relation to him. All I could think about was him. And her! God my heart ached for her. That woman handled herself so magnificently—I think I ached as much for her as I did for him. She may have had the best possible medical attention, but there is just so much anybody else can do for you. The rest of it has to come from inside and her strength was indomitable.

It was years before I could get it out of my system. I would be doing well and suddenly I would fall apart. I would force myself out of it, acting as if nothing had happened, and again the grief would take over. It would overcome me at odd moments and I would stay home for days on end. The problem was that I never let myself go completely. I stopped myself from crying it out. I knew it was best to get a hurt out of your system, but I never allowed myself to do that. I think I was afraid of what might happen. Instead of purging myself, when my insides were just wrenched, I would put music on that fed that terrible sadness aching inside of me.

After five days went by without my answering the phone, Johnny became so concerned that he had the management admit him to my room. I didn't want to see him, but he patiently resisted me, until finally I agreed to have dinner with him. Except for what I had nibbled on from room service, this was my first meal in all that time.

The next day we drove to Palm Springs and stayed at Paul Ross's place, where Johnny's girl, Dorothy Towne, joined us. The only memorable moment about that trip was the day we went to the Canyon Country Club. Frank, Dean, and about ten others were seated at a long table, and there was not one greeting from any of them. It gave me the weirdest feeling. I was with Johnny, Dorothy, and another couple, and it was as though the two groups were complete strangers. Whenever our paths crossed thereafter, I never again spoke to Frank or Dean.

Around mid-December I rented a house at 2314 San Ysidro, off Benedict Canyon, in Beverly Hills. It was a new house in a subdivision built going up a hill, on tiered lots, with the street curving at the top where it leveled off. Construction on the level part was just beginning, and that was where the FBI stationed themselves around the clock— they could look right down on me.

It was a two story house with the master bedroom upstairs, and the staircase was completely enclosed in glass on three sides. It was an impossible situation once the FBI zeroed in on me. If what the FBI did to me at that time was not a crime, then we live in a lawless land.

I became, quite literally, the victim in a Hitchcock melodrama. They were always there during the day but it was at night that they really became sinister. They made me a prisoner in my own house. Every time I went out I was accosted by agents in private and public places, intimidated and humiliated, until I was afraid to leave the house. There was always at least one car on top of the hill, and others would drive back and forth all night long, and blow their horns every time they passed my house. Others would park on the street near my house and they would turn their lights on whenever I was on the staircase. They became so aggressive that I began to fear for my life.

My brother Allen moved in with me for a while and I slept with a loaded gun on my bed. I had my mind made up. If anybody walked through that door I would fire point blank and ask questions later. Allen finally got so nervous he moved out, leaving me completely alone. After Allen left I stayed awake at night and watched the activity up and down the hill.

I became convinced they were deliberately trying to break

me down. From listening to my phone calls, and perhaps from electronic devices planted in my house, they knew that I was doing badly at this point. They were giving it that extra push to drive me over the edge. Jimmy Cantillon became very elusive, Sam was seldom available, and Johnny had vanished somewhere. (The intensity of their surveillance became apparent during Johnny's Friars trial. It came out in testimony that they knew where I was every minute of the day and night.)

Out of the blue, Johnny called to invite me to a New Year's Eve party at the Desert Inn. I jumped at the opportunity. I felt like a drowning woman being offered a life raft. The party was at the Desert Inn Country Club. I sat next to Johnny and his girlfriend—it was either Betty Mahoney or Dorothy Towne—and across from Moe Dalitz, who was introduced to me as the president of the hotel. Moe kept trying to get Johnny to tell him my name, and Johnny would laugh and not answer. I danced with Moe a couple of times and learning my name seemed to be his main preoccupation. Every time he asked me I smiled and pointed to Johnny, and it became quite a game.

The drinking was pretty heavy and it was a long noisy evening. As we were walking back to the hotel, with Johnny and his girlfriend ahead of Moe and me, I began arguing with Johnny, nothing serious, mainly taunting him about something. Moe turned me around and gently kissed me on the cheek, saying, "Come on, now, don't get so mad."

God, I hauled off and whacked him right across the face with all my might. Everybody froze as though a shot had been fired. Johnny looked at me and shook his head. "You know something," he said, "you must be crazy."

I was just as stunned as any of them. I had never done that before in my life.

Around noon the next day Johnny started banging on the connecting door to my room. When I opened it he was standing there with a big grin on his face. "Do you know who you smacked across the face last night?" I said, "I don't care who he is." Johnny doubled over laughing. "You're really crazy. Nobody smacks Moe Dalitz across the face. Christ, don't you know anything yet? Haven't you learned anything?'' He was preaching but laughing at the same time. He flopped into a chair. ''I couldn't believe it when I heard that crack,'' he howled. ''I was afraid to look. I thought he had smacked you and I would have to start picking up the pieces all over the place. Do you realize how hard you hit him? Jesus!'' He couldn't go on for a while. ''You should have seen the look on his face. You nearly knocked him flat on his ass. You pack a mean wallop, sweetheart!''

The next day I was back in my glass cage. Between January 2 and March 21 something happened to me that is almost impossible to explain. I became obsessed with the idea that the FBI would wait a certain length of time for me to commit suicide, but if I failed them, they would devise some diabolical means to kill me and make it look like suicide or an accident. I felt that any group of men capable of torturing me that way were capable of the most evil acts imaginable.

Gradually I began having difficulty going up the stairs. In the morning, after a night's vigil, I could barely lift my legs. I had to pick each leg up and place it on the next step. Later in the day I would be looser and could walk around without too much pain. My ankles swelled and turned fiery red, almost purple, and I sat and looked at them in total amazement, as though they belonged to someone else.

The periods of immobility began to last longer. Sometimes I felt so bad when I went to Dr. Jacobson's office that I couldn't lift my feet and had to take short, shuffling steps. After the shot I could move a little better, but after a while they made no difference at all.

One day I tried to brush my hair and realized I couldn't get my arm up. Another day I struggled to get my arm up but I couldn't close my fingers around the brush handle. If I gritted my teeth and really tried, the pain became excruciating. All my joints—ankles, knees, hips, shoulders, elbows, wrists, fingers—felt as though they had rusted shut. One afternoon I woke up—I had been up all night watching the activity on the hill, with the doors locked and the gun at my side—and discovered that I couldn't get out of bed. I was lying perfectly rigid. Luckily the phone was on my bed and after an enormous effort I managed to call my mother. I explained what was happening and I said, "Mom, the doors are locked but I will try to make it over to the balcony and drop the keys." It must have taken me over an hour to crawl the ten or so feet from my bed to the balcony. My mother and Allen were waiting below, their faces ashen as they watched me struggle the last few feet.

An ambulance took me to Valley Presbyterian. They recognized the symptoms right away—I had a high fever—and they put ice in my mouth, gave me a tremendous shot of Demerol, placed a cradle at the end of the bed and put a blanket over it. I couldn't stand even the weight of a blanket over me. They gave me Demerol every four hours at first, and then every three hours, which knocked me right out each time. Every so often they would change my position. The only time I was able to move by myself was during that brief moment between shots. I weighed barely a hundred pounds when I went into the hospital. For my height and bone structure, it meant that I looked like death warmed over. My normal weight then was one hundred twenty.

A neurosurgeon was called in to join a team of several doctors, and they gave me a series of tests. They found calcium deposits in all my joints, but the deposits in my ankles were so heavy that there was the possibility that I would never walk properly again.

My parents were blaming Dr. Jacobson's shots for my condition, and though I was afraid they were right, I didn't want to admit it to them. Besides I was in too much pain to think about it. After I told the doctors what I had gone through, they explained about the relationship between emotional stress and arthritis. If a person has a tendency toward arthritis, great emotional stress can sometimes trigger it.

It took five weeks for the swelling to go down, and during this entire period I was on Demerol. The day they released me my father said, "She's coming home and we're going to take care of her." He was furious at what he felt I had allowed to happen. When I left the hospital they gave me cortisone and twenty-six other kinds of pills, but no pain killers.

I began having withdrawal pains that evening and I called my doctor. "My God, do something for me, please! I'm going out of my mind." What he lacked in sympathy he made up in firmness. He said it was time for me to stop taking the pain killer. In other words, it was all right for me to scream my head off at home; in the hospital they like to keep things nice and quiet, even if it means discharging you from the hospital with a dependency created by the doctor.

For nearly two days I went through hell. Monsters came out of the walls. Cold sweat and nightmares in living color: men chasing me with daggers and guns, weird, grotesque images dancing and laughing, horror movies dredging up all the distorted fears buried in the darkest recesses of my feverish brain.

It took months for me to feel strong enough, mentally and physically, to venture out on my own. I was in pain but the unhappiness was the deepest hurt. Much of it stemmed from my inability to organize my life, to find a niche with meaning and stability. It wasn't that I wanted to relive the past. Jack was dead and Sam was out of my life. My problem was that I didn't know what or where I wanted to be. I was beginning to think that I was never going to fall in love deeply enough to ever risk marriage again. I didn't trust men. I wasn't a career woman. My most peaceful moments were when I was painting, but it takes more than peaceful moments to fulfill ones's life.

XIV

Early in January 1965, Dr. Krohn told me I was pregnant. My first thought was that it couldn't be possible, that somebody had made a terrible mistake. When it finally sank in, I thought seriously of an abortion. Friends suggested reputable doctors in Sweden and Japan. I even got my passport, but at the decisive moment I couldn't go through with it.

I went to Encinitas to stay with my sister Joan, who had recently been divorced, and I took long solitary walks on the beach, trying to gather the courage to tell my parents. Finally, I called my mother and both she and my father were unbelievable. She said, "We're coming right down to get you."

They moved me into their home and told me not to worry. They would be with me when I had my baby and they would take care of me. Despite all their concern I still became withdrawn, closing myself off in my room, not wanting to see or talk to anyone. I even stopped seeing Dr. Krohn because of the fear of running into someone I knew in his office. I became a recluse in my own home. I spent my days lying on the bed, staring up at the ceiling, my head buzzing in paralyzing turmoil. I couldn't think straight. Every thought was confused by five others. My only salvation was total blankness, which in a way is a form of self-hypnosis. I would stare at the light fixture, concentrating on one aspect of its configuration, blanking out everything else, and hours would vanish without a trace, day would turn into night. For sleep I would take Tuinal and continue that journey through my empty world.

One day when my father was out of town on business voices intruded into my blankness. It was an ominous and discordant sound. A moment later my mother opened the door and said, "Judy, two FBI men are here to see you."

My mother left the room and as I put on my robe I could feel the tightness in my chest, the trembling in my legs, that these confrontations always caused. As I came into the room, Dodge was showing my mother a picture of Johnny and the other agent was waiting to show her a picture of Sam. I went absolutely berserk. I screamed for them to leave and they just stood there. Dodge said, "All we want to do is talk to you and your mother about these men."

"Get out of here," I cried, "and if you ever bother my mother again, I'll kill you!"

My mother grabbed me before I could lunge at them. "Please, will you leave," she said, and still they stood there, with the pictures in their hands, mumbling, "But all we want to do is talk to you . . . "

I was hysterical by the time my mother got me back into my room. There is no way I can measure time for that moment. It may have been one or two days before I arrived at the crucial decision that my life was impossible. That the FBI would never leave me alone; that I could not bring up a child with the FBI hounding me; that it wasn't fair to the child to have him come into this kind of world— what would that child think of me; that I couldn't give him up. My situation had become so oppressive that I was completely irrational.

I sat on my bed, emptied a full bottle of Tuinal capsules into my hand and gulped them down. Just as I was sinking into that warm peaceful glow, my mother came into the room to say that Joan wanted to speak to me on the phone. I grinned and fumbled for the phone, my head so heavy I could barely lift it. The moment I spoke Joan knew something was wrong. That telephone call saved two lives.

I was taken to the hospital by ambulance and I remember vaguely waking up when the ambulance was backing into the hospital entry. Then I remember, again vaguely, being on a table with a huge light overhead and masked faces looking down at me. After that I was out for a day and a half.

Two months later, on May 28, 1965, my baby was born. He was a seven-month baby, but for the reasons stated in the Prologue to this book, I had made up my mind to find a good home for my son, a home where he would be protected from the hounding and persecution of the FBI.

It was a year before I could force myself to sign the adoption papers. I placed myself under the care of a psychiatrist, trying to find someone to give me the strength that would make it possible for me to give my child his chance in life. My whole family wanted to adopt him, but I knew that was no solution. I saw him only once in my whole life. One night I came to visit my mother, not knowing that he was with her, and I couldn't resist holding him. It made the final separation that much more painful, but now at least I knew that he was a sound, healthy boy, and that my suicide attempt had not harmed him in any way. That thought had tormented me for a year. My parents had told me he was fine, but I was so convinced that he was deformed I hadn't believed them.

The next day I signed the papers. My God, the terrible things my mother said to the women from the adoption agency. She wanted to kill those two women—but she was my mother and reacting as the child's grandmother.

I made my decision and I have had to live with it. I hope and pray that the sacrifice was not in vain, and that his identity will never be revealed. I have not forgotten him. I am forever longing to call the adoption agency to ask if anything has happened to him? Is he all right? Does he need anything? Can I do anything for him? Is he still alive? The anxiety is everpresent—it never leaves me. Yet I can honestly say that there are three things I know I did right in my lifetime: what I did for my child, what I did for my mother when she had cancer, and what I did for myself when I married Dan Exner.

XV

For seven months I was able to conceal from my mother the medical verdict that she was dying from cancer of the pancreas. Because her mother had died of cancer, also of the pancreas, my mother had been convinced she was going to die the same horrible death. If she had known she had cancer she would have lost her will to live. During all those agonizing months I was able to convince her that she was having trouble recuperating from a bladder operation. I never left the house. I was at her bedside every waking moment. Every morning I would find her crying and I would begin all over again to convince her that she was not dying, that she was going to be fine. Toward the end she started to vomit blood in the middle of the night. I would hold her through the convulsions and sit with her the rest of the night holding her hand. She died on April 7, 1971.

My father, who had been so strong all those years, could not accept the fact that she was dying. After she died he never forgave himself for his weakness. He would play her favorite music and collapse in tears. Not long after my mother's death, Dad was operated on for cancer of the prostate. We moved to Cardiff and I took care of him for the two years before he died. The two illnesses ruined him financially. I used all my funds and sold most of my jewelry and possessions to help defray the medical expenses.

It was in Cardiff that I met Dan. Until I met him I was a lost soul. If I could have gone to another planet to be away from all the people I had known in my lifetime, I would have gladly boarded that rocket ship. By then Dick Elwood was dead, Johnny was in prison, and Sam was living in exile in Mexico. I was alone, adrift in self-pity. I was still a night person, sleeping fitfully in the morning, and roaming the beach at night. More than once I was tempted to walk into the waves the way Renon Ross had done that night in Malibu. I would have succeeded because there was no one around to save me.

When I met Dan in the spring of 1973, he was playing golf every day, preparing to join the professional tour.

All the years of mistrust and indecision fell away when I got to know Dan. I fell in love so completely that I couldn't bear to be separated from him for a single moment. All the love that had been suppressed for so many years came pouring forth and it overwhelmed me. I had never known that love could heal aches and wounds and make you whole again.

We lived together nearly two years before we were married on May 20, 1975. He played golf every day from six in the morning until dark. Dan was accepted for the Florida minitour beginning in November. We purchased a motor home, put all of our furnishings and clothing into storage, and bought new golf wardrobes.

Dan drove the motor home to the golf course every morning, and I would sleep a little longer as he teed off at first light, long before the club was open. He would come back to the motor home around ten and I would fix something for him to eat, and then we would both go out and spend the day in the sun together. Because of the way we are with each other, it was an ideal life for the two of us. I loved every minute of it.

We were, to use a corny but apt phrase, in seventh heaven until the Senate committee issued its subpoena on September 12. There is not much sense in going over all the aggravation of the committee's intrusion into our lives, the arbitrary and belligerent attitude of their investigators and attorneys, which was equal in every way to that of the FBI and CIA agents they were supposedly investigating. As I said in the Prologue, they intimidated my sister and threatened to drag her forcefully to Washington unless she disclosed our where-abouts, creating the impression that we were in hiding when all the time were at my father-in-law's home, completely unaware of their interest in me. My name was now Exner, but that was hardly an alias.

My first awareness of the committee's existence was on June 19 when Sam was murdered in the basement kitchen of his Oak Park home. That was when I heard of his and Johnny's connection with the CIA, and the fact that Sam was killed a few days before he was to testify. I felt sorry for Sam but I never even dreamed that it could involve me.

Everything was so confused, so incredibly absurd. It would take another book to describe the sequence of events that finally resulted in our going to Washington on September 18. The next day Dan and I were ushered into a glass cubicle the size of a closet and introduced to Chief Counsel Frederick A. O. Schwarz, Jr., and Minority Counsel Curtis R. Smothers, who did most of the talking. He explained that he could not tell me exactly what it was they were going to discuss, but that it had something to do with President Kennedy, John Roselli and Sam Giancana.

After this briefing we were taken to another building and introduced to our committee-appointed attorney. Although Senator Towers had promised Dan we would have our choice of one of five prominent attorneys, there stood Henry A. Hupschman, barely out of law school, who served us well, but neglected at that moment to mention that he was with Sargent Shriver's law firm. When I told him I had a suitcase full of records and diaries covering those years, he asked if there was anything in my records relating to CIA assassination plots. I said, "Absolutely not," and he replied, "Well, then it's immaterial, and don't say anything about it." His position was that all questions should be answered with a yes or no, and nothing should be volunteered.

The next session was in Senator Towers' inner office, but Towers was not present. Schwarz, Smothers, and about six other staffers were there, but we never saw any member of the committee. I was so upset that I was sick inside. Dan held my hand and I was so grateful he was there with me. I couldn't have handled it without him.

The entire line of questioning, as best I could figure out, was directed at whether I had affairs with the men on their list. At one point, they asked Dan to leave the room because some of the questions would relate to classified documents. I could see the words TOP SECRET stamped across the papers, but the questions were the same as before. Every time they asked me about someone, the questioner would say, "Was he also a *friend?*" and the manner in which it was said left no doubt of the inference—*friend* was their euphemism for lover. I wanted to explain, but I had been warned not to volunteer information. So I answered yes or no but I knew what was going on in their heads and probably going down for the record.

That is another reason, along with those stated in the Prologue, why this book had to be written. For me, after all the years of harassment, the Senate committee was more than just another intrusion into my privacy. If they didn't start out to destroy the life we were building for each other, the result was nonetheless the same.

The notoriety that followed the committee's leaking of distorted and out of context information not only made the golf tour impossible, but it placed our very lives in jeopardy. No one really knows why Sam was murdered, or Jack, for that matter, and now Johnny. Life in the underworld of crime and the netherworld of politics is cheap. From what I have observed, it is impossible to tell the good men from the bad; all I can say is that some people are deadly serious about the games they play.

If my life has taught me anything, it is that I am a survivor. After what has happened to me, I am fortunate that I can still trust people, that I can still feel friendship and love for others. I thank God for Dan. Because of him I am stronger. The heartaches for my son, for my mother, for my father, are still there. But they are more bearable with Dan at my side. He gives me strength and hope for the future.